PERMESTA:
HALF A REBELLION

BARBARA S. HARVEY

PERMESTA:
HALF A REBELLION

EQUINOX PUBLISHING (ASIA) PTE LTD
No 3. Shenton Way
#10-05 Shenton House
Singapore 068805

www.EquinoxPublishing.com

Permesta: Half a Rebellion
by Barbara S. Harvey

ISBN 978-602-8397-38-4

First Equinox Edition 2010

Copyright © 1977 by Cornell Southeast Asia
Program Publications; renewed 2010.
This is a reprint edition authorized by the original publisher,
Cornell Southeast Asia Program Publications.

Printed in the United States

1 3 5 7 9 10 8 6 4 2

All rights reserved. No part of this publication may be reproduced, stored in
a retrieval system, or transmitted in any form or by any means, electronic,
mechanical, photocopying, recording or otherwise without the prior
permission of Equinox Publishing.

TABLE OF CONTENTS

Foreword 7
Preface 11
    I.   The National Context 17
   II.   The Regional Context: Sulawesi 39
  III.   The Charter of Inclusive Struggle 73
  IV.   From Crisis to Conflict 109
   V.   Permesta at War 143
  VI.   The End of the Rebellion 183
Conclusion 223
Appendix
    I.   Biographic Notes 229
   II.   Military Commands in East Indonesia and South Sulawesi, March 1, 1957 243
  III.   Charter of Inclusive Struggle for the Region of TT-VII Wirabuana 245
  IV.   Persons Active in Permesta, 1957-58 253
   V.   Permesta Military Organization, 1958-60 257
Glossary 259

FOREWORD

With the conclusion of Indonesia's long and arduous struggle for independence most of its people believed there would be a rapid improvement of social and economic conditions. During the early years of independence some progress was made in this direction, most prominently in education, and for the time being at least Indonesian society did become somewhat more egalitarian than in the colonial period. But the degree of improvement fell far short of expectations, and disillusionment and frustration led increasingly to an understandable tendency to blame the central government in Jakarta for the inadequate measures taken to meet the expectations that had been aroused during the revolution.

For several years, in Java as well as in the Outer Islands, disenchantment with the central government was moderated by the widely held belief that the first national democratic elections—finally actually held in 1955-56—could be counted upon to produce a genuinely representative government disposed to take, and capable of implementing, the decisive actions required to attain social and economic progress. But in fact the elections brought little change; cabinet membership was largely the same, the political parties no more disposed to cooperate with each other, and governmental capacity to bring about social and economic progress no greater than before. Once this became clear, dissatisfaction and criticism of the central government was no longer restrained and became more forcefully articulated and pointed. Especially was this so in the highly politically conscious areas of Sumatra and Sulawesi that felt slighted and discriminated against by what they perceived to be an increasingly Java-centric cast of national leadership in Jakarta.

The several movements for increased regional autonomy—culminating in open rebellion in Sulawesi and Sumatra—dominated Indonesia's political history from 1957 to 1959 and constituted a major watershed in the country's political development. As Dr. Harvey points out, they link the period between the last phase of parliamentary government and the subsequent more authoritarian and centralized system of Guided Democracy, and their ultimate failure paved the way for the firm establishment of the latter system and more generally for a substantial change in the overall pattern of power.

Partly precipitated as a reaction against the initial moves of Sukarno and the army to liquidate parliamentary democracy, the regional movements in fact set in motion a series of events that eventuated its demise. Similarly, though these movements were an attempt to reverse what was keenly felt to be the economic and administrative overcentralization of an increasingly Java-oriented national government, their failure led to an intensification of this aspect of Indonesian governance. And although the rebellions in Sumatra and Sulawesi were launched in opposition to the growth in political influence of Sukarno, the Indonesian Communist Party and the central army command, the failure of these efforts led to the further strengthening of all three. It should be noted that with the suppression of the rebellions some of Indonesia's most progressive Islamic leaders were discredited—to a point where in the country as a whole the political influence of the Modernist Islamic movement was dealt a crippling blow from which it has not yet recovered.

Regional grievances, and the ethnic particularism that often accompanied them, were also of great importance in generating the rebellions in Sumatra and Sulawesi, collectively known as the PRRI/Permesta. However, the Sumatra-based civilian Islamic leaders who were ascendant in the political leadership of these loosely linked efforts were unwilling to give full rein to these sentiments. They together with a small minority of the rebel military leaders (of whom the most prominent was Colonel A. E. Kawilarang) recognized that to have appealed in terms of regional separatism would have risked the destruction of Indonesia's national unity and involved a repudiation of the very nationalist symbols that these men themselves had helped forge. Thus, in the challenge to Jakarta the rebel military commanders on Sulawesi and Sumatra were unable to utilize the full potential of the forces of ethnic and regional particularism and were obliged to accommodate to the goal of effecting basic political changes in the government of a single all-embracing

Indonesian state. This helps account for the paradox that when in February 1958 an open break with the civilian and military leadership in Jakarta was finally made, the rebels on Sulawesi and Sumatra were constrained from making full use of those same local pressures that had earlier so powerfully increased their leverage with the central government and made possible the assertion of greater autonomy for their regions.

Although the history of both theaters of the 1958 rebellion have until now been largely unrecorded, thus far the least chronicled and the least understood has been the Sulawesi-based movement launched as the Permesta. Dr. Harvey's comprehensive account of Permesta and its aftermath more than evens the scales, her study providing a much fuller coverage of the Sulawesi-based rebellion than is available for its Sumatran counterpart. (A study of the latter by another scholar is underway, but is not yet near completion.)

It should be noted that in this monograph Dr. Harvey, a Lecturer in Politics at Monash University, brings to bear unusual qualifications. This work grows out of her long interest in Indonesia's political development and a recent focus, involving substantial periods of field research, on the political history of Sulawesi. She has done much to fill one of the major lacunae in modern Indonesian history, and readers will undoubtedly welcome her study not only for the light that it throws on this period, but also because it makes much more understandable the extensive political changes that followed.

George McT. Kahin
Ithaca, N.Y.
July 30, 1976

PREFACE

This monograph is based on research conducted in Indonesia in 1971 and 1972. At its inception the study was planned as an investigation of political integration in contemporary Indonesia, based on a comparison of North and South Sulawesi. In the course of my research I discovered that it would be possible to obtain considerable information, much of it from interviews, on two rebellions which had occurred in these areas: Darul Islam (Islamic State) in South Sulawesi; and Permesta, which began in Makassar in 1957 as part of a general regional movement affecting many parts of the archipelago, but continued in North Sulawesi in association with the Sumatra-based PRRI rebellion of 1958-1961. It seemed that a detailed study of these rebellions would cast much light on center-region relations in Indonesia, and on the nature of disintegrative impulses. In the course of writing I found it necessary to limit the dissertation based on this research to South Sulawesi, and the course and impact of the two rebellions there ("Tradition, Islam and Rebellion: South Sulawesi 1950-1965," Cornell University, 1974). This monograph is concerned with the Permesta movement and rebellion, and although some consideration is given to the inception of the movement in South Sulawesi, the focus of the study is on the course of the rebellion in North Sulawesi.

It must be noted that the perspective of this study is at the regional level, and that while it has been possible to draw on published accounts of national politics of the period, there are no local, village-level studies available to make possible a detailed assessment of the impact of the rebellion on the lives of the bulk of the people in the affected area.

The account which follows is based largely on interviews with participants in Permesta; in most cases they are cited in footnotes, but in a few instances interviewees requested that they not be identified, and these requests have been respected. I would like to thank the many people in North and South Sulawesi and in Jakarta who were so generous in sharing their knowledge and interpretations of these events with me. A number of people also made available documents and newspaper accounts which were most valuable in providing dates and factual details. In particular I would like to record my gratitude to the historian, Mr. H. M. Taulu of Manado, Mr. F. J. Tumbelaka of Jakarta, and to the staffs of the Army Military History offices in Bandung, Manado, and Makassar, for making available to me material in their archives.

The technical staff of the Monash University Department of Geography prepared the maps included in the text. Joan Kirsop and Bronwyn Fooks helped in the construction of tables, and Roberta Ludgate and Peggy Lush have been relied on for the final preparation of the manuscript. Their assistance is warmly appreciated.

Financial support for the research on which this monograph is based is gratefully acknowledged from the Fulbright-Hays Graduate Fellowship Program, the London-Cornell Project, and the Cornell University Graduate School, The Cornell Modern Indonesia Project provided both support and encouragement for the research and writing of this study.

I am particularly grateful to George McT. Kahin, Director of the Cornell Modern Indonesia Project, for his stimulation, guidance and support. This monograph could not have been written without his encouragement and patience. I would also like to thank Jamie Mackie, and Herbert Feith, who read and commented on all or parts of earlier drafts of this manuscript, and Benedict Anderson, who not only provided advice on a draft version, but agreed to see the final manuscript through to publication. Both the content and the style of the monograph have been improved by their suggestions, although they are in no way responsible for any errors or idiosyncrasies that remain.

NOTE ON SPELLING AND TRANSLATION

Spelling of Indonesian words follows the new system introduced in 1972, with the exception of quotes from documents or personal names. Names have been spelled according to individual preference insofar as this could be determined. Place names are spelled according to official Indonesian usage with three exceptions. I have retained the old spelling of Jogjakarta, which is in accordance with its usual Indonesian pronunciation. As the spelling used for the capital of North Sulawesi is inconsistent, even in official documents, I have adopted the spelling Manado, which is the spelling usually used by the provincial authorities and local inhabitants. The city of Makassar was renamed Ujung Pandang in 1971, but inasmuch as the events related in the text all occurred prior to that time, I have retained the older name of the city.

Most interviews were conducted in Indonesia; quotes are based on careful notes taken during interviews. Translations from interviews and documents are my own. I would like to thank Mr. Zainu'ddin for his help in checking and amending the translation of the Charter of Inclusive Struggle, which appears as Appendix III.

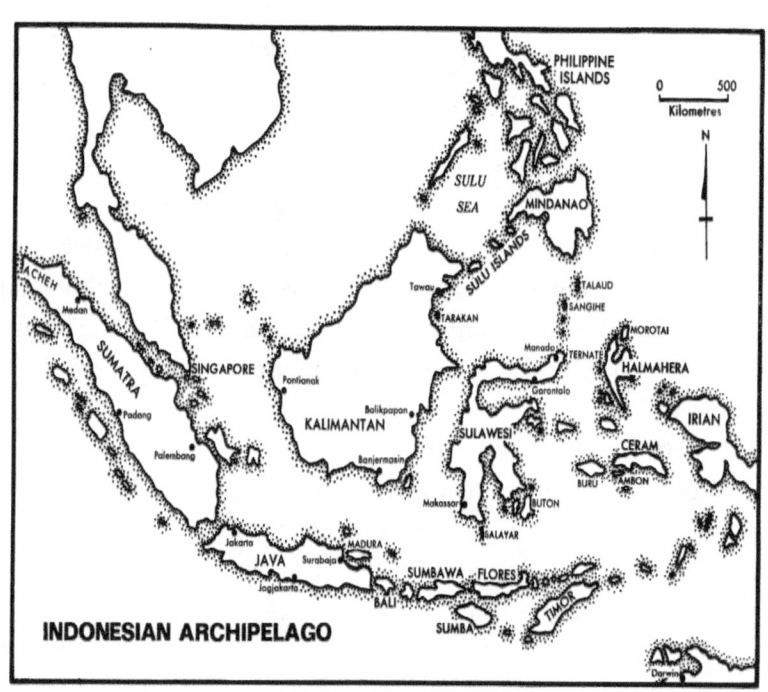

MAP I

CHAPTER ONE
THE NATIONAL CONTEXT

Indonesia's regional crisis, which first captured headlines in December 1956 and culminated in the PRRI/Permesta[1] rebellion of 1958-61, was one of several interrelated conflicts which arose out of disillusionment with the country's Western-style parliamentary democracy, and which hastened its end.[2] The disillusionment was based on a widespread sense of dissatisfaction with the existing state structure, which was widely criticized for being bureaucratic, inefficient, and corrupt. The hope and enthusiasm aroused in the revolution of 1945-49 proved difficult to sustain once independence was attained. None of the seven cabinets, all of them short-lived, of the 1949-57 period seemed able to cope with both the affective and administrative functions of government; they were either dull of ineffective. The lack of consensus on fundamental values sharpened conflicts about state philosophy and structure. The conflicts

---

1 PRRI (Pemerintah Revolusioner Republik Indonesia—Revolutionary Government of the Republic of Indonesia) was proclaimed at Padang, West Sumatra on February 15, 1958. Permesta (Perjuangan Semesta Alam—Inclusive Struggle) was the name of a charter issued in Makassar on March 2, 1957, one of whose demands was for provincial autonomy. The name continued to be used by some in North Sulawesi who joined with the PRRI in opposition to the central government. No thorough study of the rebellion has been published, although two journalistic accounts have appeared: James Mossman, *Rebels in Paradise: Indonesia's Civil War* (London: Jonathan Cape, 1961); and William Stevenson, *Birds' Nests in Their Beards* (Boston: Houghton Mifflin, 1963).
2 For the national context in which the regional crisis occurred see: Herbert Feith, *The Decline of Constitutional Democracy in Indonesia* (Ithaca, N.Y.: Cornell University Press, 1962), especially pp. 462-608; Daniel S. Lev, *The Transition to Guided Democracy: Indonesian Politics, 1957-1959*, Cornell Modern Indonesia Project Monograph (Ithaca, N.Y.: Cornell University, 1966); Herbert Feith, "Dynamics of Guided Democracy," in Ruth T. McVey, ed., *Indonesia*, rev. ed. (New Haven, Conn.: Human Relations Area Files Press, 1967), pp. 309-409; and J. A. C. Mackie, "Aspects of Political Power and the Demise of Parliamentary Democracy in Indonesia," in R. N. Spann, ed., *Constitutionalism in Asia* (Bombay: Asia Publishing House, 1963), pp. 190-214.

were between groups and individuals with different views of how the shortcomings of the political system might be overcome, and centered on questions of the basic character of the state itself: the structure of national and local governmental institutions and the relationship between them; the assertion of national control over the economy; the role of political parties and the army; and the place of Islam and communism in the polity. Because of the differing economic, cultural, and social characteristics of Java and the Outer Islands,[3] all of these questions had regional dimensions and ethnic overtones.

An appreciation of these differences is crucial to an understanding of the conflict of interests which lay behind the increasing tension between the outlying regions and the central government. Thus, the broad contrast between the socioeconomic patterns of Java and the Outer Islands will be sketched briefly.

Java, the ancient locus of wet rice-growing agricultural kingdoms, was subjected both to greater Indian cultural influence and Dutch colonial penetration than the rest of the archipelago. Islam was amalgamated into the web of existing beliefs in East and Central Java, the heartland of the ethnic Javanese, but remained a potentially divisive force in rural society. West Java, ethnically Sundanese and strongly Islamic, was one of the first parts of the island to come under Dutch control. Because its socioeconomic characteristics distinguish it from the rest of the island, West Java is often identified with "Outer Indonesia." Yet its geographical location on Java and its position as hinterland to the capital city, mean that in political terms it is often identified with the center rather than the regions.

The patterns in the Outer Islands are more diverse, although two principal configurations can be identified—coastal trading kingdoms and inland tribal groups engaged in swidden agriculture. In general the more commercially oriented peoples of the coastal areas were receptive to Islam and to its modernist reformers of the early twentieth century. The most isolated inhabitants of the interior mountains generally continued to follow their ancestral beliefs, although some were converted to Christianity during the colonial period.

---

3 Useful discussions of these patterns are in Hildred Geertz, "Indonesian Cultures and Communities," in McVey, ed., *Indonesia*, pp. 24-33; and in Feith, *Decline*, pp. 26-32.

The expansion of Dutch colonial rule at the turn of the century was followed by the development of export crops such as rubber, coffee, and copra, and of extractive industries, in particular oil and tin, in Sumatra, Kalimantan, and Sulawesi. By 1925 the bulk of the Netherlands East Indies exports came from the Outer Islands, and the collapse of overseas markets for Javanese sugar in the 1930s depression greatly aggravated that imbalance. Further, with the growth of its population, Java no longer had rice to export to the Outer Islands, and economic links between inner and outer Indonesia weakened. Java, the center of population and the center of government, became the principal consumer of imports.

Center-region relations in Indonesia are complicated by the fact that the center is located on, and often identified with, the island of Java, the most populous of the islands of Indonesia, and the home of the numerically dominant Javanese. Some two-thirds of the population of Indonesia reside in Java, and approximately half of Indonesia's people are ethnic Javanese. However, more than demography is involved. Javanese political traditions, strongly influenced by Hindu conceptions of state and authority, have identified the realm by its center. The state was seen as a series of concentric circles, defined by the diminishing power of the ruler from its highest concentration in his court and capital, through outlying districts and allied kingdoms to the world beyond his reach. A simpler conception in the same tradition divided the world into Java and Sabrang—the lands across the seas; a view reflected in the continuing use of the terminology Java and the Outer Islands. Indeed, it has been suggested that it has been difficult for the Javanese to conceive of the people from Sabrang as being equal partners in the Indonesian state.[4] For their part, the energetic entrepreneurs, traders, and cash-crop farmers of the Outer Islands lived in a world whose cultural and social values gave them little understanding of or sympathy for the Javanese whom they knew only as refined aristocrats dominating the civil bureaucracy, or as

---

4 Javanese political traditions are discussed in Soemarsaid Moertono, *State and Statecraft in Old Java*, Cornell Modern Indonesia Project Monograph (Ithaca, N.Y.: Cornell University, 1968), especially pp. 111-13; and Benedict R. O'G. Anderson, "The Idea of Power in Javanese Culture," in Claire Holt, ed., *Culture and Politics in Indonesia* (Ithaca, N.Y. and London: Cornell University Press, 1972), especially pp. 22, 29.

impoverished peasants sent as transmigrants to open up new land or to work in plantations.

Developments during late colonial rule and the Japanese occupation enhanced Java's position as the political center of Indonesia: the concentration of secondary and tertiary educational institutions on Java, the flowering there of the nationalist movement, the incipient growth of manufacturing industry, and the intense politicization of Java during the Japanese occupation (1942-45) and the national revolution (1945-49).

Thus, part of Indonesia's colonial heritage was a structural imbalance between Java, politically dominant but economically weak, and the Outer Islands, politically marginal but economically strong. This imbalance was a crucial factor in center-region relations, and complicated the attempts to solve the national crisis of 1956-57.

The National Context of the Regional Crisis

In discussing the national context of the regional movement it may be useful to begin with the 1955 elections, for the distribution of support for the principal contestants illustrates the continuing relevance of regionally based economic and cultural differences to political conflict in Indonesia. Further, disappointment with the results of the elections was directly related to the disillusionment with parliamentary democracy which was at the heart of the political crisis of 1956-57.

No party won a majority in the elections;[5] twenty-eight parties or groups won representation in the parliament. Four major parties emerged: the Indonesian Nationalist Party (Partai Nasional Indonesia—PNI), with 22.3 percent of the total vote; the modernist Islamic party, Masyumi, with 20.9 percent; the conservative Islamic scholars' association (Nahdatul Ulama—NU), with 18.4 percent; and the Indonesian Communist Party (Partai Kommunis Indonesia—PKI), with 16.4 percent of the vote.[6]

The regional basis of party support was striking. Three of the four

---

[5] Elections to the parliament were held in September 1955, and in December to the constituent assembly, whose task it was to draw up a permanent constitution for the Republic. There was little change in the overall proportion of the vote for the various parties in the two elections; unless otherwise noted, figures reported here are for the parliamentary election.

[6] Herbert Feith, *The Indonesian Elections of 1955*, Cornell Modern Indonesia Project Interim Report (Ithaca, N.Y.: Cornell University, 1957), p. 58.

major parties obtained more than two-thirds of their total vote in East and Central Java: the PNI, 65.5 percent; the NU, 73.9 percent; and the PKI, 74.9 percent. Masjumi obtained only 25 percent of its votes from these provinces. However, in nine of the fifteen electoral districts, Masjumi received between a quarter and a half of the votes. Although its vote was the most evenly spread throughout the country of any party, Masjumi was the weakest of the major parties in the Javanese heartland.[7]

Party conflict thus tended to reflect regional as well as ideological divisions. In fact, the two were intertwined. Of the major parties the PKI and Masjumi were the most strongly ideological, and it is not surprising that communism had its greatest appeal in land-poor East and Central Java, or that Masjumi's strength was greatest in the more strongly Islamic areas of outer Indonesia. The conservative Islamic party, NU, represented those opposed to the puritan modernizers of Islam, and found its constituency in syncretic Java.

The question of the place of Islam in the state was a major campaign issue, and Masjumi's advocacy of "a state based on Islam" was used by its opponents to discredit the party by linking it with the Darul Islam rebellion.[8] Masjumi, out of government for most of the campaign period, was indeed quite isolated from—and attacked by—all the other parties. On the other hand, only Masjumi directly attacked the PKI, which tended to make anticommunism rather than procommunism appear to be an extremist position. The PNI, foremost exponent of nationalism and the state philosophy of Panca Sila,[9] was able to present itself as a moderate alternative to the Masjumi and the PKI—and this may have been a key to its electoral success.[10]

One of the surprises of the election was the weak showing of the Indonesian Socialist Party (Partai Sosialis Indonesia—PSI), a frequent ally of the Masjumi, closely identified with the Western-educated

---

7 Feith, *Elections*, pp. 62, 65-66, 78.
8 Darul Islam (the Islamic state, or the world of Islam) was the name given to a rebellion centered in West Java, where it had begun in 1948, and which formed links with rebellions in South Sulawesi and Aceh in 1953.
9 The five principles may be roughly translated as: Belief in a Supreme Being, nationalism, internationalism/humanitarianism, representative government, and social justice. See George McT. Kahin, *Nationalism and Revolution in Indonesia* (Ithaca, N.Y.: Cornell University Press, 1952), pp. 122-27.
10 Feith, *Decline*, pp. 353-60; Feith, *Elections*, pp. 10-17.

intellectual elite, and a party which had frequently played an influential role in government. Quite unexpected was the strong support for the PKI. The position of the PKI as the fourth major party in the country gave it a claim to participate in government which was difficult to ignore, however threatening the party's potential social radicalism was to the national elite.

Although the election itself was treated as a solemn national ritual, the campaign which preceded it was viewed by many as damaging to national unity. Open debate on questions of state philosophy and the role of Islam had created overt conflict—in a society which values harmony and consensus. Sociocultural divisions in the villages of Java were formalized, and thus solidified, and the ethnoregional basis of ideological and political differences was made clear.

At least as important in the negative reaction to the elections was that they provided no basis for a solution to the problems of political paralysis and governmental weakness. In part the disappointment was great because the initial hopes had been so high. The elections had been looked to as something of a panacea when independence itself had not immediately ushered in the "just and prosperous society" which was as much a dream of Indonesia's people as it was a motto of its leaders. Elections, it was thought, would make the system of parliamentary democracy work. The new parliamentarians would be true representatives of the people, not appointees of the Dutch to the puppet federal council or members of the elite cliques who dominated politics in the Republic during and after the revolution. It was expected that the elections would result in a reduction in the number of parties represented in the parliament, leading to more orderly and efficient proceedings. And finally, it was expected that the party which won the majority of the votes would be able to take decisive action on questions of state structure, ideology, and policy, ending the hesitation, inaction, and instability of the past.

However, no party won a majority in the elections. The rather even balance between the four major parties, and the continued representation in parliament of a large number of minor parties, were indications that conflict would continue, and that stable and effective government might be as difficult to achieve after the elections as it had been prior to them. The cabinet was once again based on a somewhat uneasy coalition between the PNI, Masjumi, and NU. It was headed by Mr. Ali Sastroamidjojo, a Javanese PNI member, who had been the target of military and regionalist criticism prior to the elections. His re-symption of the post of Prime Minister was a symbol of how little the elections had changed the constellation of political representation.

In addition to the problems which the elections did not solve, there were problems which they could not solve. The elections could only affect the distribution of power within the existing political system; they could not ensure that there would be any significant change in that system.

The distribution of party support along regional lines made clear to the people of the Outer Islands that they were a permanent minority in a system where representation was based on population. And because decisions were made by majority vote, they had reason to fear that their interests might be sacrificed to those of the people of Java. An additional cause for Outer Island criticism of the existing parliamentary system was the fact that Java was overrepresented in the parliament—although its 66.2 percent of the population would have itself ensured Java's dominance, it held 69.65 percent of the seats.[11]

Another problem the elections could not solve was that the parliamentary system provided only limited roles for three actors who had been central to the survival of the Republic during the revolution: President Sukarno, Vice President Mohammad Hatta, and the army. As we shall see, all had ideas about what might be done. However, before turning to the remedies which they proposed, it is necessary to look at some of the issues of special concern to the regions, in particular economic policy and local autonomy.

Economic Policy

Indonesia had inherited from the period of colonial rule an economic structure often described as dualistic—with traditional, labor-intensive, subsistence peasant agriculture existing side-by-side with modern, capital-intensive, foreign owned and controlled plantation and mining enterprises.[12] The grant of political independence to Indonesia in 1949

---

11 Feith, *Decline*, p. 472.
12 The term, "dual economy," is that of the Dutch economist J. H. Boeke; the classic exposition of the concept is in his "Dualistic Economics," in *Indonesian Economics: The Concept of Dualism*

was accompanied by the stipulation that foreign economic interests would be protected, and finance, shipping, and trade remained under Dutch control. Although there was a general, if vague, commitment to socialism among Indonesia's political leaders and small band of economists, dismantling the existing capitalist structure would require the elimination (or at least tight control) of the foreign-owned enterprises which dominated the economy. Radical nationalists asserted that only by breaking foreign domination of Indonesia's economy could policies in the interest of the people of Indonesia be followed, and the state be truly independent. Pragmatic conservatives feared the disruption of the economy such action would inevitably entail, considering Indonesia's lack of trained personnel and dependence on exports for revenue.[13]

This debate too had a regional dimension. Commercial groups in the Outer Islands were inclined to fear economic deterioration if inexperienced bureaucrats came to control additional economic operations, and, as entrepreneurs, they were prepared to give "rational" economic policies priority over nationalistic pride.

However, it was basically the fact that the bulk of Indonesia's export producers—and thus revenue earners—were located in the Outer Islands that inevitably involved regional interests in the economic policies of the central government. The policies followed generally favored consumers over producers. But it was not only Java's political dominance that gave consumer interests priority. As Hans Schmitt has argued, foreign economic domination of the nonagricultural sector of the Indonesian economy limited both the opportunities and the incentives for indigenous business groups to accumulate and invest capital, and accentuated the orientation toward consumption.[14]

It was particularly on the question of the allocation of foreign exchange that the interests of consumers and producers came into

---

in *Theory and Policy* (The Hague: W. van Hoeve, 1966), pp. 165-92. Boeke recognized that the "more-or-less primitive warp is interwoven with a capitalist woof into an inseparable dualistic whole"; p. 178.

13 J. A. C. Mackie, "The Indonesian Economy, 1950-1963," in Bruce Glassburner, ed., *The Economy of Indonesia* (Ithaca, N.Y.: Cornell University Press, 1971), pp. 16-69; Bruce Glassburner, "Economic Policy-Making in Indonesia, 1950-1957," in Glass-burner, ed., *Economy of Indonesia*, pp. 70-98.

14 Hans O. Schmitt, "Foreign Capital and Social Conflict in Indonesia, 1950-1958," in Robert I. Rhodes, ed., *Imperialism* and *Underdevelopment* (New York and London: Monthly Review Press, 1970), pp. 268-80.

conflict. Although the specific mechanisms adopted varied, the various foreign exchange allocation systems in force from 1950 to 1957 tended to favor importers and consumers, largely Java-based, over producers and exporters, located primarily in Sumatra, but also in Kalimantan and Sulawesi. The tendency of Indonesian governments to maintain an overvalued exchange rate resulted in a discrepancy of about 300 percent between the official and unofficial value of the rupiah. The individual producers of export crops, who were paid at the official rate, thus received only one-third as much as they would have from direct barter trade. The consequent financial incentive to engage in such direct trade does much to explain the prevalence of smuggling in the export areas of the Outer Islands.[15]

Many in the regions justified smuggling not only in terms of the specific inequities of government foreign exchange mechanisms, but as a means of providing revenue for development projects. The central government was criticized for absorbing revenue from the regions without making an appropriate contribution in return to the financial needs of the outlying areas. The tendency to base expenditure on population worked to the advantage of Java, but it was in the Outer Islands that the infrastructure of road and rail transport was most lacking.

If Jakarta were unwilling—or unable—to carry out development projects in the regions, there were regional leaders who were prepared to do so themselves. Military officers in several regions had demonstrated since 1954 the possibilities of obtaining local revenues through sponsorship of barter trade. Their civilian counterparts argued for provincial autonomy as a means of putting both revenue and development planning under local control.

Regional Autonomy

The demand for regional autonomy was closely related to the demand for a more equitable sharing of the revenue from Outer Island exports.

---

15 J. D. Legge, *Central Authority and Regional Autonomy in Indonesia* (Ithaca, N.Y.: Cornell University Press, 1961), pp. 235-45; Mackie, "Political Power," pp. 200-204; W. M. Corden and J. A. C. Mackie, "The Development of the Indonesian Exchange Rate System," *The Malayan Economic Review*, VIII/1 (April 1962), pp. 37-60.

Increased autonomy for the regions was also seen as a way out of the dilemma posed by the weakness of the central government, and the loss of confidence in the parliamentary system.

The structure of local government had been a matter of debate from the early days of the Republic, but no unified system existed, even on paper, until the proclamation of Law 1 of 1957. There was general opposition to a federal form of government, for federalism was too closely identified with Dutch divide-and-rule tactics, exemplified by their creation in 1946-49 of various "states" to counterbalance the revolutionary Republic. The question was more the degree of autonomy—control over local decisions and finances—which might be extended to provinces and other organs of local government within a unitary system.

The design of the system was complicated by the attempt to accommodate within it both governmental administration and representation of local desires and interests. In any case, the passage of the law came too late—and was seen as conceding too little—to affect the swelling tide of regional discontent. Because of the proclamation of martial law in March 1957 it was never really implemented, and in 1959 it was suspended by presidential edict.[16]

The Military Dimension

Demands for greater regional autonomy can be seen as proposals to make government more effective—from the point of view of the regions. They were not an attack on the system of parliamentary democracy itself, although distaste for the bickering politicians of Jakarta was widely felt throughout the country.

The most direct and effective attacks on liberal democracy came principally from two sources, President Sukarno and the army. The army's attack on the parties and the parliamentary system arose from general military distrust and dislike of politicians, and scorn for the weakness and ineffectiveness of the civilian government. However, the army had

---

16 See Legge, *Central Authority*, for a discussion of the law, and of the various attempts to combine administration and representation in a local government system in Indonesia. See also, Gerald S. Maryanov, *Decentralization in Indonesia as a Political Problem*, Cornell Modern Indonesia Project Interim Report (Ithaca, N.Y.: Cornell University, 1958).

its own problems of personal rivalries, ideological divisions, and center-region tensions, which in many respects corresponded with the divisions among civilian politicians, but in certain respects also cut across them.

The army had sprung up during the revolution, essentially independent of either a central military command structure or the civilian government. The men who formed the army came from a variety of backgrounds: some had been members of the pre-war Dutch colonial army, the KNIL (Koninklijk Nederlands Indisch Leger—Royal Netherlands Indies Army); some had received military training during the Japanese occupation in the PETA (Pembela Tanar Air—Fatherland Defense Force) or other paramilitary organizations; some were town and village youths who spontaneously formed militia units to fight against the return of the Dutch.[17]

Differences of opinion within the army tended to reflect these varying backgrounds, particularly on such questions as the character of the army as a guerrilla or professional force, the relative emphasis to be given revolutionary spirit and technical qualifications in career appointments, and relations with the civilian government and political parties. In general, those officers whose initial military experience had been in the KNIL favored a professional army with high technical qualifications for its members, and had close relationships with the Western-educated intellectuals and technocrats of the PSI. Members of youth militia believed guerrilla warfare more appropriate to Indonesia's circumstances, emphasized the importance of revolutionary spirit and closeness to the people, and often had close ties with either Islamic or leftist political parties. Although most members of the PETA group sided with the ex-KNIL in favoring a technically well-qualified professional army, the group as a whole was hostile to all political influence in the army. It was a combination of PETA and KNIL groups which dominated the army leadership. Although the KNIL was drawn from a number of regions, the PETA had existed only in Java, and as it was essentially there that the revolution was fought, the army officer corps had a distinctly Javanese flavor.

---

17 On the origins of the Indonesian army see Benedict R. O'G. Anderson, *Java in a Time of Revolution* (Ithaca, N.Y. and London: Cornell University Press, 1972), especially pp. 232-68.

Personal rivalries within the army stemmed in part from the fact that it was composed of young men of approximately the same age and with similar claims to leadership positions. The weakness of the central command structure made it difficult to assert hierarchical authority. Close ties often existed between officers and the men under their command, in what is often termed a *bapak-anak buah*[18] relationship. During the revolution the men in a military unit had frequently designated their own commander, and took care to select someone who would protect their interests. The localized basis of recruitment, and sensitivity to the desire to have a "native son" (*anak daerah*) in command of local troops, also served as a constraint on the development and implementation of a national personnel policy. Selection of top officers had of necessity involved negotiation and compromise, and officers in regional commands often came to exercise considerable de facto autonomy. Symbolic of the powerful position of the commanders of the seven military regions (*Tentara Territorium*) into which Indonesia was divided, was the use of the old Malay military title Panglima to refer to them; this had been the designation of the revered General Sudirman, commander-in-chief of the army during the revolution, and implied a high degree of independent authority within their sphere.[19]

Military-Civilian Relations

Relations between the military and the civilian government had always been somewhat uneasy, and as general disillusionment with parliamentary democracy spread, some army officers advocated a return to the central political role they felt they had abandoned at the end of the revolution. In fact, the army had always exerted considerable political influence, and had played a significant role in the demise of several pre-election cabinets. In the Outer Islands, where the civilian bureaucracy was less entrenched and less powerful than in Java, the army under local "bapakist" commanders

---

18 *Bapak*—father, but also has connotation of respected leader, or patron; *anak buah*—follower. On this relationship see Anderson, *Java*, p. 43.
19 On the connotations of the title, "Panglima," Anderson comments: "It is interesting that while all other offices in the national army were given Western-derived names, the topmost one was thus endowed with the aura of ancient glory." Anderson, *Java*, p. 244.

had been an important instrument of governance and symbol of national unity.

The army, which tended to view itself as the creator and guardian of the state, resisted the imposition of civilian control over the military. Civilian politicans were believed to represent narrow partisan interests, and their bickering—in or out of government—was seen by many army officers as detrimental to national unity. Further, the exertion of political influence on the army was seen as detrimental to army unity.

However, as noted above, the army was not monolithic, and there were serious divisions within it on questions of the nature of the army and its political role. These divisions had shattered the army in the wake of the October 17, 1952 affair, an attempt by senior officers under the leadership of Army Chief of Staff, Colonel Abdul Haris Nasution, to force President Sukarno to dissolve parliament over the question of a parliamentary inquiry into army reorganization and retirement policies. This affair, with its repercussions in East Java, East Indonesia, and South Sumatra, where officers loyal to Sukarno ousted commanders loyal to Nasution, was in many respects a precursor of the regional crisis of 1956, in which rivalries within the army were a crucial factor in precipitating rebellion.[20]

Nasution lost his position as chief of staff in the aftermath of the October 17 affair, and the splits in the army left it weak and vulnerable to political manipulation and civilian control. However, at a meeting in Jogjakarta in February 1955, the army symbolically healed its divisions on the basis of a closing of ranks against ouside political influence. The resolutions of the conference, known collectively as the Jogja Charter, stressed that military appointments should be based solely on professional ability, and prohibited members of the armed forces from taking an active part in politics. The army's continuing hostility to Parliament was indicated by the statement that it would "obey all decisions taken by the Government together with the Dwitunggal (Sukarno-Hatta)."[21]

The power of the reunified army was demonstrated in June and July 1955 when its refusal to accept the government's appointee as army chief of staff brought down the cabinet of Prime Minister Ali Sastroamidjojo.

---

20 On the October 17, 1952 affair see Feith, *Decline*, pp. 246-73.
21 Feith, *Decline*, pp. 397-98. The text of the Charter, and reports of the discussions of the meeting are in Darius Marpaung, ed., *Almanak Angkatan Perang* (Jakarta: Upeni, 1956), pp. 56-69.

In October 1955, Nasution was reappointed chief of staff of the army as a compromise candidate. He was now prepared to cooperate with President Sukarno, and with his backing set out to strengthen headquarters control over the military hierarchy.

The defeated contenders for the post of chief of staff, Colonel Maludin Simbolon, commander of TT-I/North Sumatra, and Colonel Zulkifli Lubis, deputy chief of staff, led the opposition in 1955-56 to Nasution's centralizing policies, and to his willingness to work with the civilian authorities. Lubis was a vocal critic of the politicians, and an advocate of a larger role for the army in government; he was also involved in various intrigues within the army. Simbolon, one of the most senior officers in the army, was a prime symbol of regional defiance of the center for his sponsorship in May-June 1956 of large-scale smuggling in Sumatra, ostensibly to provide needed funds for troop welfare. Rivals in 1955, Lubis and Simbolon became allies in the course of the following year. The terms of that alliance had more to do with internal army politics than with the nature of the political system and the position of the army in it. It is to the military politics of center-region relationships that we will now turn.

Center-Region Relations in the Army

In the years 1952-55, the army central command was in a weak position not only vis-a-vis the civilian governments, but in relation to a number of its own territorial commanders. No major transfers took place during this period, and as a result, several of the regional commanders were firmly entrenched in their positions and operated from virtually autonomous power bases. In the post-Korean War budgetary squeeze they had been unofficially encouraged to use their own initiative to raise funds, both for routine requirements and to carry out operations against still significant rebellions in several areas. Barter trade, as the officers involved preferred to call it, of local products was resorted to, notably in Sumatra and Sulawesi. However, the scale of this smuggling was embarrassing to army headquarters when it came to light, for the army was in the habit of attacking the politicians for their corrupt behavior.

In October 1954, the commander of East Indonesia (TT-VII), Colonel J. F. Warouw, was called into court for having sponsored smuggling of copra from Sulawesi. Although he remained as panglima, several officers were transferred to non-active status, reportedly as a concession to the displeasure of the civilian leadership. Smuggling continued, however. According to the officers involved, it was necessary because they did not receive sufficient funds through official channels for either maintenance or operations. As professional military men they were in a difficult position: their careers depended on their success in subduing rebellions against the central government, to carry out operations against the rebels they had to raise funds themselves, but in their ad hoc fund-raising enterprises they were subject to censure for illegal action.

Nonetheless, control of their own finances gave the regional commanders considerable independence from army headquarters. Nasution, when he resumed his position as army chief of staff in October 1955, was determined to limit this independence, and to bring the territorial commanders under the control of the central command. He embarked on a program of territorial reorganization, transfer of regional commanders, strengthening of centrally controlled educational and training programs, and establishing a strike force at army headquarters.[22] He also proposed the "creation of separate budgets for security restoration in the regions,"[23] which would eliminate one of the pretexts for smuggling, and curb the financial independence of the panglimas.

Army reorganization involved literally cutting the regional commands down to size. Instead of seven large territorial commands (TT—Tentara Territorium), a number of smaller ones, Komando Daerah Militer (KDM—Military Area Command), were to be established. This plan would meet the demands of a number of areas—South Sulawesi the most insistent among them—for separate military status, and would at the same time lessen the power of the individual territorial commanders by reducing the number of troops at their disposal and the size of the areas under their control. Reorganization, however, was a long-range plan, and could only be instituted after the power of the existing panglimas had been broken.

Thus, the immediate step in Nasution's centralizing effort was to institute a "tour-of-duty" policy under which territorial commanders

---

22 Ruth T. McVey, "The Post-Revolutionary Transformation of the Indonesian Army," part 2, *Indonesia*, 13 (April 1972), pp. 154-75, esp. pp. 166-68, 171-73.
23 *PIA*, July 12, 1956 (A.M.), p. 1.

would be subject to regular transfers. This would inhibit the building up of local power bases in the regions, and could also be used to transfer officers whose involvement in smuggling caused not only embarrassment but a loss of revenue to the central government. When the planned transfers were announced it was clear that they were also directed toward weakening the powerful positions of Lubis and Simbolon. Simbolon, and his ally Colonel Alex Kaliwarang, commander of TT-III/ Siliwangi (West Java), were both scheduled to be transferred, as was Colonel Warouw of East Indonesia. Lubis was to replace Simbolon in Medan, headquarters of TT-I, far from his supporters in Jakarta and Bandung. There was resistance on the part of the officers involved, but after a series of alarms and maneuvers in which Lubis played a key role, both Kawilarang and Warouw handed over their commands in August 1956, and took up positions as military attache, Kawilarang in Washington, D.C., and Warouw in Peking. For his part in the attempt to block the transfers, Lubis was removed from his position as deputy chief of staff. He then tried to stage a coup against Nasution, and when that failed and a warrant was issued for his arrest, he went into hiding.[24]

His failures made those officers who had also opposed increasing centralization of army power realize the precariousness of their position, for they might be identified as followers of Lubis, and be purged with him. Thus at the anniversary reunion of the Army Staff and Command School (SSKAD) in Bandung on November 21, 1956, although the failings of the state and the armed forces were discussed, and changes were called for in the army leadership, the primary stress was on the necessity for unity within the army. Aware of their own weakness, and the need to protect themselves and their positions, the officers present invoked the Jogja Charter and the principle of the collegial responsibility of the officer corps to determine army policy and leadership. They shunted the burden of opposition to Nasution to the officers best able to resist—the panglimas in the Outer Islands. In Ruth McVey's words:

> It was because the game was up at the center that the focus of

---

24 This account is based largely on that in McVey, "Transformation," part 1, *Indonesia*, 11 (April 1971), pp. 158-73.

action in the struggle for control of the army now began to move away from Djakarta. In the Outer Islands, powerful panglima were still capable of resisting the high command's claims, and the course of events in the Lubis Affair convinced them that Nasution would not stop short of breaking their power. Moreover, it showed them that if they were going to resist they would have to do so credibly—to threaten, and be willing to carry out, a break with Djakarta.[25]

Simbolon was a key figure in the resistance to Nasution, a resistance which was at the heart of the regional crisis, and which was carried to the point of breaking with Jakarta in February 1958. Simbolon was present for the opening of a reunion of the Central Sumatra Banteng Division held in Padang, West Sumatra, November 20-24, 1956. A Banteng Council, headed by the commander of the Fourth Regiment, stationed in West Sumatra, Lieutenant Colonel Ahmad Husein, was established to urge the implementation of the meeting's call for "progressive and radical improvements" in the leadership of the army and the state. This was the first of the locally established councils which characterized this phase of the regional struggle.[26] Simbolon, Husein, and Lieutenant Colonel Barlian, the acting commander of TT-II/South Sumatra, who was also present at the Banteng reunion, acted within a few days of each other in the period December 20-24 to assume power in Central, North, and South Sumatra. Army Chief of Staff Nasution quickly staged a counter-coup against Simbolon, but Husein and Barlian had stronger local support, and Nasution negotiated with the two more junior officers for more than a year before the regional crisis erupted into civil war.[27]

---

25 McVey, "Transformation," part 1, p. 173. Nasution also says that it was because efforts against him in Jakarta and Bandung failed, that the action moved to the regions; this is quite explicit in "Djawaban tertulis Djenderal A. H. Nasution untuk (penulisan buku) H. P. Jones" (Mimeo: A-72/MPRS/III/69), p. 6, but is also implied in a Nasution speech reported in *Madjalah Angkatan Darat*, 1 (January 1958), p. 6.
26 There were reports in January 1957 of regional councils being formed in Sulawesi, a Dewan Hasanuddin in South Sulawesi [PIA, January 22, 1957 (A.M.), p. 28]; and a Dewan Manguni in Minahasa [Indonesia, Angkatan Darat, Staf Umum I, PRRI, Vol. I (Jakarta, 1962), p. 148]. Neither seems to have actually functioned, although they were both mentioned in Husein's announcement of a planned joint meeting of "revolutionary councils" in February 1957 [PIA, February 11, 1957 (P.M.), p. 1].
27 Feith, *Decline*, pp. 523-32; John R. W. Smail, "The Military Politics of North Sumatra: December 1956-October 1957," *Indonesia*, 6 (October 1968), pp. 128-87.

Civilian Critics of Parliamentary Democracy: The Dwitunggal

Important as were these dramatic events within the military in putting pressure on the government and precipitating the regional crisis, of equal significance were the actions and proposals of the civilian critics of liberal democracy. Foremost among these critics were President Sukarno and Vice President Mohammad Hatta, the Dwitunggal, the "two in one," who had led Indonesia since they together signed the declaration of independence on August 17, 1945. The parliamentary system established in the provisional constitution of 1950, when the Dutch-created federal republic was replaced by a unitary one, gave little scope to either president or vice president, and neither was satisfied to be a mere figurehead or symbol. Both were critical of parliamentary democracy and of the political parties, although the remedies they proposed were as different as their contrasting natures.

Hatta accused the parties of promoting their own interests at the expense of the people, and blamed them for much of the current disorder.[28] Sukarno criticized the parties for serving the personal interests of their leaders, and described their proliferation as a "disease." Throughout his life Sukarno spoke of the need for unity among contending groups in Indonesia; his 1926 appeal to the nationalist, Islamic, and Marxist groups to cooperate in the interests of a free Indonesia was a theme to which he often returned.[29] Democracy in Indonesia should rest on consultation and consensus, not as in the liberal democracies of the West on divisive debate and majority votes. Even before the 1955 elections the President had spoken of the need for leadership and guidance in Indonesian democracy, and this was a point to which he referred frequently in 1956. In October of that year he called for the burying of all political parties and the institution of a system of guided democracy. He did not at that time spell out the details of his plan (*konsepsi*), but promised to reveal it if party leaders did not come up with a proposal of their own.[30]

---

28 Mohammad Hatta, *Past and Future*, Cornell Modern Indonesia Project Translation (Ithaca, N.Y.: Cornell University, 1960), esp. pp. 12-13.
29 Soekarno, *Nationalism, Islam, and Marxism*, Cornell Modern Indonesia Project Translation (Ithaca, N.Y.: Cornell University, 1969); see also J. D. Legge, *Sukarno: A Political Biography* (New York: Praeger, 1972), pp. 340-42, 348-49.
30 Feith, *Decline*, pp. 514-18.

The emphasis on reviving Indonesia's traditions of consultation and consensus was shared by Sukarno and Hatta. However, Sukarno envisaged these procedures as applying in the deliberations of the national parliament, while Hatta saw them as being appropriate to vil-lage society. Hatta advocated the development of cooperatives and the granting of wide autonomy to units of local government as a means of implementing these principles. This difference in perspective was fundamental: Hatta, in building a government or a nationalist movement, emphasized patient building from the bottom up; Sukarno relied on inspired leadership from above to rouse the masses to the task at hand and to create a national consensus.

The differences between the two men encompassed perspective, substance, and style. Hatta was a Minangkabau of Sumatra, a Dutch-educated economist, pragmatic, policy-oriented, a good administrator. Sukarno described him as "careful, unemotional, pedantic," and "quite inflexible"; a man who dove "straight to the heart of the matter without preliminary pleasantries."[31] Preliminary pleasantries were part of the elaborate etiquette which defined a civilized man in the Javanese tradition, a tradition of which Sukarno was very much a part. Sukarno was romantic and emotional, vain and egotistic, an impractical dreamer. Yet it was the flexible Sukarno rather than the practical Hatta who had a keener sense of political timing and the limits to maneuver, and who survived longer as a political force.

During the national revolution Sukarno's dynamism and Hatta's determination had been joined in the struggle for independence. Their union, as the Dwitunggal, was symbolic of the unity of Indonesia, of the bringing together of Java and Sabrang in the new Republic. As that unity came under threat from the rising tide of regional and ethnic discontent, the symbol of the Dwitunggal took on increasing importance, and there were many who looked to renewed cooperation between Sukarno and Hatta as a way out of the national crisis. However, the two men had grown apart, and in July 1956 Hatta announced his intention of resigning from the vice presidency. He was not prepared to continue in a position

---

31 *Sukarno: An Autobiography*, as told to Cindy Adams (Indianapolis: Bobbs-Merrill, 1965), pp. 117-18.

where he had no power to affect government policy, but might be held responsible for it. He would not, he said, be "the prisoner of other men's policies."[32]

On December 1, 1956, Hatta submitted his resignation. He was a symbol of responsible administration and rational economic planning, and to those in the regions concerned about economic development and regional autonomy, this was a disturbing sign. Following the military coups in Sumatra in mid-December, opposition to the cabinet of Ali Sastroamidjojo grew, and voices were heard, Masjumi's among them, calling for its replacement by a Hatta-led cabinet. To dramatize their belief that a new cabinet should be formed which would be capable of working out a solution to the burgeoning regional crisis, the five Masjumi members of the cabinet resigned on January 9, 1957.[33] The withdrawal of the party with the greatest strength in the Outer Islands was seen as a further diminution of regional influence in the national government.

Sukarno then took the political initiative by revealing, as he had promised the previous October, the details of his plan for dealing with the malaise gripping the country. In a speech on February 21, 1957, he outlined his konsepsi. There were two main elements. First, the cabinet was to be based on all four major parties: the PNI, Masjumi, NU, and—for the first time—the PKI. Second, a presidentially appointed National Council (Dewan Nasional), composed of representatives of regions and functional groups, was to be established to advise the cabinet.[34]

The enunciation of the konsepsi was the first step in the process of Sukarno's assumption of a more active political role, which culminated in July 1959 in the return to the 1945 constitution and the official inauguration of Guided Democracy. The konsepsi also laid the foundations for the more active role of Sukarno's partners in Guided Democracy—the army and the PKI. The proposal that the PKI be included in the cabinet was an attempt to accommodate the increasingly powerful communist party within the institutions of government. The proposal that the National Council be based on functional groupings provided a means for the

---
32 In an interview with the American journalist Louis Fischer, reported in his *Story of Indonesia* (New York: Harper & Row, 1959), p. 287.
33 Feith, *Decline*, pp. 533-34.
34 Feith, *Decline*, pp. 538-42; Legge, *Sukarno*, pp. 282-285.

direct participation of military representatives in the civilian organs of government.

The reaction to the President's konsepsi in the regions was critical. The National Council was no substitute for a Senate based on territorial representation, and the proposed inclusion of the PKI in the cabinet met fierce hostility.

The initiative now shifted back to the regional leaders. As the next step was taken in East Indonesia, it is to that region that we will now turn our attention.

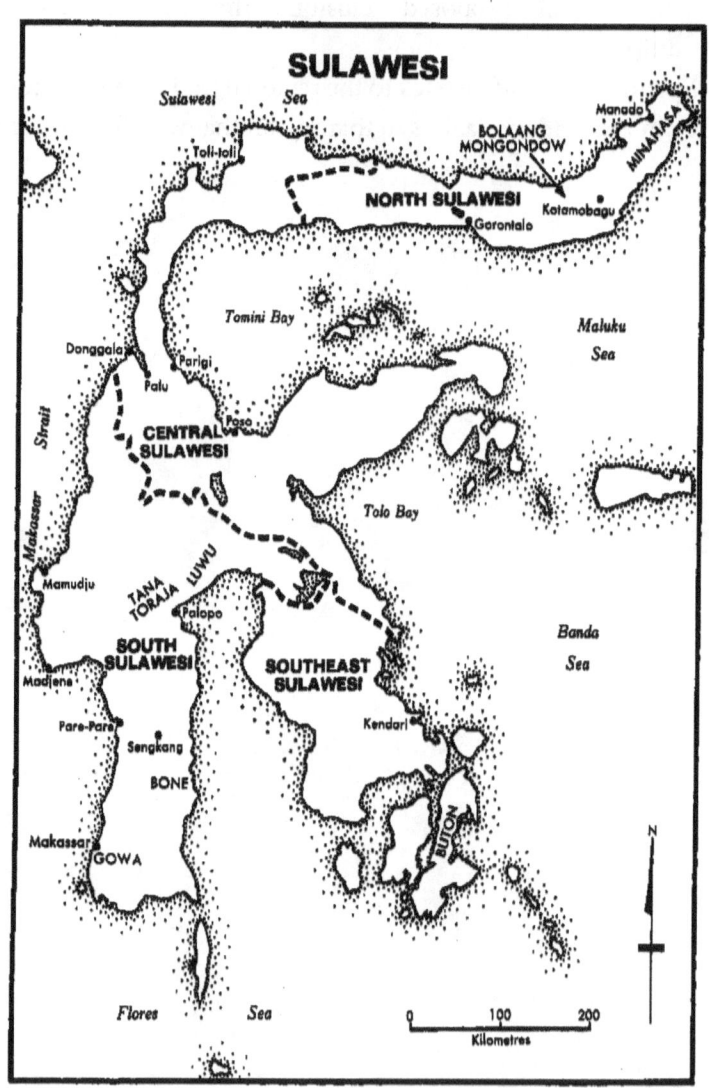

MAP II

CHAPTER TWO
THE REGIONAL CONTEXT: SULAWESI

East Indonesia, the site of the next move in the regional crisis, is an area of great cultural and ethnic diversity (see Table 1). In 1956 it contained three functioning administrative provinces—Sulawesi, Maluku, and Nusa Tenggara; plus West Irian, which was still under the control of the Dutch. The entire area comprised a single military territorial command, TT-VII/Wirabuana, with headquarters at Makassar, South Sulawesi. There were four infantry regiments within the command, all with territorial as well as operational responsibility: RI-23, based in Pare-Pare, South Sulawesi; RI-24, based in Manado, North Sulawesi; RI-25, based in Ambon, South Maluku; and RI-26, based in Den Pasar, Bali, Nusa Tenggara.

Both within and between these civilian and military administrative units there were rivalries and tensions which made intraregional relations as important in the political dynamics of the area as relations between East Indonesia and Jakarta. Indeed, it is an oversimplification to consider East Indonesia as a unified region in either the civilian or the military sphere.

It was, however, in the name of East Indonesia that the challenge to the central government which came to be known as Permesta, was formally issued in March 2, 1957, in Makassar. The heartland of Permesta was in Sulawesi: in Makassar where the planning for the proclamation was centered, and in Minahasa at the northern tip of the island where within a year people prepared to fight the central government under the banner of Permesta.

It is, then, to Sulawesi that we will turn, to consider briefly the social and political history of the island, and the rivalry between the principal contenders for regional influence—the Buginese/Makassarese of the South, and the Minahasans of the North.

Sulawesi

The island of Sulawesi is almost as diverse as the region of East Indonesia of which it is a part (see Table 2). Prior to the arrival of the Dutch in the early seventeenth century, the island had contained a large number of small kingdoms and tribal groupings. Dutch rule was first exerted in the area around Makassar in the south following the defeat of the kingdom of Gowa in 1667. Gorontalo and Minahasa in the northern peninsula, and the Sanghe Islands offshore were brought under Dutch control through treaties of friendship signed between 1677 and 1679. It was only in the first decades of the twentieth century that much of the rest of the island, including the greater part of the populous southwestern peninsula, was effectively incorporated into the Netherlands East Indies. Sulawesi was then divided into two adminis tratively distinct units: the Government (in 1938 Residency) of Cele-bes and Dependencies in the south and southeast, and the Residency of Manado in the north and part of the center (see Map 2).

During the colonial period Minahasa came under strong Dutch influence as a directly ruled area. The population was by 1930 more than 90 percent Christian,[1] and Minahasans were strongly represented in the colonial civil and military services. In 1930 the Residency of Manado had the highest student-to-population ratio, and the highest literacy rate, in the Netherlands East Indies (NEI).[2] It was the existence of a large number of private schools, both vernacular and Dutch-medium, many of them mission-run, which gave Minahasa its educational advantage over other parts of Sulawesi (see Table 3). The importance of the private, particularly church, schools is clear in a comparison of literacy rates in the predominantly Christian areas of Minahasa and Sangihe-Talaud, with those in the predominantly Islamic area of Gorontalo, the Central Sulawesi districts of Poso and Donggala, and the entire Residency of Celebes and Dependencies (see Table 4).

---

1 According to the 1930 census, Minahasans were 90.9 percent Protestant and 5.8 percent Roman Catholic. *Volkstelling 1930*, Vol. V, pp. 91-92.
2 Dutch East Indies, Hollandsch-Inlandsch Onderwijs Commissie, No. 7, *De Geografische Verspreiding van het Onderwijs in Nederlandsch-Indie en de nog Wachtende Taak op Onderwijsgebied* (Weltevreden; G. Kolff, 1930), p. 54; Dutch East Indies, *Algemeen Verslag van het Onderwijs in Nederlandsch-Indie*, 1936-37, part 1, p. 71.

No strong local aristocracy had ever developed in Minahasa. The district was granted a local council in 1919, one of the first non-municipal councils to be approved by the NEI government. Its political heritage, thus, was colonial democracy rather than indigenous feudalism.

Table 1
Population—East Indonesia

	1930		1961
	Indonesians	Total	Total
North ξ Central Sulawesi	1,110,386	1,138,655	2,003,211
(Residency of Manado)			
Sangihe-Talaud	155,709	158,729	194,253
Minahasa/Manado	365,204	379,753	581,836
Bolaang-Mongondow[a]			150,217
Gorontalo	183,056	186,038	383,748
Donggala	169,058	172,713	373,075
Poso	237,359	241,422	320,082
South ξ Southeast Sulawesi	3,063,217	3,093,251	5,076,138
(Celebes ξ Dependencies)			
Southeast Sulawesi	399,239	400,401	559,594
Bali	1,092,037	1,101,393	1,782,529
West Nusatenggara	-	-	1,807,830
Lombok	696,806	701,290	1,300,234
Sumbawa	311,287	314,843	507,596
East Nusatenggara	-	-	1,967,297
Sumba	181,593	182,326	251,126
Flores	715,244	717,300	901,772
Timor ξ Islands	437,977	442,907	814,399
North Maluku (Ternate)	486,803	492,758	238,966
South Maluku (Ambon)	389,325	400,642	-
Central Maluku (Ambon)	-	-	352,070
Southeast Maluku	-	-	198,498

[a]Included in district of Manado in 1930.

Dutch East Indies, Departemen van Economische Zaken, *Volkstelling 1930*, Vol V (Batavia: Landsdrukkerij, 1936), pp. 121-24; Indonesia, Biro Pusat Statistik, *Sensus Penduduk 1961 Republik Indonesia: Angka² Sementara* (Jakarta, 1963), pp. 12-13.

Table 2
Major Ethnic Groups in Indonesian Population of Sulawesi—1930

	Sangirese & Talaudans	Minahasans	Bolaang-Mongondow	Gorontalese	Banggai group	Tominiers	Toraja
Residency of Manado	183,563	254,947	63,724	222,989	80,363	29,064	184,685
Sangihe-Talaud	154,905	473	21	68	-	-	17
Manado	27,089	250,094	62,522	14,003	68	44	310
Gorontalo	246	1,241	295	178,138	4	-	74
Donggala	612	1,136	667	20,716	8	9,532	113,317
Poso	711	2,003	219	9,998	80,280	19,488	70,967
Celebes & Dependencies	226	1,823	-	-	-	-	372,823
Makassar	132	896	-	-	-	-	429
Bonthain	-	-	-	-	-	-	144
Bone	-	-	-	-	-	-	4,094
Pare-Pare	-	142	-	-	-	-	12,147
Mandar	-	169	-	-	-	-	60,765
Luwu	-	352	-	-	-	-	293,923
Buton & Laiwui (Southeast)	-	154	-	-	-	-	1,321

	Buginnese	Makassarese	Mandarese	Salayerese	Tolaki	Butonese	Bajo	Javanese ξ Madurese
Residency of Manado	29,046	1,630	1,571	189	1,360	3,909	9,096	8,389
Sangihe-Talaud	-	-	-	-	-	-	-	33
Manado	1,380	339	-	-	-	380	34	5,430
Gorontalo	953	-	-	-	-	-	167	1,449
Donggala	16,791	625	1,136	104	-	-	2,323	905
Poso	9,858	623	403	38	1,359	3,507	6,572	572
Celebes ξ Dependencies	1,384,671	630,144	175,271	67,510	101,259	300,301	9,147	7,762
Makassar	142,718	487,012	6,262	2,265	38	634	1,253	5,014
Bonthain	137,974	139,825	61	64,895	69	5,959	1,658	420
Bone	643,928	370	29	17	55	159	443	421
Pare-Pare	351,794	1,413	569	19	2	17	9	655
Mandar	15,644	520	168,244	16	-	21	5	501
Luwu	73,824	377	86	54	24,646	56	196	402
Buton ξ Laiwui (Southeast)	18,789	627	20	244	76,449	293,455	5,583	604

Volkstelling 1930, Vol. V, pp. 163-70.

Table 3
Education—Sulawesi—1928

	Public Schools				Private Schools				Total
	Number of Schools	Pupils			Number of Schools	Pupils			
		European	Indonesian	Foreign Asian		European	Indonesian	Foreign Asian	
Residency of Manado									
Vernacular primary education	345		38,030		546		38,323		76,353
Dutch primary education	14[a]	388	1,826	635	30[b]	105	3,081	620	6,655
Celebes & Dependencies									
Vernacular primary education	515		31,141		91		5,236		36,377
Dutch primary education	14[c]	341	1,491	580	3[d]	115	82		2,609

[a] 10 in Manado/Minahasa, 4 in Gorontalo
[b] 20 in Minahasa, 3 in Gorontalo, 2 in Sangihe-Talaud, 1 in Bolaang-Mongondow, 1 in Poso, 3 unidentified.
[c] 9 in Makassar.
[d] All in Makassar.
Algemeen Verslag Onderwijs, 1928, part 1, pp. 161 ff.; part 2, pp. 22-27, 30-31, 38-39.

South Sulawesi, on the other hand, with the exception of the city of Makassar, had been lightly touched by Dutch influence. The proportion of students to population in South Sulawesi in 1936-37 was one in fifty-five, compared to a ratio of one in nineteen in the Residency of Manado.[3] Although there was an expansion of Western-type education during the period of Dutch rule, few private schools were established in South Sulawesi, and Dutch language education was much less available there than in Minahasa. Literacy rates in South Sulawesi in 1930 were among the lowest in the Netherlands East Indies.

The Buginese and Makassarese population of South Sulawesi was overwhelmingly Islamic, and during the 1930s a network of schools and organizations sponsored by the modernist Islamic movement, Muhammadiyah, spread throughout the area.

The local aristocracy retained much of its traditional prestige, influence, and wealth, in both the directly and the indirectly ruled areas. It had in general escaped the onus of collaboration with the colonial regime, for the power of that government was largely exercised through the civil service, and it was the Minahasans and Ambonese whose Dutch language education qualified them for positions in the administrative hierarchy.

Table 4
Literacy—Indonesian Population of Sulawesi—1930

	Total Literates						Literate in Dutch					
	Total		Males		Females		Total		Males		Females	
	Number	%	Number	%	Number	%	Number	%	Number	%	Number	%
Residency of Manado	243,361	21.91	147,649	26.41	95,612	17.34	10,805	.97	6,181	1.11	4,624	.84
Sangihe-Talaud	54,410	34.94	30,758	39.84	23,652	30.13	1,038	.67	594	.77	444	.57
Manado[a]	142,312	38.97	80,796	43.84	61,516	34.01	8,396	2.30	4,637	2.52	3,759	2.08
Gorontalo	14,133	7.72	10,217	11.49	3,916	4.16	776	.42	528	.59	248	.26
Donggala	10,969	6.49	9,400	11.09	10,969	1.86	210	.12	149	.18	61	.07
Poso	21,437	9.03	16,478	13.30	4,959	4.37	385	.16	273	.22	112	.10

---

3 *Algemeen Verslag Onderwijs*, 1936-37, part 1, p. 71.

Celebes & Dependencies	128,321	4.19	109,603	7.29	18,718	1.20	3,398	.11	2,744	.18	654	.04
Makassar	30,020	4.61	26,675	8.17	3,345	1.03	1,843	.28	1,430	.44	413	.13
Bonthain	17,155	4.88	15,158	8.78	1,997	1.11	249	.07	217	.13	32	.02
Bone	28,615	4.40	23,300	7.37	5,315	1.59	511	.08	488	.14	63	.02
Pare-Pare	15,105	4.11	13,038	7.25	2,067	1.10	223	.06	184	.10	39	.02
Mandar	11,175	4.50	9,811	7.96	1,364	1.09	101	.04	79	.06	22	.02
Luwu	18,480	4.68	14,656	7.41	3,824	1.94	274	.07	217	.11	57	.03
Buton-Laiwui (Southeast)	7,771	1.95	6,965	3.71	806	.38	197	.05	169	.09	28	.01

^aIncludes Minahasa and Bolong-Mongondow.
Volkstelling 1930, Vol. v, pp. 201-8.

The rather sparsely populated interior of the island, home of the Toraja people, was split in the colonial period between the two Sulawesi residencies. In the late nineteenth and early twentieth centuries the Toraja were the subjects of an active Christian missionary effort, in which Minahasan Protestants participated as teachers in mission schools.

Southeastern Sulawesi, with the exception of the island of Buton, was an area of largely uninhabited jungle. Its political significance was negligible.

Economically Sulawesi was dependent on copra. It has been estimated that copra provided the major source of income for 70 percent of the population of Sulawesi (and East Indonesia) in the early 1950s.[4] Forced planting of coconut palms began some time after the turn of the century. The producers were virtually all (95 percent) small holders, with an

---

4 Boyd R. Compton, "The Fall of the Copra Foundation,"*Institute of Current World Affairs Newsletter,* BRC/44 (June 16, 1956), p. 5. A similar estimate is given by Major John Rahasia in "Masalah Kopra," *Gaja Pergolakan,* 2/10 (June 30, 1956).

average yearly production of one ton of copra.⁵ By 1920 copra was the most valuable export crop in both North and South Sulawesi, and by 1939, copra accounted for 86 percent of total exports from Manado and 57 percent of Makassar's exports. (See Tables 5 and 6 for production and export figures.)

South Sulawesi was much less a one-crop economy than was the North, for it produced an estimated annual surplus of 60,000 to 70,000 tons of rice for export to other parts of the archipelago. However, a rebellion broke out in South Sulawesi in 1950, and by 1955 controlled so much of the interior that the government was unable to purchase any rice at all.⁶

Sulawesi: Civilian Administration and Political Relationships

The island of Sulawesi was first effectively constituted as a single administrative unit in 1950. As noted above, during the colonial period it had been divided into two residencies. During the Japanese occupation, 1942-45, a single Celebes Civil Administration Department was established, with headquarters at Makassar, and a branch office at Manado.⁷ However, because of the brief duration of the occupation and

---

5 Karl J. Pelzer, "The Agricultural Foundation," in McVey, *Indonesia*, pp. 120, 150. According to Pelzer, one hectare of swidden land is usually planted with 100 to 120 coconut palms, yielding 1,000 to 1,200 kilograms (one ton) of copra a year. The estimate of average yearly production as one ton is from a memorandum written by J. M. J. Pantouw, January 27, 1969, p. 6.
6 The following figures on government purchases of rice in Sulawesi are illustrative:

	Planned (tons)	Results	
		tons	% of plan
1953	60,000	56,701	94.5
1954	60,000	35,300	58.8
1955	60,000	--	--
1956	30,000	--	--

Bank Indonesia, *Report for the Year*, 1953-54, p. 99; 1954-55, p. 113; 1955-56, p. 119; 1956-57, p. 133.

7 "Outline of the Conduct of Military Administration in Occupied Areas," March 14, 1942, in Harry J. Benda, James K. Irikura, and Koichi Kishi, eds., *Japanese Military Administration in Indonesia: Selected Documents*, Southeast Asia Studies, Translation Series, no. 6 (New Haven, Conn.: Yale University, 1965), pp. 27-28.

the exigencies of war, an integrated civilian administration for the island hardly had an opportunity to develop.

Table 5
Copra Production Estimates
(tons per year)

	1940	1950	1954[a]
South & Southeast Sulawesi	47,000	54,000	(28,277)
Makassar			392
Bonthain			5,572
Bone			480
Pare-Pare			283
Mandar			9,878
Luwu			5,257
Southeast Sulawesi			6,415
North & Central Sulawesi	(300,000)	306,000	(262,695)
Minahasa	85,000		56,464
Gorontalo	47,000		37,213
Bolaang-Mongondow	—		24,719
Sangihe-Talaud	29,000		29,072
Donggala	35,000		56,676
Buol/Toli-Toli	25,000		—
Poso	37,000		58,551
Banggai (Luwuk)	42,000		--
Maluku		84,000	
Ternate	60,000		
Ambon	27,000		

[a]Jajasan Kopra Purchases.

For 1940, J. M. J. Pantouw, memorandum of January 27, 1969, p. 8; for 1950, Usman Ambo Tuwo, "Tataniaga Kopra di Daerah Sulawesi Selatan" (M.A. thesis, Faculty of Agriculture, Hasanuddin University, Makassar, 1969), p. 6; for 1954, John Rahasia, "Masalah Kopra."

Table 6

Copra Exports

	South Sulawesi (Makassar)		North Sulawesi (Manado)	
	Value (Gold)	Weight (kilos)	Value (Gold)	Weight (kilos)
1920	27,464,653	58,852,261	10,835,167	21,245,426
1925	23,811,668	82,109,202	22,990,474	79,277,494
1938	16,101,331	231,719,666	5,598,579	85,917,279
1939	9,914,949	211,660,165	4,454,668	93,694,174

Statistiek van den Handel en de in- en uitvoerrechten in Nederlandsch Indie, 1920, part 3, pp. 265-77, 292; *Jaaroverzicht in- & uitvoer*, 1925, part 3, pp. 81-83; 1939, Part 4, pp. 128-31.

At the start of the revolution in August 1945, Sulawesi was made one of the eight provinces of the Republic of Indonesia. Makassar was to be its capital, and a nationalist leader of Minahasan origin, Dr. G. S. S. J. (Sam) Ratulangie, was appointed its governor. However, the Republican administration never functioned, initially because of Allied prohibitions, and then because of the Dutch arrest of Ratulangie and senior members of his staff in April 1946. Within a year the Dutch-sponsored State of East Indonesia (Negara Indonesia Timur—NIT) was formed with headquarters at Makassar. Sulawesi was again split, this time into five regions, within a larger administrative area.[8] Only after the dissolution of the NIT in 1950, following the transfer of sovereignty, did Sulawesi function as a single province. Named as governor was Sudiro, a Javanese, whose appointment was in part occasioned by the desire of the central government to avoid exacerbating ethnic rivalry in Sulawesi.

During the Japanese occupation and the revolution a basis was laid for cooperation between the Minahasans of the north and the Buginese-Makassarese of the south. In the closing months of the Pacific War, the Japanese decided to encourage Indonesian nationalism against the Allies and the return of the Dutch, and began to set up in other parts of the

---

8   The thirteen regions of the NIT were: South Celebes, North Celebes (Gorontalo and Bolaang-Mongondow), Central Celebes (Donggala and Poso), Minahasa, Sangihe-Talaud, Bali, Lombok, Sumbawa, Flores, Sumba, Timor and islands, South Maluku, North Maluku.

archipelago the sorts of nationalist organizations they had earlier founded in Java. In June 1945 they established in Makassar the organization known as SUDARA (Sumber Darah Rakjat—Source of the People's Blood; in Japanese Kenkoku Doshikai—Nation Founding Friendship Association). Appointed as chairman was the most prestigious southern aristocrat, Andi Mappanjukki, son of the last Rajah of Gowa and himself the Rajah of Bone, a man who had fought against the Dutch takeover in 1906. Dr. Sam Ratulangie, who had been taken from Java to Makassar in 1944 as an adviser to the Japanese naval administration of East Indonesia, was named vice chairman of SUDARA. Whatever tensions may have existed between these two leaders and the groups which they represented, SUDARA did give them a basis for cooperation in the early months of the revolution. It was Andi Mappanjukki who led the effort to raise support for Dr. Ratulangie and the Republic among the aristocracy of South Sulawesi. SUDARA's successor, the Pusat Keselamatan Rakjat (PKR—Center for People's Welfare), which was in effect a surrogate Republican provincial office, survived the arrest and exile of these two leaders in 1946. After being banned in September 1946, the PKR reemerged two months later as the Partai Kedaulatan Rakjat (People's Sovereignty Party), and later formed a key element in the federation of pro-Republican parties in the NIT parliament.[9] Although in the proliferation of political parties after 1950 it lost a number of its members to national parties, and won few votes in the 1955 elections (see Table 7), the PKR continued to provide a focus for cooperation between the ethnically mixed intellectuals of the city of Makassar and progressive members of the Buginese and Makassarese aristocracy of South Sulawesi. A Makassarese PKR member, Lanto Daeng Pasewang, succeeded Sudiro as governor of Sulawesi in 1954, and was himself replaced in July 1956 by another PKR member, Andi Pangerang Petta Rani, the eldest son of Andi Mappanjukki.

Although the PKR formed an organizational link between some of

---

9 SUDARA is mentioned in Koichi Kishi, Shigetada Nishijima, et al., eds., *Japanese Military Administration in Indonesia*, U.S. Department of Commerce, Joint Publications Research Service (Washington, D.C.: U.S. Government Printing Office, 1963), p. 430; and in George Sanford Kanahele, "The Japanese Occupation of Indonesia: Prelude to Independence" (Ph.D. thesis, Cornell University, 1967), pp. 225-26. On the PKR see Indonesia, Kementerian Penerangan, *Republik Indonesia; Propinsi Sulawesi* (Jakarta, 1953), pp. 224, 511; and Indonesia, Kementerian Penerangan, *Kepartaian dan Parlementaria Indonesia* (Jakarta, 1954), pp. 197-209.

the political leaders of North and South Sulawesi, it affected relatively few people. More important was the fact that the Buginese-Makassarese of the South and the Minahasans of the North experienced the revolution in quite different ways. Groups opposing the Dutch and favoring the revolutionary Republic were active in Minahasa in 1945-46, and a KNIL unit rebelled against its Dutch officers and held much of Minahasa for the Republic from February 14 to March 11, 1946.[10] Nonetheless, the area was subdued without much difficulty or bloodshed, and pensioned KNIL veterans provided a solid bloc of pro-Dutch opinion in Minahasa. In South Sulawesi, on the other hand, the Dutch had to mount a bloody "pacification" campaign to eliminate the resistance to their resumption of control. Under the notorious Captain "Turk" Westerling, guerrilla resistance was stamped out in three months (December 1946-February 1947) in which villages were burned and large numbers of people were killed or imprisoned.[11] Only then was it possible for the Dutch to proceed with the formation of the State of East Indonesia (NIT), the first step in their plan for a federal Indonesia as a counter to the Republic. The fact that many of the civil servants who worked with the Dutch in the NIT (as in the pre-war bureaucracy) were Minahasan—and continued to hold their positions after independence- -was a cause of resentment and ill-feeling among many people in the south.[12]

---

10 B. Wowor, *Peristiwa Patriotik (Merah-Putih): 14 Pebruari 1946 di Manado, dalam rangka revolusi kemerdekaan bangsa Indonesia* (Manado: Jawatan Penerangan Republik Indonesia, 1972).
11 The number killed is a matter of some dispute; several Indonesian sources speak of 40,000 "victims"; Dutch sources admit to 3,000 to 4,000 deaths in the course of the pacification campaign. *Propinsi Sulawesi*, pp. 243-48; Sjamsuddin Lubis, *Sulawesi Selatan*, I (Jakarta: Analisa, 1954), pp. 61-93; Netherlands, Tweede Kamer der Staten-Generaal, Zitting 1968-69, *Nota Betreffende het Archiefonderzook-naar gegevens omtrent Excessen in Indonesia begaan door Nederlandse Militairen in de periode 1945-1950* (The Hague, 1969), Appendix 2, pp. 2 and 11. Westerling's own description of his "cleansing" of South Sulawesi is in Raymond ("Turk") Westerling, *Challenge to Terror* (London: William Kimber, 1952), pp. 88-123.
12 See, for example, Raymond Kennedy, *Field Notes on Indonesia: South Celebes, 1949-50* (New Haven, Conn.: Human Relations Area Files, 1953), p. 24.

Table 7
1955 Parliamentary Elections
Percentage of Votes Received by Important Parties in Sulawesi

	Parties[a]								
	PNI	Masyumi	NU	PKI	PSII	Parkindo	Katolik	PSI	PKR
North & Central Sulawesi	13.60	25.02	2.86	4.39	22.93	19.08	2.26	1.23	0.41
Sangihe-Talaud	23.36	1.53	0.02	6.18	7.81	51.66	0.88	1.31	0.53
Minahasa	21.13	2.95	0.16	10.99	3.98	25.97	7.00	2.71	0.38
Manado (city)	8.68	8.52	0.61	13.63	16.24	27.21	5.56	2.83	1.26
Bolaang-Mongondow	8.88	35.27	0.37	3.33	31.81	14.08	0.55	2.94	0.03
Gorontalo	12.45	37.35	11.27	0.78	35.78	0.50	0.04	0.15	0.23
Donggala	6.51	36.71	1.21	0.25	46.13	6.97	0.09	0.15	0.96
Poso	8.94	42.49	1.80	0.93	16.86	26.24	1.07	0.27	0.02
South & Southeast Sulawesi	4.15	39.98	14.26	1.60	10.29	10.65	0.81	0.61	1.93
Makassar (city)	3.87	32.73	15.51	5.77	13.27	9.22	2.13	1.30	2.29
Makassar	1.66	33.98	39.30	0.58	10.13	0.25	0.08	0.32	1.80
Bonthain	5.41	63.16	13.95	0.86	9.07	0.23	0.05	0.03	0.95
Bone	2.22	53.98	20.87	0.40	9.76	0.22	0.04	0.21	1.77
Pare-Pare	3.03	43.33	1.24	2.20	34.69	0.98	0.18	2.59	4.24
Mandar	3.22	51.06	15.32	1.70	3.93	15.73	0.03	0.01	0.08
Luwu	5.44	17.55	0.43	3.16	6.32	56.49	3.17	0.06	2.77
Southeast	8.06	41.16	0.55	0.25	1.11	0.55	0.56	0.41	0.06

[a] A total of 53 parties or groups ran candidates for the DPR; see Kementerian Penerangan, *Tjalon-tjalon Dewan Perwakilan Rakjat untuk Pemilihan Umum I, 1955*, pp. 175-88.

"Pemilihan Umum DPR dan Konstituante Sulawesi Tenggara/Selatan," document from Kementerian Dalam Negeri, obtained by Daniel S. Lev.

Following independence, the people of Minahasa for their part felt it rather a decline in prestige to be incorporated into a single province with the capital at Makassar, for Manado had been on a par with Makassar as a residency capital in the colonial period. Particularly when members of the Buginese/Makassarese aristocracy began to demand and get an increasing share in provincial positions, sentiment grew in Minahasa for the division of Sulawesi into two provinces. Such a plan was announced by the Ministry of the Interior in January 1956,[13] and in September of that year Governor Andi Pangerang held hearings in Manado to ascertain the view of political parties in North Sulawesi on the proposal. It was reported in the Manado press that all parties favored the division of Sulawesi into two provinces, and that there would be no problem in carrying out the separation, as branch offices for a province of North Sulawesi were already prepared.[14]

The people of the South had mixed feelings about the separation of the island into two provinces. They would welcome a diminution of the Minahasan domination of the civil service, which might result if a separate provincial administration were set up and staffed in Manado. On the other hand, the present and previous governors were men from the South. Further, under the circumstances of the insurgency, in which the government in the South controlled only the towns, it did not have the resources to be an autonomous province on its own. Thus, the leadership in the South tended to favor autonomy for the province as a whole, an autonomy which could be based on the revenue from the copra trade of North and Central Sulawesi. For the South, provincial autonomy was seen not only as providing a symbol of local control useful in countering the protests of the rebel leaders against Javanese domination (see below), but was also seen as necessary for stimulating economic activity and providing jobs which might attract the rebels in from the jungle.

---

13 *Marhaen* (Makassar), January 7, 1956.
14 *Suara Revolusi* (Manado), September 25, 1956; *Pikiran Rakjat* (Manado), October 8, 1956.

Sulawesi: Military Cooperation and Rivalries

Although the revolution was more a divisive than a unifying experience for the people of Sulawesi, some links between the North and the South were forged not only in the Makassar-based PKR, but among the youth from all parts of the island who fought in Java against the Dutch. The most famous of the organizations in which Sulawesi youth participated was the KRIS (Kebaktian Rakjat Indonesia Sulawesi—Loyalty of the Indonesian People from Sulawesi), established in Jakarta on October 8, 1945. Among those involved in its founding were A. "Zus" Ratulangie, daughter of the Republican Governor of Sulawesi, who was its head, and Qahhar Mudzakkar, a young man in exile from his native Luwu in South Sulawesi, who was its first secretary.[15] Although young people from the South, such as Manai Sophian and Saleh Lahade, were active in its political arm, the KRIS militia was composed exclusively of Minahasan youth. It retained a sense of separate identity even after being incorporated into the national army (TNI—Tentara Nasional Indonesia) in 1948. At that time irregular units composed of youth from Kalimantan and East Indonesia were formed into Brigade XVI. Rivalries among them for leadership positions were involved in the opposition of some of the South Sulawesi units, under Qahhar Mudzakkar, to the initial appointment of a Minahasan former KNIL officer, Lieutenant Colonel Lembong, as commander of Brigade XVI. However, in a compromise settlement, another Minahasan officer, Lieutenant Colonel J. F. Warouw, was appointed commander, with Qahhar Mudzakkar as his deputy. Major H. N. "Ventje" Sumual, from KRIS, was made chief of staff, with another Buginese officer, Saleh Lahade, his deputy.[16]

At the conclusion of the revolution, neither Warouw nor Qahhar Mudzakkar was given a position in the territorial military administration set up for East Indonesia; both were relegated to positions in the general staff at army headquarters in Jakarta. This was a time when education, technical qualifications, and discipline were all emphasized as criteria

---

15 On KRIS see Anderson, *Java*, p. 261, n. 55; Hardjito, ed., *Risalah Gerakan Pemuda* (Jakarta: Pustaka Antara, 1952), pp. 123, 126-27; *Antara*, October 25, 1945; B. C. J. Waardeburg, "KRIS," *NEFIS Publikatie*, no. 16 (July 23, 1946).
16 See biographic notes in Appendix I.

for appointments. Qahhar Mudzakkar was obviously ill-qualified on all counts; it was possibly Warouw's earlier association with the radical Pesindo that disqualified him. Selected to head the military commission to accept the transfer of responsibility from the Dutch commander of East Indonesia was Lieutenant Colonel A. J. Mokoginta, a member of an aristocratic family from Bolaang-Mongondow, and a graduate of the KNIL academy in Bandung. He had been carefully chosen as a person who would be acceptable both to the predominantly Christian Minahasans of the North and the predominantly Islamic Buginese and Makassarese of the South, as well as to members of the smaller ethnic groups who might be fearful of domination by either of these. Mokoginta was succeeded in April 1950 by Colonel A. E. (Alex) Kawilarang, a Minahasan, and a highly respected officer of West Java's Siliwangi Division. Kawilarang was appointed commander of TT-VII/East Indonesia, and of an expeditionary force sent to South Sulawesi to cope with an attempt by the Dutch-sponsored NIT government to forestall the landing of TNI forces in Eastern Indonesia.[17] Warouw was included in the staff of the expeditionary forces, and after serving briefly as commander of the unit stationed in Manado (RI-24's predecessor), was in November 1950 made commander of RI-23 in Pare-Pare, South Sulawesi. In March 1952 he was appointed chief of staff of TT-VII.

Qahhar Mudzakkar had no such powerful friends. Indeed, his ambition to be named commander of South Sulawesi was opposed not only by army headquarters, but by unsympathetic Buginese/Makassarese officers such as Saleh Lahade and Andi Mattalatta, old rivals in Brigade XVI in Java. Andi Mattalatta commanded a battalion of Buginese/Makassarese troops in the expeditionary forces, and Saleh Lahade, a member of the original mission under Mokoginta, was the assistant for civic and territorial affairs on the TT-VII staff. However, many of the young men who had fought as guerrillas against the Dutch in South Sulawesi during the revolution looked on Qahhar Mudazakkar as their champion. In early 1950 they were demanding recognition as freedom fighters by being incorporated into the TNI. Qahhar was sent to negotiate with them in June 1950;

---

17 This incident, known as the Andi Azis Affair, is described in detail in *Propinso Sulawesi*, pp. 249-300; a shorter account is included in Bardosono, *Peristiwa Sulawesi Selatan 1950* (Jakarta: Jajasan Pustaka Militer, 1955), pp. 11-20.

instead he joined them, and began a struggle which was to last until his death in 1965.[18]

In 1951 an agreement was reached to grant the guerrillas temporary reserve status (in the Corps Tjadangan Nasional—CTN—National Reserve Corps) prior to their acceptance into the TNI or demobilization. However, the agreement broke down, and Qahhar and about half of the guerrilla forces returned to the jungle. Those who were accepted into the TNI in 1951-52, were formed into five battalions, under their own commanders. They remained almost as troublesome to the local and national army commands as their erstwhile colleagues who stayed in the jungle. By 1953 Qahhar Mudzakkar and the men who followed him were formally linked with the Darul Islam rebellion of West Java, and by 1956 they controlled most of the countryside of South Sulawesi. Although Qahhar's rebellion was in part a struggle for power within South Sulawesi, it fed on opposition to Javanese and Minahasan domination of the civil and military services, and on resentment of the Javanese troops sent to subdue it.

The pattern of ethnic competition within the military, as in the civilian administration, was indeed complicated, and involved rivalry between and within three major groups: the Buginese/Makassarese, the Minahasans, and the Javanese. These rivalries were important not only in the rebellion led by Qahhar Mudzakkar, but in Permesta and the events which led to its proclamation. And as the October 17, 1952 affair in Jakarta (described above) was a prelude to the regional crisis in the army, so the reaction to it in Makassar was a prelude to Permesta.

On November 16, 1952, Warouw, as chief of staff of TT-VII, ousted the Javanese commander, Colonel Gatot Subroto, who had made clear his support for Nasution and the challenge to the President. Warouw's action, in turn, was encouraged by Sukarno, and seems to have had at least tacit support from Governor Sudiro (Javanese and a member of the PNI). The popular reaction in Makassar to the confinement to quarters of Gatot and the largely Javanese military police (CPM—Corps Polisi Militer), captures the essence of the regional dimension of the incident: "The

---

18 For details on the rebellion of Qahhar Mudzakkar, see Barbara S. Harvey, "Tradition, Islam, and Rebellion: South Sulawesi 1950-1965" (Ph.D. thesis, Cornell University, 1974).

Minahasans have disarmed the Javanese." Minahasan support for Warouw seems to have been solid, both among officers at TT-VII headquarters in Makassar, and among those assigned to RI-24 in Manado. South Sulawesi officers either supported Gatot, or were uninvolved. This alignment can be explained in terms of the specific interests of the officers from the two areas at the time. The Minahasan officers, proud of the military heritage of their area, but aware of the fact that as a Christian minority which had been favored by the Dutch they were often looked on with suspicion by the Islamic majority, may have seen in Gatot's appointment as panglima a threat of Javanese intrusion into an area which they believed should be rightly their domain. They may also have feared a conspiracy of Javanese and South Sulawesians against them. The Buginese and Makassarese officers, on the other hand, were fewer in number, and more poorly educated in general. They could not at that time hope to hold their own unaided against their rivals from the North. They may have thought it in their own interest to work with the Javanese to prevent Minahasan domination of TT-VII.[19]

Although Warouw was not officially confirmed as commander of TT-VII until August 1954, Minahasan control over positions on the TT-VII staff did tighten in the wake of Gatot's ouster. The most senior staff officer from South Sulawesi, Saleh Lahade, who had led the support for Gatot and been arrested with him, was placed in inactive status from November 1952 until October 1956. Lieutenant Colonel Andi Mattalatta, the senior battalion commander from South Sulawesi, was continually given combat duties in the field until April 1954, when he was made Makassar city commander, a position which had previously been held by more junior officers. Further, some officers from the North were assigned to positions with the former CTN battalions, which had hitherto been considered the virtually exclusive domain of their original commanders.

An attempt to gain more equitable representation for South Sulawesi officers in TT-VII staff and command positions was made in 1955, following a reunion of Brigade XVI, the unit in which Sulawesi men had fought in Java during the revolution. A manifesto issued at the reunion urged that the core of officers of TT-VII be composed of former members

---

19 See Harvey, "Rebellion," pp. 275-87.

of Brigade XVI and the *laskar seberang* (outer island militia). The South Sulawesi officers were apparently successful in convincing Panglima Warouw that the spirit of the manifesto required that they should regain the command of the ex-CTN battalions. However, South Sulawesi officers continued to be excluded from staff positions in TT-VII, and their effort to have Andi Mattalatta appointed to succeed Warouw as Panglima of TT-VII in 1956, with Saleh Lahade as his chief of staff, came to naught.

As noted above, Warouw was scheduled to be transferred in August 1956, in accordance with Nasution's new tour-of-duty policy, but was reluctant to leave his post. Thus, despite the sentiment in South Sulawesi favoring his replacement with Andi Mattalatta, army headquarters may have thought it wise to replace Warouw with another Minahasan officer. This might facilitate obtaining Warouw's agreement to his transfer, and might help to soothe the feelings of the Minahasan officers, whose three most senior men were all scheduled for transfer: Colonel Alex Kawilarang from panglima of TT-III/Siliwangi (West Java) to military attaché in Washington, D.C.; Warouw from panglima of TT-VII/Wirabuana (East Indonesia) to military attaché in Peking; and Major H. V. Worang from commander of RI-24 in Manado to commander of Regiment 6 in Tanjungkarang, South Sumatra.

In May 1956, Lieutenant Colonel H. N. V. Sumual, who had been Warouw's chief of staff in Brigade XVI, was appointed to that position in TT-VII. He became acting commander almost immediately when Warouw left to accompany President Sukarno on a trip to the Soviet Union and China, and on August 22 Warouw formally transferred his command to Sumual. At about the same time Major D. J. Somba, a Minahasan officer on the staff of TT-VII, was appointed to replace Worang in Manado; the transfer was effected in December 1956 after Worang had been involved in yet another copra smuggling incident.[20]

Although the Minahasan officers continued to control the central TT-VII command structure, in general the direction of Nasution's plans for

---

20 The transfer ceremonies were reported in *PIA*, August 24, 1956 (a.m.), PP. 5-6; and *Antara*, December 29, 1956. The smuggling incident, which involved conflict between Worang and the commander of Battalion 714, Major Dolf Runturambi, was reported in *Suara Revolusi*, September 6, 8, and 14, 1956, and *Pikiran Rakjat*, September 7, 8, 15, and 19, 1956. The bad feelings between Worang and Runturambi which resulted from this incident may help to explain why Worang did not join the Permesta rebels in 1958, for Runturambi was prominent among them.

army reorganization was favorable to the interests of the officers from South Sulawesi: a splitting of TT-VII into smaller territorial commands would free them from the Minahasan domination of the regional command, and the new emphasis on education and training would better equip the officers and men—the majority of whom were ex-guerrillas accepted into the army in the post-CTN compromise of 1952—for competition for promotions and positions. Conversely, the new policies were somewhat threatening to the officers from Minahasa: Warouw would be transferred from his lucrative post as panglima of TT-VII, and if the territorial reorganization were carried out, his successor would have substantially less authority and autonomy. Many of the Minahasan officers already had quite high levels of education and training; indeed, this was one of the factors which had enabled them to dominate the command structure of TT-VII.

Both the plans for the army's territorial reorganization and those for strengthening its education and training programs were particularly associated with Colonel Ahmad Yani, who became first deputy to Nasution in December 1956, some months after his return from a year's training at the U.S. Army Staff and Command School at Fort Leavenworth, Kansas. While in the U.S., Yani had come to know a young Buginese officer, Major Andi Muhammad Jusuf Amir. Jusuf was the first officer from South Sulawesi to attend the Indonesian army staff college (SSKAD) in Bandung, and the first to be trained abroad. He had been quick to recognize the importance of education in the professional army. He was also quick to realize the importance to his own plans for the future of the policies which Nasution and Yani began to implement in 1956. His friendship with Yani also provided him with valuable backing at army headquarters.

Jusuf is said to have felt strongly that because of the dangers to Indonesian unity of the involvement of ethnic overtones in the insurgency in South Sulawesi, responsibility for ending it must be given to those from the area themselves. Because most of the troops fighting the insurgents were Javanese, Qahhar had used anti-Javanese slogans to attract support for the rebellion. His demand that South Sulawesi be run by its own native sons (*anak daerah*), was also directed against the Minahasans who filled so many high positions in the military and civilian services. To Jusuf, the problem was not only the presence of Javanese troops in South

Sulawesi, but the privileged position of the Minahasans, especially in TT-VII. Jusuf's views on the necessity for the anak daerah to control their own region were strengthened by his own experience. When he returned from Fort Benning, Georgia in mid-1956, he was informed that there was no position open for him in TT-VII. This was a decision which the new commander, Sumual (a classmate of Jusuf's at SSKAD in 1952), may later have had cause to regret.

Sulawesi: Regional Issues

Thus, by mid-1956, as the national political crisis intensified and regional demands on Jakarta mounted, civilian and military rivalries within Sulawesi were exacerbated. The announced plan to divide Sulawesi into two provinces, although welcomed in the North, not only threatened the position of Governor Andi Pangerang, but would cut the South off from the only source of revenue—the copra trade—which could finance local autonomy. The reorganization plans of army headquarters threatened to break the East Indonesia command into smaller districts, under the control of local officers, and although welcomed in the South, would tend to limit the career opportunities of the Minahasan officers by confining them to a much smaller area than that which they had hitherto dominated. In each case those who lacked control over the larger administrative area argued for a splitting into smaller units under local people, while those who held top positions in the province or regional command opposed diminution of their territory.

These were not the only differences between North and South Sulawesi, although these were to prove significant in the course of the Permesta movement. The people of the two areas interpreted the objectives of Permesta in terms of their own particular interests: in the South, ending the rebellion of Qahhar Mudzakkar, and in the North, gaining control over the revenue of the copra trade. Although military officers in the South seem to have been somewhat ambivalent about the desirability of ending the insurgency—which provided justification for the retention of a sizeable number of men in the TNI in Sulawesi and kept their rivals in the jungle—the primary concern of the civilian leadership, and the people, who were its chief victims, was that peace should be restored.

North Sulawesi, on the other hand, had been able to confine its insurgency problem to dimensions just large enough to justify the retention of a regimental headquarters in Manado. The only guerrilla group of any significance in North Sulawesi was the Pasukan Pembela Keadilan (PPK—Defenders of Justice Army), active in southern Minahasa under the leadership of a former KNIL soldier, Jan Timbuleng. It had a few thousand members at most, sparsely armed, and although it carried out occasional raids, it was more an irritation than a threat to security.[21]

The problem in the North centered on copra, in particular on the control and use of revenues from its export. The people of Minahasa felt that these revenues, under the existing government regulations, were not being used to meet their needs but were being wasted on dubious projects in Jakarta. They wished to maintain their high levels of education and literacy, but central government financing of schools was inadequate. The city of Manado had been badly damaged by Allied bombing, but the central government seemed deaf to requests for a share in the forthcoming Japanese reparations money. Roads had been neglected and were often impassable; interisland shipping could not be relied on. Yet, many believed, if the revenues from the export of copra could be controlled by Minahasa itself, many, if not all, of these needs could be met.[22]

Because the issue of the control of the copra trade was at the heart of Minahasan dissatisfaction with the central government, and played a crucial role in political rivalries within Sulawesi, some discussion of how the copra trade was carried out, and what the complaints of the regions were, is in order.

---

21 A number of civilians in Minahasa suggested in interviews with the author that the TNI deliberately permitted the rebellion to smolder on; this is denied by both the TNI and the PPK. Estimates of the size of the PPK vary widely. A former member, Gerson Sankaeng (Goan), numbered its supporters at 38,000 persons, and said that there had been 15 battalions of 1,000 persons each; interview, Manado, November 20, 1971. TNI sources estimate its strength as having been no more than 1,000 men, with 10-20 weapons. Press estimates in early 1957 were from 1,000 to 3,000 members, with no figures given for weapons; *PIA*, February 4, 1957 (a.m.), p. 6; March 12 (a.m.), p. 10, March 15 (a.m.), p. 15.

22 For a summary of the situation in Minahasa and complaints of regional leaders, see *PIA*, August 6, 1956 (a.m.), pp. 4-7; and February 4, 1957 (p.m.), pp. 4-6 which reports on representations from a Minahasan delegation to the central government. That these views were widespread was confirmed in a number of interviews in North Sulawesi during 1971 and 1972.

Copra

The buying and selling of copra in East Indonesia was a monopoly of the government's Copra Foundation (Jajasan Kopra). Initially established by the Netherlands East Indies government in 1940, the Foundation continued to function after the transfer of sovereignty with essentially the same structure and regulations, although headquarters were moved from Makassar to Jakarta, and Indonesian nationals replaced the Foundation's Dutch personnel. The minimum quantity of copra which the Foundation would purchase from a person or enterprise was lowered from fifteen to three tons. This did tend to make it possible for some Indonesian copra farmers, cooperatives, and merchants to compete with the Chinese and Arab merchants who had earlier dominated the middleman role. The figures in Table 8 on copra purchases by the Foundation in East Indonesia illustrate this trend.[23]

The Copra Foundation maintained the pre-war split of the archipelago into free market and monopoly zones. The free market zone included Java, Bali, Sumatra, and part of Kalimantan, where copra production was lesser in quantity and quality than in East Indonesia and was destined primarily for domestic consumption. Although the copra of East Indonesia was of superior quality—and was more important to the economy of the area—producers in East Indonesia received a far lower price for their copra than did those in the free market area. The difference was particularly striking at the time of the Korean War boom, when producers in East Indonesia received Rp. 140 per quintal from the Copra Foundation, while the price in Java and Sumatra was as high as Rp. 245 per quintal.[24] As noted above, the overvalued exchange rate of the period was detrimental to exporters, and this intensified the feeling of discrimination in export areas of the outer islands, such as Sulawesi.

---

23 Both Pantouw and Compton note that the figures in Table 8 are misleading, because many foreign merchants acquired Indonesian partners, often their wives, or set up front companies to disguise their control; Pantouw memorandum (January 27, 1969); Compton, "Copra Foundation," pp. 9-10.

24 Rahasia, "Masalah Kopra"; similar figures are given by Compton, "Copra Foundation," p. 8.

Table 8
Sources of Copra Purchases by Copra Foundation in East Indonesia

	1949	1950	1951	1953	1954
Chinese merchants	72.14%	68.48%	54.75%	46.26%	42.87%
Plantations	4.62	3.50	3.37	3.86	3.63
Indonesian merchants	14.00	17.17	24.93	30.75	35.61
Cooperatives	6.07	5.14	8.55	8.97	7.15
Copra Foundation cooperatives	-	-	-	-	.40
Farmers	3.03	5.67	8.37	10.15	10.31
Other	.14	-	-	-	.03
(Total—tons)	(336,364)				(381,954)

Compton, "Copra Foundation," p. 9; Pantouw memorandum, p. 10.

The copra trade was seriously affected by the 1954 decision of the first Ali Sastroamidjojo cabinet to end the monopoly (enjoyed since 1940) of the KPM (Koninklijke Paketvaart Maatschappij—Netherlands Steamship Company) on shipment of copra within Indonesia, and to give some coastal shipping routes to Indonesian firms. In particular, Copra Foundation shipments from the North Sulawesi ports of Manado and Bitung were to be carried by Indonesian flag ships. Some of the Indonesian firms, notably Perindo, a Manado-based company which had handled feeder shipping for KPM since 1947, were experienced and efficient. Others, however, were not. Shipping schedules became confused, and copra piled up in warehouses in Sulawesi.[25]

In addition to criticizing government policies which disrupted shipping and penalized exporters, regional copra interests accused the Foundation of mismanagement, of delayed payment to copra producers, of obtaining an unjustifiably large profit margin, and of misusing these profits to finance political party activities and to build luxurious homes for the Foundation staff in the new Jakarta suburb of Kebayoran. In

---

25 Compton, "Copra Foundation," p. 8; *Bahtera*, July/August 1954; letter to author from Howard Dick, The Australian National University, July 27, 1975.

fact, the Foundation had spent substantial sums on such projects as Bitung harbor, opened in July 1954, and the purchase of copra loading vessels. The criticisms directed against the Foundation indicate that the underlying issue was indeed that of control over copra trade and revenue, and the fundamental complaint of the regions was that decision making was overcentralized in Jakarta. As reported by Boyd Compton:

> Representatives of the copra-producing regions have played no determining role in making decisions on prices, selling policy, transportation, and the disbursal of funds for Copra Foundation wharves, buildings, automobiles and equipment. There is no conclusive evidence that decisions in these fields worked to the detriment of the copra-producing area, but regional critics were passionately certain that such was the case. . . . Yet the regional critics had no opportunity to act, for policy decisions in the giant monopoly were made by the Directorate of the Copra Foundation, which was in turn controlled directly by the Ministry of Economic Affairs.[26]

Three incidents in Sulawesi illustrate the discontent with government and Copra Foundation policy, and all contributed to the regional crisis which was building up throughout the country by 1956.

The first incident, referred to briefly above, occurred in September 1954. With the stated purpose of calling to the attention of the central government the need for a reform in the structure and operations of the Copra Foundation, the military commander of East Indonesia, Colonel J. F. Warouw, openly sponsored the illegal export of copra in the Muang Bama (a Burmese ship) and the South Breeze incidents. These incidents are said to have followed contacts with Lieutenant B. Wantanea, a junior Minahasan officer assigned to army headquarters, on load to TT-III/Siliwangi (West Java) at the time; and to have taken place with the foreknowledge of the deputy chief of staff of the Army, Colonel Zulkifli Lubis. The Navy, however, acted to stop the smuggling, and a number of those involved, including Colonel Warouw, were investigated by the

---

26 Compton, "Copra Foundation," p. 9.

attorney-general. After an appearance in court, several officers were discharged or placed in inactive status, including Wantanea and Warouw's intelligence officer, Major J. M. J. (Nun) Pantouw, a man whose name became inextricably entwined with copra, smuggling, and Permesta.[27]

The second incident, or series of incidents, began in Manado in January 1955, when a group of local businessmen, copra farmers, and army veterans seized control of the local office of the Copra Foundation, and proclaimed the establishment of a Minahasa Coconut Foundation (Jajasan Kelapa Minahasa). With strong support from local civil and military officers they were able to obtain government recognition of the Coconut Foundation, and in February the assets of the Copra Foundation were officially turned over to it.[28] Similar action was taken on November 10, 1955, in Sangihe-Talaud, Bolaang-Mongondow, and Gorontalo; although only the Sangihe-Talaud foundation was recognized by the central government.[29] This was followed in April 1956 by the seizure of the East Indonesia headquarters of the Copra Foundation in Makassar by a group, largely composed of army veterans, calling itself the Action Committee for the Decentralization of the Copra Foundation.[30] This was the final blow to the Copra Foundation, now hovering on bankruptcy and in debt some Rp. 59,000,000 to copra producers in East Indonesia for copra already delivered to it. On May 25, May 1956, the government decided that the Copra Foundation would be formally dissolved on July 26, 1956, and would be replaced a year later by a Central Copra Cooperative.[31]

Finally, the Bitung Harbor incident in June 1956 demonstrated substantial popular support in Minahasa for copra smuggling in defiance of the central government. Between February and April 1956 at least six

---

27 Angkatan Darat, *PRRI*, I, pp. 149-52; *Pikiran Rakjat*, November 16, 1954; interviews: A. C. J. Mantiri, Airmadidi (Manado), November 5, 1971, and J. M. J. Pantouw, Jakarta, January 23, 1972.
28 Bank Indonesia, *Report for the Year*, 1954-55, p. 125, and 1955-56, p. 131; Compton, "Copra Foundation," pp. 13-14; Rahasia, "Masalah Kopra," which says that the government recognized the Minahasa Coconut Foundation on February 4, 1955; the seizure itself seems to have occurred in January.
29 Compton, "Copra Foundation," p. 16; Rahasia, "Masalah Kopra." The takeovers in Sangihe and Gorontalo were reported in *Marhaen*, November 11, 1955.
30 Compton, "Copra Foundation," pp. 16-17.
31 *Ibid.*, p. 18.

foreign ships took a total of 25,000 tons of copra from Bitung Harbor without proper authorization from the central government. According to rumor, however, the export was being carried out with the consent and protection of local army units, who received a share of the imported barter goods—rice, textiles, machinery, jeeps, and automobiles. The government acted on June 1 to curb the smuggling by closing Bitung Harbor to ocean shipping. The storm of protest in Minahasa united the area against Jakarta under the slogan, "Reopen Bitung Harbor or Face Revolt." The government was not prepared to face a revolt—at this time— and on June 10 the cabinet announced that it had acted only because certain legal technicalities had not been met in the formal opening of Bitung as an international port, and that the government had no intention of closing the harbor permanently.[32] A further conciliatory move was made in July, when Army Chief of Staff Nasution participated in a ceremony in Manado for the symbolic division of the barter goods to various government offices for further distribution throughout North Sulawesi. Nasution's participation in this ceremony was designed to give the affair an aura of legality, and thus obviate the need to discipline the officers involved, with whom, as noted above, he was in the midst of delicate negotiations for the transfer of their commands. Nonetheless, his participation undoubtedly lessened the effectiveness of his earlier order that the smuggling be stopped.[33]

Each of these incidents indicated the degree to which regional leaders in Sulawesi were prepared to take matters into their own hands in defiance of the central government, and the Bitung Harbor incident illustrated the extent of popular support for these actions.

However, it must be noted that the unilateral transfer of control over Minahasa's copra to the locally based Minahasa Coconut Foundation did not end the complaints of the producers. The new Foundation did pay the producers approximately Rp. 10 per kilo more than the official Copra Foundation price, and in its first year of operation (1955) is estimated

---

32 *Ibid.*, p. 15; similar slogans are reported in Feith's account of the incident, *Decline*, pp. 494-95. See also *Marhaen*, June 5 and 8, 1956. A list of the ships involved in the smuggling is in Angkatan Darat, *PRRI*, I, pp. 149-50.
33 *Marhaen*, July 17 and 20, 1956; *PIA*, July 15, 1956 (a.m.), p. 13; July 17 (a.m.), p. 5; July 20 (a.m.), p. 5.

to have purchased about 59,000 tons of copra, a slightly larger amount than its predecessor had purchased the previous year.[34] By 1956, however, there were again complaints that copra was piling up in warehouses, and that producers were not being paid. In May, Warouw assigned his former intelligence officer, Nun Pantouw, to be director of the Minahasa Coconut Foundation, and sometime later that year Pantouw opened an office in Singapore, under the name of Eastern Produce Agency, to sell Minahasa's copra.[35]

Criticism, reminiscent of that directed at the Copra Foundation, was leveled at the Minahasa Coconut Foundation by members of the regional assembly in November 1956. One of the sharpest critics was a PKI member, Karel Supit, who accused the local foundation of paying its thirteen directors lavish honoraria although it owed copra producers some Rp. 20,000,000 for copra already delivered. He was one of three members appointed to a committee to investigate the Coconut Foundation.[36] The Foundation responded that it regretted the manner in which the assembly had discussed the problem of copra and opposed its suggestion that the Foundation be made responsible to the district government. Foundation arrears were only Rp. 3,000,000, it said, and blamed its problems on shipping difficulties caused by the central government.[37]

Blaming the central government for the problems of the copra producing areas—not entirely without reason—was indeed the defense of those in Sulawesi who had taken matters into their own hands. Colonel Warouw, in his final press conference in Makassar (August 13, 1956) before his transfer, accepted full responsibility for the smuggling of copra via Bitung. He added that the problem was a deeper one, and that the Bitung incident was only the visible manifestation of the regional struggle. While the point of view at the center might be "the regions are smuggling copra," from the viewpoint of the copra producing area of

---

34 Estimates given in Bank Indonesia, *Report for the Year*, 1955-56, p. 129; the Copra Foundation is said to have purchased 56,464 tons of copra in Minahasa in 1954 (Rahasia, "Masalah Kopra"). Total yearly production in Minahasa is variously estimated at from 85,000 to 100,000 tons.
35 Interviews, J. M. J. Pantouw, Jakarta, January 23 and February 6, 1972.
36 *Pikiran Rakjat*, November 8, 1956. The other members of the committee were Mr. Wantah, of the Catholic Party, who had initially proposed that the assembly discuss the operations of the Minahasa Coconut Foundation; and Mr. Kullit, of the PSI, a director of the Perindo shipping firm. I have seen no report of the outcome of the committee's investigation.
37 *Pikiran Rakjat*, November 12, 1956.

North Sulawesi, according to Colonel Warouw,

> it is the center which carries out smuggling, not the people in the regions. That is to say the center has "smuggled" the proceeds of the people's copra in the interests of other parties not in the interests of the region in which the people who produce the copra live.[38]

A New Military Rival

Although demands for a more equitable sharing of export revenue and for increased local autonomy were at the heart of the regional movement in Sulawesi, it was rivalries within the military which sparked off the challenge to central authority.

Rivalries between Buginese/Makassarese and Minahasan officers have been discussed above, as well as the anti-Javanese feeling involved in the Darul Islam rebellion of Qahhar Mudzakkar and the ouster of Panglima Gatot Subroto in November 1952. The military situation in South Sulawesi was further complicated in July 1956 by the establishment of a new command for operations in South Sulawesi, the South and Southeast Sulawesi Pacification Command (KoDPSST—Komando Pengamanan Sulawesi Selatan Tenggara) (see Appendix II). Appointed as commander was Colonel R. Sudirman, who had been panglima of the East Java Brawijaya Division since 1952. KoDPSST was directly responsible to army headquarters, not to TT-VII, and had operational control over twenty of the twenty-one TNI battalions stationed in the area. Only one battalion in South Sulawesi (702), stationed in the city of Makassar and predominantly Minahasan in composition, remained under the operational authority of TT-VII. KoDPSST's twenty battalions included nine on loan from TT-V/Brawijaya; the four which comprised RI-23, three of which were originally from Brawijaya and one from TT-IV/Diponegoro (Central Java); the five ex-CTN battalions of former south Sulawesi guerrillas; and two battalions of South Sulawesi men who had been in Battalion Mattalatta in 1950 or were accepted into the TNI during screening of guerrillas that year. KoDPSST was also to have under its command members of two rebel

---

38 *Marhaen*, August 13, 1956.

groups, the Tentara Keamanan Rakjat (TKR—People's Security Army) and the Tentara Republik Indonesia (TRI—Republic of Indonesian Army), who had agreed to end their rebellion in June 1956. During a transitional period while arrangements were worked out to integrate the TKR and TRI units into the national army, they were to be designated as auxiliary combat troops.[39]

The presence of all these military units in South Sulawesi—many of which were hardly distinguishable from the Darul Islam rebels they were supposed to be fighting, and many of whose commanders were relatively autonomous war lords—made the problems of command and discipline extraordinarily difficult. A start was made in October 1956 when the seven south Sulawesi battalions were formed into a reserve unit under KoDPSST, KRU-Hasanuddin (Komando Reserve Umum—General Reserve Command), to be given intensified training in preparation for recognition as an infantry regiment. Major Jusuf was commissioned as commander of KRU-Hasanuddin on October 5th. At the same time the two most senior South Sulawesi officers were appointed to the KoDPSST staff: Lieutenant Colonel Andi Mattalatta as deputy commander (concurrently with his position as Makassar city commander), and Lieutenant Colonel Saleh Lahade as chief of staff.[40]

Although these officers accepted positions within KoDPSST, they did not relinquish their hope for the eventual establishment of a South Sulawesi military command under their own control. By the end of the year, a number of South Sulawesi officers came to feel that, contrary to their expectations, they were still denied the role they deserved in security operations in their area. The South Sulawesi battalions were more involved in training than in fighting, and their members felt that they were looked down on by the Javanese troops engaged in operations against the rebels. Further, Sudirman's efforts to negotiate a settlement with Qahhar are said to have aroused the apprehensions of some of the South Sulawesi officers,

---

39 On the establishment of KoDPSST see *PIA*, July 13, 1956 (p.m.), pp. 2-3; and July 17 (a.m.), p. 5; also, Harvey, "Rebellion," pp. 313-20. On the TKR and TRI see *Marhaen*, June 22 and 28, 1956; *PIA*, June 23, 1956 (a.m.), pp. 2-4, and July 20 (a.m.), p. 2; see also Harvey, "Rebellion," pp. 295-304.
40 "Pembentukan K.R.U. 'Hasanuddin'" (October 5, 1956), Dinas Sejarah Militer-Angkatan Darat (hereafter DSM-AD), File—PUL ₹ PAN, T, III, no. 334; source—Sejarah Ringkas Resimen Infanteri HASANUDDIN 1957/1960.

who had ambivalent feelings about ending the insurgency—particularly if it were to be done on Qahhar's terms.

The civilian leadership and general population, on the other hand, welcomed and cooperated in Sudirman's efforts to bring peace through negotiations, although his policy of "Peace through Metaphysics," which relied principally on appeals to faith, was not notably successful.[41] Community criticism of KoDPSST and its commander were directed more against the special economic and commercial privileges which Sudirman is said to have given to businessmen from East Java, in preference to local entrepreneurs. There are also said to have been apprehensions about a rumored plan of the Brawijaya Division to open South Sulawesi to Javanese transmigration once the area had been pacified.

The attitude of the Minahasan TT-VII staff officers toward the KoDPSST had also become increasingly critical. Sumual, although he publicly supported the establishment of the KoDPSST as a means to increase the efficiency of military operations, was known to be displeased at the loss of operational control of all but one battalion of troops in South Sulawesi, the site of his headquarters.

Opposition to the continued existence of the KoDPSST, Javanese-led and staffed by Javanese troops, provided a basis for cooperation between the officers of North and South Sulawesi. This was the "minimum program" shared by those officers who came together in the early months of 1957 in the planning for what came to be known as Permesta.

Although it was this rather narrow issue which provided the immediate impetus for Permesta, the movement incorporated broader aims and objectives. Demands for provincial autonomy, and opposition to the leftward trend of Jakarta politics united civilian and military leaders in Sulawesi, and East Indonesia.

The regional movement assumed the proportions of a national crisis in 1957-58 when civilian and military discontent merged into a single powerful surge of protest against actions and policies being pursued by the central government. Civilian and military participants used and were used by each other. Without military support the claims of the civilians

---

41 R. Sudirman, *Keamanan dengan Metafisika* (Makassar: Jawatan Penerangan RI Propinsi Sulawesi, [?1957]).

received little attention from the central government; without the cover of the political demands of the civilians, the officers involved would have appeared to be acting purely in their own selfish interests. In fact, interests and ideals were mixed in both. What would benefit a particular region would also benefit those who led it; and men and women with visions of a better tomorrow saw themselves as the instruments for bringing it about.

CHAPTER THREE
THE CHARTER OF INCLUSIVE STRUGGLE

The complexity of what is known as the regional movement, and the difficulty which the central government had in coming to terms with it, is in part a reflection of the diversity of the regions of Indonesia and of the interests of those making demands on the central leadership. The complexity is also a reflection of the fact that both civilians and military leaders were involved at regional and national levels, and their interests and actions were not always harmonious.

While the internal contradictions of the regional movement posed difficulties for those in the national leadership trying to find solutions to the mounting discontent, these same contradictions provided opportunities to weaken the regional challenge by playing on the divisions among the challengers.

The account of the Permesta movement which follows will attempt to portray the conflicting interests and objectives of the participants as the regional challenge moved toward civil war.

The story of Permesta is in part that of the narrowing of the territorial base of the movement from all of East Indonesia to the culturally and religiously homogeneous district of Minahasa at the northernmost tip of the island of Sulawesi. In part the story of Permesta is that of the struggle of the people of Minahasa to protect the position of dominance in the Eastern islands which they had inherited from the colonial period.

The story begins, however, in Makassar, the capital of the province of Sulawesi, with the planning for the Proclamation of March 2—The Charter of Inclusive Struggle.

The Civilian Planners

The civilians who formed the nucleus of the planners of' Permesta were members of the PKR (Partai Kedaulatan Rakjat—People's Sovereignty Party), the party which had brought together urban intellectuals and progressive aristocrats during the revolution to support the Republic within the NIT parliament. Despite its weak showing in the 1955 elections, PKR members held important positions in local government: Andi Pangerang Petta Rani as governor of Sulawesi; Andi Burhanuddin, a Resident on the Governor's staff; J. Latumahina, head of the political section in the Governor's office; Mrs. Milda Towoliu-Hermanses, chairman of the Makassar City Council.

In early February 1957 Governor Andi Pangerang went to Jakarta to discuss with central government officials a number of issues similar to those later incorporated into the demands of the Permesta Charter. According to press reports at the time, the Governor presented to the Prime Minister and the Minister of the Interior demands that the province of Sulawesi be given autonomous status within one month; that money be made available for development projects in the province; and that priority be given to a division of revenues from the province, with the region retaining 70 percent of the income, and 30 percent going to the central government. The Governor was quoted as saying that he had discussed with the Minister the desire of the people of Sulawesi to have the island divided into two autonomous provinces, and that the Minister promised to send a commission to Sulawesi later that month to study the matter. Speaking about conditions in Sulawesi, the Governor said that it would be preferable to appoint people from Sulawesi to fill administrative posts in the province, because local people were more aware of local customs and traditions, enabling work to proceed more smoothly. He also said that he had requested some Rp. 400,000,000 to carry out construction plans for the province as a whole. In reply to a question, Andi Pangerang admitted that there were feelings of discontent in Sulawesi, but said that such feelings would not be permitted to burst into radical action, but would be directed through the proper legal channels.[1]

---

1 *PIA*, February 9, 1957 (a.m.), p. 8.

For some months prior to this, PKR members had been meeting informally to discuss the situation in Sulawesi and the mounting national crisis. In mid-February they organized themselves into an association, the Konsentrasi Tenaga Untuk Keselamatan Rakjat Sulawesi (Concentration of Forces for the Welfare of the People of Sulawesi). The officers, all members of the PKR were: Chairman, Resident Andi Burhanuddin, Vice-chairman, J. Latumahina; Secretary, Henk Rondonuwu (general chairman of PKR, and a journalist in Makassar); Treasurer, Mrs. Milda Towoliu-Hermanses. Assistants were designated from other political parties: Achmad Siala, PNI; A. Tadjuddin, PSII; and Abdul Muluk Makkatita, Masjumi. According to one report, they stated in a press conference on February 20 that their purpose was to work together with the local government to obtain a better understanding on the part of the central government of the demand of the people of Sulawesi for provincial autonomy. Their aim in demanding autonomy was to promote the welfare of the people of Sulawesi, not to separate themselves from the unitary Republic, for which so many of them had striven during the revolution. They specified that the term autonomy included the division of revenue between the central and the regional governments. Toward the end of February a delegation was sent to Jakarta, composed of Andi Burhanuddin, Henk Rondonuwu, and Achmad Siala, to support the Governor's earlier demand for autonomy.[2]

In addition to the PKR-initiated group, a number of youth organizations had been engaged in discussions of local and national issues over the previous months. In a meeting on February 3, 1957, the Sulawesi Youth Council (Dewan Pemuda Sulawesi) was formed, with seventy-seven individual members, and the support of forty-seven youth groups. Indicative of the inclusive nature of the organization is that regional, religious, and political groups belonged, among them federalist, nationalist, Islamic, socialist, and communist youth organizations.[3] The

---

2 Based particularly on interviews in Makassar with Saleh Lahade, October 4 and 9, 1971, and Henk Rondonuwu, June 9, 1971.

3 Named as chairman was Nurdin Djohan, a young veteran and a friend of Major Jusuf; secretary-general was R. M. Amin Daud, who had been active in guerrilla organizations during the revolution. "Manifest Dewan Pemuda SeSulawesi di Makassar" (February 3, 1957, mimeo). Other information on pemuda participation in Permesta is from interviews in Makassar with Husain Achmad, October 11, 1971; Abdul Muis, October 18, 1971; Ismail Habi, March 4, 1972; R. Amin

Dewan Pemuda Sulawesi met again on February 20, 1957, and approved organizational guidelines and a detailed political, economic, and cultural program. The first item on the program was a demand for provincial autonomy. Other proposals included: a five-year development plan for the province; expansion of educational facilities from kindergarten to the Hasanuddin University; material and "moral" guarantees for surrendering rebels; turning over land owned by the old kingdoms to the province, to be used to provide a living for the unemployed; formation of agricultural and fishing cooperatives; protection of local businessmen and local industry from the grip of capitalism, whether foreign or "national";[4] elimination of unemployment, illiteracy, and corruption; improvement of communications; and promotion of local culture and protection of it from harmful foreign influences.[5]

During February there were contacts between the youth groups, the older civilians, and local military officers. Lieutenant Colonel Saleh Lahade, who had been an (unsuccessful) PKR candidate in the 1955 election, was one of the key figures linking the civilian and military groups, for he also had close contacts with several of the Dewan Pemuda leaders.[6]

The Military Make Plans

The senior military officer in East Indonesia, the commander of TT-VII, Lieutenant Colonel H. N. V. (Ventje) Sumual, had attended the SSKAD reunion in Bandung in November 1956, where the state of the army and the nation were discussed, and where the call for unity within the army was a cover for opposition to Army Chief of Staff Nasution's policies for increasing the power of army headquarters (see above, p. 12). Sumual was apparently in contact with the dissident Sumatran colonels, Simbolon and Husein, and sympathized with them, but felt that

---

Daud, March 9 and 22, 1972; and Nurdin Djohan, March 28, 1972.
4 The phrase used was "jang berkedok nasional" (those masquerading as national); the implication would be naturalized Indonesian citizens of Chinese descent.
5 Dewan Pemuda SeSulawesi, "Program" (February 20, 1957, mimeo).
6 Indonesia, Kementerian Penerangan, *Tjalon-tjalon Dewan Perwakilan Rakjat untuk Pemilihan Umum I, 1955* (Jakarta, 1955), p. 179. Interviews, Makassar: Husain Achmad, October 11, 1971; Abdul Muis, October 18, 1971.

he could do nothing to support them because he had only one battalion of troops under his operational authority in South Sulawesi, where his headquarters was located. Sumual was also in touch with civilian leaders in Minahasa, including Mr. A. C. J. (Abe) Mantiri, a director of Perindo, whose shippint interests gave him frequent cause to travel to Makassar and Jakarta. Although only recently appointed to replace his fellow Minahasan, Warouw, as commander of TT-VII, Sumual was well aware of the discontent in his native region which simmered close to the surface, ready to erupt as it had on the closing of Bitung Harbor in June 1956.[7] (See above, p. 37).

Thus, the military initiative in East Indonesia was taken by officers from South Sulawesi. Lieutenant Colonel Saleh Lahade, the senior officer from the South, and Major Andi Muhammad Jusuf Amir, commander of the recently established Hasanuddin Reserve Command (KRU-Hasanuddin) , had met with Army Chief of Staff Nasution on January 7 and 8, 1957, at his request, to discuss the situation in Sulawesi and the reaction there to the recent events in Sumatra. In the meeting Saleh Lahade warned that the same factors which had led to the Sumatran movements were present in Sulawesi, and that to prevent the occurrence of a similar incident in Sulawesi steps should be taken in four areas: (1) military—KoDPSST should be replaced by a Military Area Command (Komando Daerah Militer—KDM) for South and Southeast Sulawesi, as a division-level command, directly responsible to army headquarters; (2) security—policy should be consistent, not fluctuating as it had in the past between offers of amnesty and threats of annihilation; a full mandate should be given to local civil and military authorities to reach a solution, and an adequate budget should be supplied; (3) government—the province of Sulawesi should be given autonomy in accordance with the provisional constitution; (4) development—serious attention should be given to development, both in drafting a five-year development plan, and in providing funds through a division of revenue between the center and the region of 30 percent to 70 percent. Nasution is said to have replied that only military and security matters were within his competence. In the military field, the Yani Commission had already prepared a reorganization plan to establish

---

7 Interview, H. N. V. Sumual, Jakarta, March 9, 1971.

military area commands (KDM), and with regard to security policy, the government would continue to follow that of "amnesty and abolition"— abolition of charges against surrendering rebels, and immunity from prosecution.[8]

At this meeting it was also agreed that in preparation for the formation of the South and Southeast Sulawesi area command (KDM-SST), the KRU-Hasanuddin would be commissioned as a regular infantry regiment, and that Infantry Regiment 23 (RI-23) would be reorganized, with the four Javanese battalions under its command being returned to their areas of origin. In accordance with this agreement, KRU-Hasanuddin was formally commissioned as RI-Hasanuddin on January 20, 1957, still under the command of Major Jusuf.[9]

Thus, it appeared that the military demands of the South Sulawesi officers were being met. The more intractable problems of provincial autonomy and regional development, however, still claimed the attention of military as well as civilian leaders in the region. Saleh Lahade was as much a political as a military figure in South Sulawesi, and as noted above, he was in touch with both the civilians of the PKR group and the Dewan Pemuda Sulawesi who had also been discussing these matters .

However, it was Jusuf, although not yet a figure of significance on the local scene, who in a radio broadcast of February 9 called for the holding of a meeting of representatives of parties, mass organizations, students, the press, and other groups in Makassar to explain the results achieved thus far in efforts to restore internal security and to discuss "what's wrong with the country." Nonetheless, at the same time, he cautioned that

---

[8] This policy had been worked out at a meeting in Cipayung (Tjipajung), West Java, in December 1955; in accordance with it, rebel groups in South Sulawesi (TKR and TRI), numbering some 35,000 persons (including civilian followers) ended their rebellion in June 1956. The agreement (Persetudjuan Tjipajung) is mentioned in the report of the meeting between Nasution, Saleh Lahade, and Jusuf: "LetKol Saleh Lahade dan Majoor Andi Jusuf mengadjukan 4 Usul Kepada KASAD" (January 7-8, 1957), DMS-AD, File-PUL & PAN, T, III, no." 334, Source—Doc. SEMDAM XIV/HN, no. 0011/57. Based also on interviews with Saleh Lahade, Makassar, October 1, 4, and 9, 1971. General Nasution did not recall this specific meeting, as he had met with many officers during this period, but he did say that South Sulawesi had been the strongest voice asking for its own military command; interview, Jakarta, May 17, 1972.

[9] Kementerian Pertahanan, Staf Angkatan Darat, *Himpunan Peraturan dan Maklumat A.D. jang Penting-penting dari KSAD*, Kwartaal II, 1957, pp. 35-36; "Pembentukan/Peresmian Res. Inf. Hasanuddin" (January 21, 1957), DSM-AD, File—PUL & PAN, T, III, no. 334, Source—Doc, SEMDAM XIV.

military men should not become politicians or merchants, as this could have a bad effect on security measures.[10]

Formal planning for the March 2 proclamation began at a meeting of senior officers from North and South Sulawesi on February 25, 1957, which both Saleh Lahade and Jusuf attended. The meeting was held at the home of Dr. O. E. Engelen, chairman of the Officers' Association for East Indonesia (Ikatan Perwira Republik Indonesia—Indonesia Timur).[11] He and the secretary of the Association, Captain Bing Latumahina,[12] spoke to the assembled officers, as did Saleh Lahade and Jusuf. Saleh Lahade, as the senior officer present, seems to have taken the primary role in explaining the critical situation which the Governor and people of Sulawesi were facing in their relations with the central government. He analyzed the background of the Sumatran incidents, and pointed out the similarities in the situation in Sulawesi: the feelings of dissatisfaction that the government did not operate efficiently, that development was stagnating, and that these circumstances were favorable to the spread of communism. Others seemed more concerned that these same conditions would lead to a disaster through encouraging separatist movements, such as the "Twa-Pro" in Minahasa, which was said to be enjoying a resurgence of popularity.[13] Inasmuch as there was a divergence of interest between the northern and southern officers on military matters, care was taken to limit discussion in this area to a "minimum program" on which both could agree—the dissolution of the KoDPSST. Military backing for

---

10 This last statement may have been an effort on Jusuf's part to distinguish himself from Saleh Lahade, who had been deeply involved in the TT-VII organized barter trade. *PIA*, February 11, 1957 (a.m.), P. 4, mentions only the explanation of the results of the security policy; *Waspada*, February 13, 1957, provides the other details.
11 On the IPRI, see McVey, "Transformation," I, p. 155. It is not clear whether Engelen called the meeting on his own initiative or after discussion with Jusuf; the two officers were apparently on good terms. Indeed, Engelen, a Minahasan, seems to have maintained cordial relations with officers from both South and North, although he was well aware of the tensions between the two groups. Information on this meeting is based on interviews in Makassar: Saleh Lahade, October 4 and 9, 1971; and in Jakarta: Arnold Baramuli, January 14, 1972; Bing Latumahina, January 14 and 19, 1972; and Dr. O. E. Engelen, February 1, 1972.
12 Bing Latumahina was first assistant (intelligence), on the TT-VII staff; his father, J. Latumahina, was head of the political section in the governor's office, and was himself an active participant among the Permesta civilians.
13 "Twa-Pro"—twelfth province—was a political party in Minahasa during the NIT period which favored joining the Netherlands Union as a twelfth province. Its resurgence at this time was mentioned by Bing Latumahina, interview, Jakarta, January 14, 1972.

the civilian demands for provincial autonomy and regional development would provide a cover for the proposed proclamation of martial law in East Indonesia which would place all military units in East Indonesia under TT-VII, thus effectively depriving KoDPSST and its commander, Colonel Sudirman, of jurisdiction in South Sulawesi. Accounts differ as to whether or not policy toward Qahhar Mudzakkar, including proposals that *anak daerah* (local people) try to negotiate an agreement with him, was also discussed at this meeting, or whether it grew out of later discussions at a working committee set up at that time.

It was agreed that Panglima Sumual (who was not present at the meeting) should go to Jakarta to convince the central government of the seriousness of the situation in East Indonesia, and to support the demands of the Governor and the civilian leaders for provincial autonomy. An eleven-man committee was established to make contingency plans—which would almost certainly be put into effect—should the demands of the Governor and the Panglima for the granting of provincial autonomy by the first of March not be met. Saleh Lahade headed the committee, and he, with the assistance of Captain Bing Latumahina and Captain Lendy Tumbelaka, drew up the Piagam Perdjuangan Semesta Alam (Charter of Inclusive Struggle—Permesta), which summarized the complaints, demands, and proposals of the officers and people of Sulawesi. Major Jusuf was designated operations officer. Other members of the committee included: Lieutenant Colonel Andi Mattalatta, Makassar city commander and deputy commander of KoDPSST; Major Her Tasning, deputy commander, CPM (Military Police Corps), East Indonesia; Major J. W. (Dee) Gerungan, fourth assistant (Logistics), TT-VII; Major Sjamsuddin, chief of staff, Makassar city command; Major Eddy Gagola, TT-VII; and Lieutenant Colonel Dr. O. E. Engelen.[14]

Following the meeting Jusuf and Saleh Lahade contacted Panglima Sumual, and informed him of the decisions taken at the February 25 meeting. Jusuf is said to have offered the support of his seven RI-Hasanuddin battalions to prevent the Brawijaya battalions under KoDPSST from taking action against the proposed challenge to it and

---

14 The eleventh member was either Arnold Baramuli (provincial and army attorney-general), Captain John Ottay (commander of Battalion 702), or Captain Arie Supit (TT-VII staff).

to the central government. Sumual, whose sympathy with the dissident officers in Sumatra and whose distaste for the establishment of a separate operational command in South Sulawesi has already been noted, readily accepted Jusuf's offer of support. Sumual agreed to go to Jakarta to support the civilian demands for provincial autonomy and regional development, and to consult with sympathetic officers at army headquarters to warn them of plans underway in East Indonesia. Of the work of the committee of eleven, Sumual told Jusuf and Saleh Lahade, "You make the plans, I will sign the proposals."[15]

Sumual did go to Jakarta for a two-day visit, accompanied by Jusuf and Arnold Baramuli, the provincial/military attorney-general, to meet individually with sympathetic officers there. While in Jakarta, Sumual met with Lieutenant Colonel Minggu, commander of RI-26 in Nusa Tenggara and informed him of TT-VII's plans. He also cabled the other regimental commanders in TT-VII, Major D. J. Somba, RI-24 in Manado, and Lieutenant Colonel Herman Pieters, RI-25 in Ambon.[16] Somba came to Makassar on February 28, and in Sumual's absence met with Major Gerungan and Major Gagola, who explained the contents of the charter which was being drawn up. He returned to Manado on March 1.[17]

On the afternoon of the first of March, Jusuf and Sumual returned to Makassar. On the same plane was the civilian delegation headed by Andi Burhanuddin and Henk Rondonuwu, which had been in Jakarta unsuccessfully urging the central government to grant autonomy to Sulawesi. Later that afternoon Sumual and Saleh Lahade met with the members of the civilian delegation, and with Governor Andi Pangerang, and the civilians were briefed on the contingency plans which were about to go into effect.

---

15 Interviews, H. N. V. Sumual, Jakarta, March 9, 1971, April 13, 1972.
16 Interviews, Jakarta: H. N. V. Sumual, April 13, 1972; Arnold Baramuli, January 14, 1972.
17 Interview, D. J. Somba, Jakarta, August 15, 1971.

The March 2 Proclamation[18]

At midnight on the first of March, prominent civilians in Makassar were roused from their beds by uniformed soldiers bearing invitations to a meeting at the Governor's residence, to which they would be taken immediately. Although the escorts had been chosen with care, and most seem to have been acquaintances of the invitees, many of those so rudely awakened were startled and frightened. Some feared that they were being kidnapped by guerrillas and one hysterical wife is said to have clung screaming to the jeep that bore her husband away, thus denying Mrs. Towoliu the distinction of being the only woman present at the gathering. Passing through the heavily guarded streets of the city—with armed men from RI-Hasanuddin stationed at every corner—did little to lessen the aura of danger. Only when the invitees reached the well-lit safety of the Governor's residence, and were greeted by Andi Pangerang himself, did the tension ease.

Some fifty persons were assembled for the meeting, which was officially opened at 3:00 a.m. by TT-VII commander, Sumual. He read the proclamation of a State of Emergency in East Indonesia. Martial law was being instituted, according to the declaration, "in the interest of the unity of the Republic of Indonesia, and for the sake of the safety and well-being of the Indonesian people in general and the people of East Indonesia in particular." It concluded, "necessary changes and adjustments will be carried out in the shortest possible time, and should not be interpreted as a separation [of East Indonesia] from the Republic of Indonesia."

Saleh Lahade then read the *Piagam Perdjuangan Semesta Alam* (Permesta—Charter of Inclusive Struggle).[19] (For the text of the charter

---

18 This account is based on documents in *Proklamasi 2 Maret 1957 dan Program Perdjoangan Semesta* (Makassar: Panitya Pusat Kongres Bhinneka Tunggal Ika, 1957), many of which are included in Indonesia, Kementerian Penerangan, *Pemberontakan "Permesta" di Sulawesi* (Jakarta, 1962); and on reports in *PIA*, March 3, 1957 (a.m.), pp. 1, 8-9; March 4 (a.m.), p. 1; March 5 (a.m.), pp. 1-6; and March 6 (a.m.), p. 9. Additional information is from the following interviews: Makassar—Henk Rondonuwu, June 9, 1971, and February 23, 1972; Mrs. M. Towoliu, September 30, 1971; and Saleh Lahade, October 4 and 9, 1971; Jakarta—H. N. V. Sumual, March 9, 1971, and April 13, 1972; Bing Latumahina, January 14 and 19, 1972; and Dr. O. E. Engelen, February 1, 1972; Gorontalo—Sun Bone, November 23, 1971.

19 According to Saleh Lahade the term "semesta" was chosen to indicate that the struggle included all sectors (*bidang*) and regions (*wilayah*); interview, Makassar, October 4, 1971.

see Appendix III.) Regional level objectives included the granting of autonomy to the province; more attention to regional development; a more equitable allocation of revenue and foreign exchange; authorization of barter trade; and, in accordance with the program of TT-VII, the development of East Indonesia as a territorial defense area and the granting of a mandate—and financial and material support—for the settlement of internal security problems. On the national level the charter called for the elimination of centralism, "the basic cause of bureaucratism, corruption and stagnation in regional development," and the restoration of "dynamism, initiative and responsibility" through decentralization. It further demanded that the cabinet and the proposed national council (Dewan Nasional) be led by the Sukarno-Hatta duumvirate, "as a symbol of unity, dynamism, and responsibility," and that the leadership of the armed forces be completely changed in accordance with the Jogja Charter.[20] In conclusion, the Permesta Charter stated that the intention of its signatories was not to separate themselves from the Republic of Indonesia, but to strive to improve the welfare of the people of Indonesia and to complete the unfinished national revolution.

There was no discussion of military objectives or problems, although apparently some who asked why it had been necessary to hold the meeting in the middle of the night were told that it was to avoid a clash with the Brawijaya troops of KoDPSST. The Charter was apparently accepted without dissent, or even discussion, the atmosphere hardly being conducive to either. All fifty-one persons present signed it. The meeting was closed with a statement by Governor Andi Pangerang calling on the people to carry on their normal activities, to remain calm, and to follow the military regulations then in effect.

Accompanying the proclamation of martial law was an Order of the Day which instructed members of the armed forces and other government servants to: hold firmly to discipline and order, guard unity to the utmost in accordance with the Jogja Charter, pledge good cooperation between representatives of the government and the people, protect the people and villages, and not to aggravate ethnic tensions or take arbitrary actions. Specific regulations were also issued (perhaps not at the meeting itself

---

20 On the Jogja Charter and its implications, see above, p. 10.

but the following day), limiting the amount of money that could be taken out of the area, prohibiting the hoarding or sending out of the area of essential goods and commodities (rice, sugar, kerosene, etc.), and placing sea and air communications under official supervision.

Similar regulations—and calls for the people to be calm, carry out their normal tasks, and obey orders of the military government—were issued in Manado on the second and fourth of March.[21]

The day following the proclamation, the shape of the military government that was being set up under martial law became clear. At its head was Panglima Sumual as military administrator, assisted by Saleh Lahade as chief of staff. In addition to a military government staff and a private staff, a "Team of Assistants" organized into eight functional sections, and a Central Advisory Council (Dewan Pertimbangan Pusat—DPP) of 101 members were attached to the military government. Four military governors were designated, and made responsible to Sumual as military administrator:

1. South and Southeast Sulawesi—Andi Pangerang Petta Rani (Governor of Sulawesi)
2. North Sulawesi—Major D. J. Somba (Commander of RI-24, Manado)
3. Maluku and West Irian—Lieutenant Colonel Herman Pieters (Commander of RI-25, Ambon)
4. Nusa Tenggara—Lieutenant Colonel Minggu (Commander of RI-26, Bali)

A South and Southeast Sulawesi Command (KoSST) was formed and made organizationally responsible to TT-VII; Andi Mattalatta was appointed its commander. This new command was given responsibility for coordinating security/pacification matters in the area. The prior existence of the KoDPSST was noted, but its relationship with the new KoSST, or with the new military government, was not mentioned.

Andi Pangerang was formally installed as military governor of

---

21 "Peraturan Kekuasaan Militer," Nos. PKM-021/24/1957 and PKM-02/24/1957, both dated March 2, 1957 and signed by D. J. Somba; and copy of "Order of the Day," March 4, 1957, signed by D. J. Somba. Reported in *Pikiran Rakjat*, March 6, 1957.

South and Southeast Sulawesi, with full authority for security policy, on March 8.²² In a ceremony in Manado in March 11, Panglima Sumual commissioned Major Somba as military governor of North and Central Sulawesi.²³

Initial Reactions: The Avoidance of Violence

The proclamation of martial law in East Indonesia was a dramatic challenge to army headquarters and to the central government. The immediate danger, however, was that fighting would erupt between the Brawijaya and Hasanuddin troops in South Sulawesi. Indeed, army headquarters may have been tempted to use the East Javanese units of KoDPSST to put down the regional challenge.²⁴ The commander of KoDPSST, Colonel Sudirman, recognized that the aim of the March 2 proclamation was to "liquidate" KoDPSST, but he opposed taking military action against Permesta, although the preponderance of force among the TNI battalions in South Sulawesi was on his side. (See Appendix II.) Sudirman has a reputation as a man who dislikes violence, but his restraint was also based on the consideration that with the insurgency led by Qahhar Mudzakkar at the peak of its strength, it was too dangerous to risk yet another civil war. Sudirman ordered units under his command to take no action in response to the March 2 proclamation, and to guard the safety of the troops and people. He also cabled Chief of Staff Nasution that a settlement between the proclaimers of the Permesta Charter and the KoDPSST could be satisfactorally effected only by the central government, and that he and his staff were willing to sacrifice their own prestige and positions to avoid deleterious effects.²⁵

---

22 "Pelantikan Gubernur Militer Sulawesi Selatan Tenggara bertempat di Lapangan Karebosi, Makassar, tanggal 8 Maret 1957, djam 15:30". (typescript of speeches of Sumual and Andi Pangerang); reported in *PIA*, March 8, 1957 (a.m.), pp. 9-10.
23 *Pikiran Rakjat*, March 11, 1957. I have seen no references to the dates of installation of Pieters in Maluku or Minggu in Nusa Tenggara.
24 Feith, *Decline*, p. 546. Nasution said only that he had been in touch with Brawijaya, and that these troops were the only ones in the area on which he could rely at that time; interview, Jakarta, May 17, 1972.
25 Radiogram, number T.R. 25/1957, March 3, 1957, from Panglima KDPSST to KSAD (text in Angkatan Darat, *PRRI*, I, p. 165); "Pendjelasan Pa Penad KODPSST Sekitar Proklamasi 2 Maart 1957" (March 20, 1957, typescript). Interviews, Jakarta: H. N. V. Sumual, March 9, 1971, and April 13, 1972; R. Sudirman, May 13, 1972.

Although there was no direct contact between Sudirman and the Permesta officers, couriers were exchanged. Immediately after the March 2 meeting Sumual sent a Javanese officer on Bing Latumahina's staff to inform Sudirman of what had transpired.[26] Sudirman refused to see Sumual, but did ask Saleh Lahade to meet him. When Saleh Lahade sent back a message that he was ill, Sudirman, undoubtedly concerned about the regulations on finance and communications issued in connection with the proclamation of martial law, sent a three-point ultimatum to Sumual: (1) not to stop or interfere with the finances of KoDPSST, (2) not to close communications, (3) not to try to occupy Mandai [airport]. If any of these demands were infringed upon, KoDPSST would not be responsible for the consequences.[27]

Both Sumual and Sudirman received a radiogram from Chief of Staff Nasution on March 2, ordering them to make no organizational changes in their commands, and to avoid taking any action which might endanger the safety of the troops or the community. Should any violence occur, full responsibility would fall on the commander of TT-VII (Sumual). For several days army headquarters would say publicly only that it was in contact with both men, and refused either to justify or to condemn Sumual's action.[28]

To ensure compliance with his order that there be no change in the status quo, Nasution despatched a mission, composed of former chief of staff of TT-VII, Colonel Kretarto, and the army spokesman, Lieutenant Colonel Rudy Pirngadie, to Makassar on March 7.[29] At the same time the Brawijaya commander, Colonel Sarbini, went to Makassar, and on March 14 it was announced that he and Sumual had reached agreement on directives to be issued to the troops of their respective commands.[30]

---

26 Although Sudirman was aware of the January meeting of Saleh Lahade and Jusuf with Nasution, and had felt that something was in the offing, he had not been informed in advance of the plans for March 2. According to Sudirman, it was a staff member of KoDPSST who first brought the news of the March 2 proclamation to him. Possibly he was informed by Azis Taba, chief of staff of RI-Hasanuddin, for Maros, where KoDPSST headquarters was located, was in the sector for which he was responsible. Sudirman himself, however, had spent the night in the city of Makassar. Interview, General R. Sudirman, Jakarta, May 13, 1972.
27 Angkatan Darat, *PRRI*, I, pp. 165-66.
28 *Ibid.*, pp. 164-65; *PIA*, March 4, 1957 (a.m.), p. 14; March 6 (p.m.), p. 11.
29 For the mission and press conference on its conclusion see *PIA*, March 8, 1957 (a.m.), pp. 1-2; March 9 (a.m.), pp. 1-3; and March 9 (p.m.), p. 8.
30 *PIA*, March 14, 1957 (a.m.), p. 10; March 15 (a.m.), p. 4.

Justifications and Explanations

While all parties—TT-VII, KoDPSST, and army headquarters—sought to avert violence in the wake of the March 2 proclamation, the Permesta leaders were also concerned to justify their action to army headquarters, and to organize popular support for the demands encompassed in the charter. Although the immediate objective of the military participants in Permesta was to liquidate KoDPSST, as Sudirman recognized, and the proclamation of martial law was designed to give Sumual a legal right to issue the necessary decrees, the formal and public explanations of the action were made in terms of the demands of the charter for regional autonomy and development, and for changes in national policies which were detrimental to the interests of the regions. It was consistently stressed that no separation of Indonesia from the Republic was intended, but merely a "correction" of the national government. A justification particularly stressed in internal army communications, and which Sumual emphasized in his initial report to Chief of Staff Nasution on March 2, was that President Sukarno's konsepsi, the proposal to include representatives of the PKI in the government, was unacceptable to the strongly religious people of East Indonesia (both Islamic and Christian), and might provoke a reaction from Indonesia's anticommunist neighbors—the Philippines, Australia, and the Dutch in West Irian—all of which bordered on East Indonesia. Interesting, in view of later developments, is that Sumual added that the United States might become involved in subversive activities in Indonesia in an effort to block the growth of the "red danger."[31]

There was no mention of the KoDPSST in this initial report, but in a briefing paper dated March 24 for a meeting of civil and military officials from East Indonesia, the necessity to disband KoDPSST is given as one of the reasons for the March 2 proclamation of martial law, KoDPSST's reliance on "metaphysical" operations against the Darul Islam rebels had given Qahhar Mudzakkar an opportunity to consolidate his position, and spread his activities to Southeast Sulawesi. Further, Qahhar had responded to Colonel Sudirman's overtures by proposing negotiations on a state-to-

---

31 The text is in Angkatan Darat, *PRRI*, I, p. 158. A similar explanation was given to the Pirngadie/Kretarto mission, as reflected in their press conference (see above, footnote 29).

state basis, and this was extremely dangerous to the nation and the army. Also mentioned is the failure of the central government to provide the funds necessary to implement the June 1956 agreement with the TKR and TRI rebels, and the lack of understanding among some army units of the reasons for the agreement. However, the principal justification given for the proclamation of martial law was the anticipated negative reaction, domestic and foreign, to the President's konsepsi.[32]

Organization of Civilian Support

After the proclamation of March 2, 1957, the military government under Sumual and Saleh Lahade moved quickly to organize civilian support and arouse popular enthusiasm for their undertaking. The Team of Assistants, which included both military and civilian members, was installed on March 4. One hundred and eleven members of a Central Advisory Council (Dewan Pertimbangan Pusat—DPP) were appointed on March 7 and installed the following day. Civilian participation in Permesta was channeled through both of these organizations, which had considerable overlap of membership. Support from youth groups was organized primarily through the Dewan Pemuda Sulawesi, which on March 5 announced its support for the Permesta proclamation and renamed itself the Dewan Pemuda Indonesia Timur.[33]

Although the DPP's principal function was to advise the Permesta military government, it also served as a working group to plan for public rallies and an East Indonesian congress to demonstrate popular support for the demands of the March 2 proclamation. Reports at the time, and later discussions with participants, indicate that there was initially considerable enthusiasm for the initiatives of the Permesta leaders. It must be noted, however, that the civilians involved in Permesta were made quite aware of the dominant role of the military in the movement. For example, at the conclusion of the first meeting of the DPP, Saleh Lahade spoke critically of the hesitancy he had perceived in some of the

---

32 Markas Besar Komando Pemerintahan Militer TT.VII Wirabuana, "Instruksi Bekerdja Pemerintah Militer diseluruh Wilajah Terr. VII" (March 24, 1957). The meeting was reported in *PIA*, March 29, 1957 (a.m.), p. 4; April 10 (p.m.), p. 9.
33 Dewan Pemuda Se Sulawesi, "Pernjataan" (March 5, 1957).

members to follow a "new road," and warned of the seriousness of the military in facing the problems of East Indonesia, and of Indonesia as a whole. "Together with you, or by ourselves," he concluded, "we who have ignited the spark, will bear all the consequences."[34]

Members of the DPP were among the eight speakers who addressed a mass rally in Makassar's Karebosi Square on March 10, attended by an estimated 100,000 persons. Of those who spoke, Mrs. Fachruddin Daeng Romo (of Polongbangkeng, an area to the south of the city which had been a center of opposition to the Dutch during the revolution) seems to have given most vivid expression to the concerns of the people:

> Those who opposed independence are those who now benefit most from it, while our youth, who were hunted down and jailed for fighting for freedom, are cast aside. This is what has upset us, has forced us to take action, to present demands...
>
> But the central government only disappoints us: if the regions ask for money for the restoration of security there is none; but money can always be found to build a picnic ground in Bandung or Jakarta...
>
> If people in Jakarta are corrupt they are protected; but if people in the regions try to solve their problems on their own initiative, that is considered an offense...
>
> We oppose the inclusion of those who are antireligious in the government...Moslems are not permitted by their God to sit at the same table with people whose principle it is that religion is the opiate of the people.

The chairman of the Dewan Pemuda, Nurdin Djohan spoke of the suffering of the people, and the absence of justice. "You call us rebels," he said, directing his remarks to the central government, "but you at the center of corruption are a band of robbers." Sumual spoke briefly, noting that as a responsible instrument of the state his efforts were directed toward the completion of the revolution—building a just and prosperous

---

34 Dewan Pertimbangan Pusat, Pemerintah Militer TT-VII, "Rapat Dewan Pertimbangan Pusat untuk Memilih Ketua, Ketua I dan II, pada tgl. 9 Maret 1957, Bertempat di Panti Penghibur, Makassar." The quoted phrase is on p. 13. Interview, Datulolo, Makassar, September 28, 1971.

state. Saleh Lahade, as was his wont, spoke at length. Permesta, he said, "is not a shooting revolution, but is a revolution aimed at work, a revolution for reviving the dynamic spirit of youth, a revolution inspired by love for the region and aimed at improving the present untenable situation." He said that although the central government had no money to fight the deplorable poverty and lagging development efforts in the region, "funds are available for the construction of big buildings in Jakarta, for receptions and for traveling abroad." One of the "sacred" aims of the proclamation, said Saleh Lahade, was the restoration of peace and security in the region. He appealed to Qahhar Mudzakkar and his men to meet with Andi Pangerang, himself, or Andi Mattalatta to end through peaceful negotiations the present situation, which causes thousands of people to suffer. He concluded by denying separatist intentions: "We continue to be one nation, one language, and one country, Indonesia."[35]

The DPP was also used to make representations to the central government on behalf of Permesta. On March 14 a delegation, designated by Sumual and approved by the DPP, went to Jakarta to "clarify" the background of the March 2 proclamation to the President and the central government. With unintentional irony, Saleh Lahade explained to the DPP that the purpose of this "goodwill mission" was to provide information to those who had reacted to the proclamation of March 2 with the "slander that those who had signed the Charter did so at the point of a bayonet."[36]

The delegation met separately with Sukarno and Hatta, and with members of Parliament and the Constituent Assembly from East Indonesia. At first reserved, Sukarno is said to have been relieved by the assurances of the delegation that they were neither separatists nor

---

35 "Rapat Raksasa di Lapangan Karebosi" (March 10, 1957). Mrs. Fachruddin Dg. Romo's speech, pp. 2-5; Nurdin Djohan, pp. 5-6; Panglima Sumual, pp. 10-11; Saleh Lahade, pp. 11-14. The rally, and Saleh Lahade's speech, were reported in PIA, March 12, 1957 (p.m.), pp. 2-4. The final quote is the 1928 Youth Pledge, a well-known nationalist symbol in Indonesia.

36 The delegation was headed by Henk Rondonuwu and Mrs. M. Towoliu, both members of the working committee of the DPP, and included the chairman of the DPP, Haji Makkaraeng Daeng Mandjarungi, Sun Bone (Masjumi), Achmad Siala (PNI), J. Latumahina and Andi Burhanuddin (PKR and the Governor's office). Dewan Pertimbangan Pusat, Pemerintah Militer "Wirabuana," "Risalah Sidang ke-III DPP Pern Mil. TT.VII" (March 12, 1957), p. 5. Members of the delegation are listed in Angkatan Darat, T.T. VII/Wirabuana, Pemerintahan Militer, "Mandaat" (March 13, 1957); attachment to "Notulen Rapat Pleno ke:5 Dewan Pertimbangan Pusat Pemerintahan Militer TT.VII Tgl. 2/4 di Panti Penghibut." Delegation is also mentioned in PIA, March 15, 1957 (p.m.), p. 9.

federalists, and ended by wishing them well in their endeavor provided no damage was done to the unity of the state. Hatta, according to the report of the delegation, had read the March 2 Charter carefully, and seemed to be impressed with it, although he advocated the granting of autonomy to second- rather than first-level regions (*kabupaten* rather than provinces). Hatta too, they reported, disapproved of Sukarno's "konsepsi" and the proposed national council.[37]

The DPP held nine meetings by the end of April, including special sessions to discuss the demands of the Charter, problems of the economy (particularly copra), and the problem of security (ending the rebellion led by Qahhar Mudzakkar). The members of the various sections of the Team of Assistants met frequently and drew up proposals for economic development, for taking over foreign enterprises in the area, for improving education, and for coping with a wide variety of problems. (The supply of mimeograph paper in Makassar must have been near exhaustion.)

Representatives of all the major political parties were included in the original membership of the DPP. However, the rising tone of anticommunism and opposition to the President's konsepsi did result in the withdrawal from the DPP of a PKI representative, Paiso, and the departure of the Pemuda Rakjat from the Dewan Pemuda.[38] On the whole, however, popular enthusiasm for Permesta—albeit with some prodding—seems to have remained high during the two months following the proclamation.

Efforts to Reach a Solution: Military

As the immediate crisis caused by the March 2 proclamation was a military one, the initiative in meeting it came from army headquarters. Initial instructions to TT-VII and KoDPSST, as noted above, were to maintain the status quo and to avoid action which might result in violence.

---

37 Reports of the delegation members to the DPP: "Notulen Rapat Pleno ke:5 DPP"; interview, Henk Rondonuwu, Makassar, June 9, 1971.
38 *PIA*, March 14, 1957 (a.m.), p. 8; March 15 (a.m.), p. 4. Mentioned in Dewan Pertimbangan Pusat, Pemerintah Militer "Wirabuana," "Risalah Sidang ke-III DPP Pem./ Mil. TT.VII" (March 12, 1957). Interview, Nurdin Djohan, Makassar, March 28, 1972.

Although the March 2 action was in part directed against Army Chief of Staff Nasution—one of the demands of the Charter was for a complete change in the leadership of the armed forces—the army seems to have been determined to settle its own internal problems itself, with as little interference from the civilian government as possible. The army leaders, no less than the dissident colonels, called on the principle of army unity in an attempt to silence opposition and force acceptance of their own views. While each side was prepared to use civilians as allies, effective decision making on military matters was to remain a prerogative of the armed forces.

In order to strengthen their authority to work out a solution to the problems created by the declarations of martial law in East Indonesia and in North Sumatra, Nasution and his deputy, Colonel Gatot Subroto, persuaded President Sukarno to declare a nationwide State of War and Emergency. This was done on March 14, 1957, the same day on which the Ali cabinet returned its mandate to the President.[39]

From March 15 to 22 the territorial commanders (with the exception of Central Sumatra's Husein) met at army headquarters in Jakarta; Colonel Sudirman was also included. The conference began with a courtesy call on President Sukarno. Discussions at the meeting itself revolved around developing and improving the army, and protecting it from political influence, which could only be harmful to army unity. No solution was devised for the regional crisis, but agreement was worked out on the structure of military government to be authorized under the national State of War and Emergency. The system of military governors in TT-VI and TT-VII would be accepted temporarily, and if a commander thought it necessary he could establish a team of assistants and a civilian advisory council. During the conference Nasution stated that "the crisis did not stem from the Army itself, but from developments outside the Army."[40]

At the conclusion of the meeting the army spokesman commented on the situation in TT-VII:

---

39 Feith, *Decline*, pp. 547-48.
40 *PIA*, March 18, 1957 (p.m.), p. 3. Other details are from Saleh Lahade's report on the conference to the Dewan Pertimbangan Pusat in "Notulen Rapat Pleno ke:5 DPP," pp. 5-7. Other stories on the conference are in *PIA*, March 13, 1957 (p.m.), p. 1; March 15 (a.m.), p. 16; March 15 (p.m.), p. 1; March 16 (p.m.), p. 4.

...the Army command understands and apprehends the "March 2 proclamation" but in the interests of maintaining law and order can not legalize the course taken. The Army command is of the opinion that the wishes and desires of the proclamation can be channelized through existing institutions.[41]

Sumual met with Nasution and his staff both before and after the conference. During the final discussions Nasution informed Sumual that he (Sumual) would be required to transfer his command to the Army Chief of Staff (Nasution). Sumual replied, "If you do that, there will be a war."[42] Their meeting ended on that note, although there were continued efforts on the part of Nasution, Gatot, and Yani to negotiate a solution.[43] Gatot and Yani accompanied Sumual back to Makassar for further discussion on the "dual command question" with the two officers involved. In statements on their arrival at Mandai airport both Sumual and Gatot stressed the necessity to preserve and strengthen the unity of the Indonesian people and state.[44]

The following month (April 26-28) military administrators and civilian governors from throughout Indonesia met in Jakarta to discuss solutions to the problems facing the country. They concluded that if cooperation between Sukarno and Hatta could be achieved, some solution to national problems might be found. They also recommended that the proposed National Council be composed of provincial representatives, that a consistent policy be followed toward insurgent groups, that administration be improved and corruption eliminated, that provincial development be accelerated, and that the problems within the army be settled by peaceful means, without neglecting "military and disciplinary norms."[45]

The broader issues discussed at this meeting were not within the

---

[41] *PIA*, March 22, 1957 (a.m.), pp. 6-8.
[42] Interview, H. N. V. Sumual, Jakarta, April 13, 1972.
[43] According to Nasution, Sumual was concerned that he would still have a position; interview, Jakarta, May 17, 1972. Nasution also noted that he used Gatot and Yani in discussions with the dissident officers because he realized they were closer to the regional commanders than he himself; Nasution had always served at army headquarters, never in a territorial command.
[44] *PIA*, March 25, 1957 (p.m.), p. 8; March 27 (p.m.), p. 11; March 28 (p.m.), pp. 3-4.
[45] *PIA*, April 29, 1957 (a.m.), pp. 1-5.

competence of the army to solve. However, the army leadership did move to settle its own problems.

Nasution realized that in East Indonesia it was objections to the existence of KoDPSST which had precipitated the proclamation of martial law on March 2: TT-VII officers were unwilling to have a second command operating in their area, and South Sulawesi officers wanted to have their own military area command. The limited nature of the objectives of many of the South Sulawesi participants in Permesta, objectives which were in any case in line with the proposed territorial reorganization of the army, meant that it was relatively easy for army headquarters to meet their desires and gain their loyalty. Thus, Nasution was prepared to recognize the four military commands established by Permesta as official military area commands (Komando Daerah Militer—KDM). At the same time he was determined to dissolve both KoDPSST and TT-VII. KoDPSST had demonstrated little success with its "metaphysical" operations against Qahhar's rebels, and it could be disbanded with little effect on the security of the region. Nasution seems also to have been convinced by Jusuf's arguments that greater success would be achieved by giving responsibility for negotiations with and operations against the rebels to local people (anak daerah).[46] At the same time, elimination of TT-VII would leave Sumual with no official position, and the whole elaborate structure of the Permesta military government would be left without either a head or a base. The four military area commands in East Indonesia would be placed directly under the authority of army headquarters, and Nasution could then negotiate directly with their commanders.

These decisions were announced in army communiques of May 5 and 27, which stated that TT-VII and KoDPSST would be unified into a single command under the supervision of the Army Chief of Staff, and that consequently both Sumual and Sudirman would be transferred to other, unspecified, positions. At the same time, army spokesman, Lieutenant Colonel Rudy Pirngadie, said that the army was proceeding with its plans for territorial reorganization, by dividing East Indonesia into four military regions: South and Southeast Sulawesi, North and Central Sulawesi, Maluku and West Irian, and Nusa Tenggara. Sulawesi

---

46 Interview, A. H. Nasution, Jakarta, May 17, 1972.

Governor, Andi Pangerang Petta Rani, was appointed military governor of South and Southeast Sulawesi, with the rank of titular colonel, effective April 1, 1957. The appointment of military governors in the other areas was still under consideration, the communique concluded.[47]

Both Sumual and Saleh Lahade reacted to these announcements—which abolished the commands in which they held official positions without granting recognition to the Permesta military government for East Indonesia which they had established—by stressing that it was essential that those who had pioneered the new initiatives of the Permesta Charter remain in the area to fulfill the goals it had set forth.[48]

In Manado, Major Somba issued a statement that he did not agree with the decisions announced in the army communique, which represented a policy of divide and rule dangerous to the unity of the army as a whole as well as to the unity of TT-VII. He specifically noted that he did not agree with the decision to remove Sumual from his post. He would not be responsible, he added, for the consequences of these decisions, which had come as a shock to the community.[49]

On the other hand, Andi Pangerang, whose position as military governor of South and Southeast Sulawesi had been confirmed, emphasized on his return in early May from the Jakarta meeting of governors and military administrators, that the central government "was paying due attention to the problems faced by the regions." While continuing to decry the bureaucratism and centralism of the national government, Andi Pangerang warned against those in the regions who said they were working in the interests of the people, but were in fact not doing so.[50]

The Waning of Civilian Support

The recognition of Andi Pangerang as military governor of South and Southeast Sulawesi was a deliberate move on the part of Nasution and the

---

47 Kementerian Pertahanan, *Himpunan Peraturan dari KSAD*, Kwartaal II, 1957, pp. 22-24, and Kwartaal III, 1957, pp. 163-64. Reported in *PIA*, May 6, 1957 (a.m.), pp. 5-6; and May 27 (p.m.), pp. 1, 6.
48 *Marhaen*, May 7, 1957.
49 *Pikiran Rakjat*, May 9, 1957.
50 *Marhaen*, May 3, 1957; *PIA*, May 3, 1957 (a.m.), p. 6.

central government to ensure the loyalty of respected local leaders, with the further hope that they would influence those junior to them.[51] A similar move was the designation of Andi Mappanjukki, the most senior and most respected aristocrat in South Sulawesi, as Sulawesi representative to the National Council (Dewan Nasional) which had been proposed as part of Sukarno's konsepsi in February 1957 and was set up the following May. There is no record of further criticism of the Council in South Sulawesi, although voices continued to be raised against it in the North.[52]

By May 1957, Andi Pangerang's differences with the military leaders of Permesta were obvious. Indeed, he had expressed reservations in private about what was being done under the banner of the March 2 Charter almost as soon as he had signed it. A further indication of his wish to distance himself from Permesta was his absence from the Kongres Bhinneka Tunggal Ika (Unity in Diversity Congress), where delegates from all of East Indonesia met in Makassar, May 8-12, 1957, to discuss the aims of the Charter proclaimed in March 2.

Although the Congress was in many respects the high point of Permesta activity in East Indonesia, it also marked the point at which public enthusiasm for the movement began to wane. In the weeks before the Congress the Permesta Central Advisory Council (DPP) sent goodwill missions to Manado, Ambon, and Kupang (Timor) to arrange for delegates to come to the meeting. All areas of East Indonesia were represented among the 122 persons who attended the Congress, and in the membership of the new Central Advisory Council and its 64-member Executive Committee selected at the Congress to advise the Permesta military government.[53] Discussions were held and resolutions passed

---

51 Interview, A. H. Nasution, Jakarta, May 17, 1972.
52 According to some press reports, Mrs. Towoliu, the head of the Makassar city council and one of the original signers of the Permesta Charter, was also to be appointed as a Sulawesi representative to the National Council, but refused because of pressure from people in North Sulawesi, as well as general aversion to the Council among Permesta supporters. Opposition to the National Council from North Sulawesi was further indicated when the North Sulawesi branch of Parkindo announced its opposition to having a Parkindo member, Drs. W. J. Rumambi, sit as a representative of the Protestant group to the Council. See *Marhaen*, June 15 and July 23, 1957; *Pikiran Rakjat*, July 5, 15, and 18, and September 7, 1957; Lev, *Transition*, p. 27.
53 According to the records of per diem paid, the number of delegates and the areas which they represented was as follows: South Sulawesi—47, Central Sulawesi—12, Gorontalo—6, Bolaang-Mongondow—6, Minahasa—6, Manado—6, Sangihe-Talaud—6, North Maluku—5, South and Central Maluku—5, Ambon—7, West Irian—8, Bali—7, Flores—1. Reports of the Congress are

supporting the demands of the Permesta Charter. A number of delegates warned that the bureaucratism and centralism of Jakarta not be moved to Makassar or Manado. The Permesta leaders responded that the holding of Congress was itself a step toward abolishing centralism within the area of East Indonesia. However, the Advisory Council met only once following the Congress, in August 1957, unlike its predecessor, which had met frequently.

Although a number of national leaders had been invited to the Bhinneka Tunggal Ika Congress (Sukarno, Hatta, Prime Minister Djuanda, former Chief of Staff of the Armed Forces Major General T. B. Simatupang) none attended. The Sumatran colonels, Simbolon and Husein, also sent their regrets. Andi Pangerang's absence has already been noted. There was some embarrassment at the opening session of the Congress when Major Jusuf, who had been scheduled to give a speech on security matters, also failed to appear.[54]

The apparent lack of enthusiasm for the Permesta movement on the part of a number of local and national leaders may have contributed to the declining popular support for it. However, the Congress itself was seen by some who had originally supported the movement as demonstrating a greater concern for show than for substance, and the atmosphere of luxury of the Congress was criticized as being inappropriate in the midst of the suffering of the people, and not in accordance with the aims of the March 2 Charter.[55]

The Bhinneka Tunggal Ika Congress may have represented more show than substance in the effort to attract civilian support for Permesta. A more substantial effort to gain popular sympathy was the allocation of Rp. 2,000,000 to each of the second-level districts (kabupaten) in East Indonesia. The money for this purpose was withdrawn by the Permesta

---

in *Marhaen*, May 10, 1957, pp. 1-2; *PIA*, May 4, 1957 (a.m.), p. 4; May 8 (p.m.), p. 2; May 10 (a.m.), pp. 5-7; May 15 (a.m.), p. 13; May 16 (a.m.), p. 5; May 18 (p.m.), pp. 2, 5. Additional information is from documents issued by the Congress, and from interviews in Makassar with Henk Rondonuwu, June 9, 1971; Datulolo, September 28, 1971; and Andi Baso Amier, September 23, 1971.

54 *PIA*, May 10, 1957 (a.m.), p. 6; interviews, Makassar: Henk Rondonuwu, June 9, 1971; Datulolo, September 28, 1971.

55 Letter from Corps Pemuda Pembangunan Indonesia Bahagian Timur, no. 013/CPP/ IBT/57 (April 21, 1957), signed by Husain Achmad, general chairman. Also interviews in Makassar in 1971 and 1972.

military government in May 1957 from the Makassar and Manado branches of the Bank Indonesia. The money was used in a variety of ways: markets in Makassar and Bonthain, buildings for Christian youth organizations in Ambon and Flores, a housing complex in Ternate, a stadium in Gorontalo. Additional money was allocated for the construction of military office buildings and barracks in Makassar, Malino, and Pare-Pare. Although some of the funds channeled via Permesta seem to have been well used, the criteria by which the money was disbursed came in for criticism, as it was noted that some of those associated with the movement seemed to be prospering, while a number of worthwhile projects were neglected.[56]

Military Reorganization

Army Chief of Staff Nasution arrived in Makassar on May 30 to install the new South and Southeast Sulawesi Military Command (KDM-SST), and to discuss settlement of other issues with Sumual, the provincial authorities, and the regimental commanders in East Indonesia. He was accompanied by a team of officers who were to work out solutions to financial and economic problems in the area, and he was prepared to remain in Makassar until both Sumual and Sudirman had relinquished their commands to him. The atmosphere in Makassar was tense, for Sumual had not yet agreed to transfer his command, and had made a number of public statements indicating his determination not to do so. Although Sumual said he welcomed official recognition of the four subordinate area commands (KDM) in East Indonesia, he opposed the abolition of TT-VII and its replacement by a regional command with only coordinating, not operational, authority.

What Nasution describes as a "war of nerves" ensued. The first engagement was a clear victory for Nasution and army headquarters,

---

56 Rp. 15,000,000 was withdrawn from the Manado branch on May 18, 1957, and Rp. 100,000,000 from the Makassar branch on May 22; some accounts also report that Rp. 12,000,000 was withdrawn from the Ambon branch of Bank Indonesia by Permesta. See *PIA*, May 28, 1957 (a.m.), p. 6; May 30 (a.m.), pp. 5-6; June 8 (a.m.), p. 11. No complete record of the use of the money seems to exist. Projects listed were mentioned in *Marhaen*, July 23 and August 2, 1957, and in interviews with Saleh Lahade, Makassar, October 4, 1971, and Bing Latumahina, Jakarta, January 19, 1972. Misuse of funds was mentioned in a number of interviews.

for on the first of June 1957 the KDM-SST was formally established, with Lieutenant Colonel Andi Mattalatta as commander, and Major Her Tasning as acting chief of staff. Military Governor Andi Pangerang and Colonel Sudirman attended the ceremony; Sumual flanked Nasution. In a statement to the press, Mattalatta welcomed the placing of the responsibility for settling Sulawesi problems in the hands of people from the area, and appealed to the local population not to aggravate ethnic tensions, but to work together for peace and development.[57]

Then, accompanied by Andi Pangerang, Mattalatta, Jusuf, and others, Nasution traveled to Pare-Pare, Pinrang, and Polewali, where he explained to army units in the interior, many of them from Brawijaya, that KDM-SST had been formed in accordance with the "territorial warfare" system, and for the purpose of stabilizing the security situation in the area.[58]

While waiting for agreement from Sumual on the transfer of his command, the negotiation team which accompanied Nasution discussed financial and economic problems with local officers and civilians. The team, headed by Colonel Dahlan Djambek, remained in Sulawesi for several weeks, and visited Manado as well as Makassar in its investigation of local economic matters, such as the copra trade. The focus of its investigation, however, was on TT-VII's withdrawal of money from the Bank Indonesia branches in East Indonesia. In communiques issued on May 29 and 31 and June 6, TT-VII had explained that the withdrawals were "business loans" or "emergency loans" which would be repaid in accordance with an agreement between the bank management and the Panglima, that the money would be used to finance construction and development projects, that Rp. 2,000,000 had been given to each kabupaten for these purposes, and that money circulation in the area had remained normal. It was not until June 23 that a "solution" was reached; in a speech in Makassar Nasution announced that he had assumed responsibility for the matter

---

57 "Pengresmian Ko.D.M.S.S.T. dan Pelantikan Komandan-nja," DSM-AD, File—PUL ξ PAN, T, II-5, no. 326; source—report of Ltd. J. A. Tumengkol, Kepala Biro Sedjarah, TT-VII/Wirabuana, dated June 3, 1957. Reported in *Marhaen*, June 1, 1957; PIA, June 3, 1957 (a.m.), pp. 1-2; June 4 (a.m.), pp. 1-2. Additional information, interviews: Saleh Lahade, Makassar, October 4, 1971; H. N. V. Sumual, Jakarta, April 13, 1972; A. H. Nasution, Jakarta, May 17, 1972.

58 *Marhaen*, June 3, 1957; *PIA*, June 5, 1957 (a.m.), pp. 10-12. For Nasution's views on territorial warfare see his *Tjatatan2 Sekitar Politik Militer Indonesia* (Jakarta: Pembimbing, 1955), pp. 199-200.

in the interest of good relations between the central government and the region.[59]

In the meantime, Nasution had won the war of nerves with Sumual, and obtained his agreement to the dissolution of TT-VII. Nasution's victory was made possible by the shift in support of key South Sulawesi officers from Permesta to the army leadership.

Following the formal installation of KDM-SST, Sumual and the officers who had originally planned the March 2 proclamation met on the night of June 4-5 to discuss what their next step should be. Reports on the meeting differ, but there is general agreement that the discussion was heated, and that it was clear that there was a difference of opinion between Sumual and Saleh Lahade on one side and Jusuf on the other. Jusuf is said to have believed that from the standpoint of technical capability, the army in South Sulawesi was not prepared to fight the central government. He is said to have argued that the priorities should be education and training, building up the military organization and its territorial control, settling the problem of security in South Sulawesi (that is, ending the rebellion of Qahhar Mudzakkar), and only then would it be possible for development to occur. Further, he was satisfied with what had been achieved thus far: the KoDPSST would be dissolved; a separate command for South Sulawesi, headed by a local man, had been established; and a beginning had been made on the withdrawal of the Javanese troops. He was prepared to accept the Yani reorganization plan, in which the military districts would be under the authority of army headquarters, and in which there would be only a regional coordinator. Sumual, who stood to lose if this proposal were implemented, wanted to hold out for regional command authority at the division level over the four KDMs. He is said to have proposed that those present resign from the TNI and prepare to fight in the jungle. Sumual himself says that Jusuf proposed moving the headquarters of Permesta to Pare-Pare, but that this was merely a tactic in order to have an excuse to arrest Sumual in the presence of Nasution and Yani should Sumual actually leave the city. When Jusuf and Her Tasning were seen to go directly from the meeting to the governor's guest house

---

59 *PIA*, May 30, 1957 (a.m.), pp. 5-6; June 3 (a.m.), pp. 5-6; June 7 (a.m.), p. 7; June 8 (a.m.), p. 11; June 14 (a.m.), p. 8; June 19 (p.m.), p. 1; June 25 (a.m.), pp. 1-2; *Marhaen*, June 1, 1957; *Pedoman Rakjat*, June 24, 1957.

where Nasution and Yani were staying, the Permesta leaders decided to stay in Makassar, and fight there should it come to that. The South Sulawesi officers wanted neither to fight in the city, nor to retreat to the jungle. They were only too aware that Qahhar controlled the interior, and that if a decision were made to fight for Permesta in South Sulawesi it would have to be on the basis of an agreement with Qahhar, an agreement the terms of which Qahhar would be able to dictate.[60]

Realizing that he no longer had the crucial support of Jusuf, who commanded the RI-Hasanuddin troops, Sumual on June 5 met with Nasution and worked out a compromise agreement. Sumual would be made chief of staff of a unit to plan for the formation of an East Indonesia Coordinating Command (Staf Komando Indonesia bagian Timor/ Koordinasi Antar Daerah); the planning unit, which had no commander, would be established immediately and would continue in existence for one month.[61]

On June 8 a ceremony was held in Makassar at which both TT-VII and KoDPSST were officially dissolved, and responsibility for East Indonesia was placed with the Army Chief of Staff. At the same ceremony Nasution delegated responsibility for security in South and Southeast Sulawesi to Andi Pangerang, in his capacity as military governor; Andi Mattalatta, as commander of KDM-SST, had operational authority. A liaison officer from the Brawijaya Division was attached to the military governor's office in connection with the tactical use of Brawijaya troops in the new KDM-SST area.[62]

There was sharp reaction in North Sulawesi to the dissolution of TT-VII and to Sumual's ouster from command of East Indonesia. In a radio broadcast of June 13, Major Somba announced that he would continue to support Sumual as Panglima of TT-VII, and repeated his May 8 statement to that effect. "We are convinced," he said, "that the Proclamation of

---

60 How openly this was discussed is not known. Interviews, Makassar: Saleh Lahade, October 4, 1971; Jakarta: Bing Latumahina, January 19, 1972; Her Tasning, February 1, 1972; H. N. V. Sumual, April 13, 1972. Additional information on Jusuf's attitude is from an interview with Azis Taba, Jakarta, February 3, 1972.
61 Kementerian Pertahanan, *Himpunan Peraturan dari KSAD*, Kwartaal II, 1957, pp. 37-38. Interviews, Jakarta: H. N. V. Sumual, March 9, 1971, and April 13, 1972; A. H. Nasution, May 17, 1972.
62 *PIA*, June 7, 1957 (a.m.), p. 7; *Marhaen*, June 8, 1957.

March 2 represents a new road and a starting point for the achievement of the security and welfare of the people of East Indonesia." He continued, "It is difficult for the central government to criticize the Proclamation of March 2, because it realizes that the Proclamation contains truth and justice, unlike the regulations of the central government which always in the past have brought suffering and disunity." This, he implied, was the reason the central government was now following a tactic of divide and rule, and was transferring Lieutenant Colonel Sumual away from East Indonesia.[63]

There was no public reaction from Nasution or army headquarters to Somba's statement. Then on June 19, Lieutenant Colonel Jonosewojo, former chief of staff of TT-VII, who had been assigned with Sumual to the planning staff for the East Indonesia coordinating command, announced that Sumual had completed his work with the planning staff and had gone to Manado to explain to Major Somba the June 8 agreement on the dissolution of TT-VII.[64]

Army headquarters proceeded with the establishment of the other regional military commands in East Indonesia. Lieutenant Colonel Herman Pieters was installed as commander for Maluku and West Irian on June 26, and on July 5, Lieutenant Colonel Minggu was installed as commander for Nusa Tenggara. Also on July 5, Pieters, Minggu, and Somba were appointed as military administrators of their territories in accordance with martial law provisions; Andi Pangerang, who had been appointed military governor of South and Southeast Sulawesi in April was also made military administrator in July.[65] Not until September 28, after the holding of the National Conference (Musjawarah Nasional—MUNAS) on the regional crisis, was Major Somba installed by Nasution as commander of North and Central Sulawesi (KDM-SUT).[66]

The new Inter-Regional Command for East Indonesia (KADIT—Komando Antar Daerah Indonesia bagian Timur, later KOANDA-IT) was established on August 20, 1957. Jonosewojo was named acting chief

---

63 *Pikiran Rakjat*, June 13, 1957. *Marhaen*, June 7, 1957, mentions a radio address on Somba on May 29 with a similar tone; I have seen no other reference to it.
64 *Marhaen*, June 19, 1957.
65 *PIA*, July 6, 1957 (a.m.), p. 4.
66 *Pikiran Rakjat*, September 28, 1957; *Marhaen*, September 30, 1957, p. 2.

of staff, but no commander was appointed until February 1958.⁶⁷ In accordance with the Yani plan, KADIT was responsible to the army chief of staff for the coordination of the four military area commands (KDM) in East Indonesia, but had no operational authority over these commands or their troops. The power of army headquarters was thus very much increased, and that of the regional command very much diminished. The fact that the commander of the Inter-Regional Command was designated as a deputy to the army chief of staff and was stationed at army headquarters in Jakarta demonstrates the shift away from regional autonomy toward central control.

South Sulawesi: Focus on Security

The military settlement of June 1957, which gave local men control over military and security matters in South Sulawesi, was welcomed in the Makassar press as "approaching perfection."⁶⁸ With the formation of the South and Southeast Sulawesi command in Makassar, attention of most of the Buginese and Makassarese officers turned to the question of ending the rebellion of Qahhar Mudzakkar. To some of the officers, Jusuf in particular, eliminating TT-VII and KoDPSST was the first step, and establishing the separate military command under officers from South Sulawesi, the second step, toward ending the rebellion. Only if *anak daerah* were in control of the civilian and military government of the area would it be possible to negotiate successfully with Qahhar; and only if the troops used to combat the rebels were anak daerah could the ethnic hostility toward the Javanese which fueled the rebellion be eradicated. However, in order to rely on local troops, the former TKR and TRI rebels would have to be integrated into the TNI units which made up KDM-SST, and the training and discipline of all the local units would have to be improved. To these matters—improvement of local forces to meet the military threat of the rebellion, and negotiations with Qahhar's Darul

---

67 Sumual, and Jonosewojo, had been engaged in the planning for this new command, but Sumual never held a position in KADIT. KADIT was without a commander until the appointment of Brigadier General Gatot Subroto on February 4, 1958. *Marhaen*, August 20, 1957; *PIA*, August 21, 1957 (a.m.), p. 1. The date of Gatot's appointment (Surat Keputusan KSAD no. 82/2/1958, February 4, 1958), supplied by Sejarah Militer, KOWILHAN IV (Sulawesi).
68 Editorial, *Marhaen*, June 11, 1957.

Islam rebels—the officers of KDM-SST now turned their attention.

Negotiations with Qahhar Mudzakkar had been a topic of discussion at a meeting of the Permesta Advisory Council on April 16, 1957,[69] and there had been press reports in mid-March that a senior officer of RI-Hasanuddin (later identified as Major Jusuf) had met with Qahhar to discuss "preliminary arrangements" for Qahhar's "eventual surrender."[70] While some doubt has been expressed that such a meeting did take place, public appeals to Qahhar to negotiate with the anak daerah now in positions of responsibility were made as early as Saleh Lahade's speech to the Permesta mass rally on March 10. Shortly after assuming full responsibility for security in South Sulawesi, Andi Pangerang and Andi Mattalatta broadcast on June 12 an appeal to Qahhar, and to all rebels still in the jungle, to return to the fold. They repeated these appeals in Independence Day speeches on August 17. Both emphasized that responsibility for local matters was now being handled entirely by anak daerah, and that the door was open for those still in rebellion to return and devote themselves to the development of the area.[71]

There were a number of reports from July through September that the situation was quiet, and that the guerrillas had reduced their activities. Some attributed this to the designation of Andi Pangerang as military governor with responsibility for security policy, others to the recognition of the guerrillas that the chief victims of the insurgency were the people of the area themselves. Some suggested that any continuing disturbances were being caused by groups for which Qahhar Mudzakkar was not responsible.[72]

However, in October and November heavy fighting broke out in Southeast Sulawesi; major battles took place in Kasepute (near Kolaka),

---

69 Dewan Pertimbangan Pusat, Pern. Mil. TT.VII/Wirabuana, "Risalah Sidang Pleno DPP Ke VII (Tgl. 16 April 1957)."
70 *PIA*, March 15, 1957 (a.m.), p. 15; March 17 (a.m.), p. 4; April 2 (a.m.), pp. 4-5. It is difficult to say whether or not such negotiations actually did take place. Many who were in the area at the time suggest that the reports might have been part of Jusuf's "psy-war" against Sudirman and the KoDPSST, to demonstrate that the anak daerah could handle negotiations with Qahhar themselves. On the other hand, there is an official report on the meeting in army archives: "Pertemuan Kahar Muzakar dengan Kmd. R.I. Hasanuddin Majoor A. Jusuf cs" (March 12, 1957), DSM-AD, File—Peristiwa Penting Lainnja; Source—Doc. SEM DAM XIV/HH.
71 *Marhaen*, June 13, 1957, and special broadsides of August 17 speeches.
72 *Marhaen*, July 23, August 14 and 20, September 11, 1957.

the largest transmigration center in the province (at Konda) was burned, and the city of Kendari itself was threatened by a Darul Islam offensive.[73] The insurgency in the South was far from over.

As noted above, the policy for coping with the rebellion did not rely solely on negotiations, but also on strengthening the local TNI units, so that they could assume responsibility for security operations. On August 17, 1957, 6,228 former TKR and TRI rebels were formally accepted into the TNI, nearly doubling the manpower under the command of KDM-SST. To provide training for these men, and "upgrading" courses for the ex-CTN battalions (who were also former guerrillas), a training center (Pendidikan Pendahuluan Ulangan Perwira—Preliminary and Refresher Officer Training) was opened in Malino, south of Makassar, on October 28, 1957. Mattalatta and Jusuf, who spoke at the opening ceremony, said that within thirty months all officers in KDM-SST would have had a three-months course at the center.[74]

With the increase in the number of troops assigned to KDM-SST, and the presumed improvement in their ability through training, the officers of KDM-SST, Jusuf in particular, pressed for the return to Java of the one Diponegoro and three Brawijaya battalions which had been stationed in South Sulawesi since being sent as part of the Expeditionary Forces in 1950. In accordance with the agreement made at the January 1957 meeting between Saleh Lahade, Jusuf, and Nasution, these units were administratively transferred from RI-23 to TT-IV/ Diponegoro and TT-V/Brawijaya in August; part of one Brawijaya battalion left immediately, and the others were withdrawn in the course of the next several months.[75] There remained the nine Brawijaya battalions, which since the dissolution of KoDPSST were under the tactical authority of Military Governor Andi Pangerang, although their use was coordinated with a Brawijaya liaison officer attached to the staff of the Military Governor. Following a serious fight in the city of Makassar in December 1957 between Battalion 718 of RI-Hasanuddin and Brawijaya Battalion 513, it was decided to withdraw the remaining nine Brawijaya battalions.

---

[73] *Marhaen*, October 19, November 7 and 8, and December 14, 1957.
[74] *Marhaen*, August 19, 1957, p. 2, and October 21, 29, and 30, 1957; *PIA*, October 30, 1957 (p.m.), pp. 8-9.
[75] *Marhaen*, September 13, 1957; *Bara*, January 20, 1958; *PIA*, March 8, 1958 (a.m.), p. 4.

By July 1958 all had been withdrawn.[76]

KDM-SST was now composed entirely of units made up almost completely of anak daerah. On January 22, 1958, these units were divided between the Makassar city command, RI-Hasanuddin, and RI-23.[77]

With the establishment of the KDM-SST and the start of the withdrawal of Javanese troops from South Sulawesi, Jusuf had achieved his primary objective. He had made clear at the June 4 meeting of the officers who had initially planned Permesta his satisfaction with the agreements reached with Nasution. From then on, Jusuf was clearly the leader of the anti-Permesta group. He was strongly supported by the chief of staff of KDM-SST, Major Her Tasning.[78] Saleh Lahade, the South Sulawesi officer most closely identified in public with Permesta, was clearly the leader of the pro-Permesta forces there. The position of other officers, including Andi Mattalatta, commander of KDM-SST, was more ambiguous.

A number of the Permesta officers whose jobs had disappeared with the dissolution of TT-VII and KoDPSST were apparently offered study assignments, or appointment to nonfunctional staff positions with no real duties. Because study assignments had often been used to get rid of undesirable or unqualified officers, they were frequently viewed with distaste. Nor were the nonfunctional positions desired, for they usually meant the effective end to a military career. Officers who received such positions, in a play on the Indonesia words, were termed "officers who are made ghosts."[79]

---

[76] The incident was reported in *Marhaen,* December 23, 24, 26, and 27, 1957; and *PIA,* December 25, 1957 (a.m.), pp. 1-3; December 27 (a.m.), pp. 2, 4; December 30 (a.m.), pp. 10-11; January 13, 1958 (a.m.), p. 8.

[77] The city command remained at the strength of one battalion; RI-Hasanuddin retained three TNI battalions, and added four companies of ex-TRI rebels, two of ex-TKR, and three other companies; RI-23 received three TNI battalions, plus six companies from other TNI battalions (including some of those being returned to Java), and ten companies of ex-TKR rebels. "Pembagian Pasukan2 jang Administratif Masuk R.I. HN, dan Organiek KDM-SST" (January 1, 1958), DSM-AD, file—PUL ξ PAN, T, III, no. 334; source—Doc. SEM DAM XIV. Reported in *Marhaen,* January 22, 1958.

[78] Her Tasning, although a member of the planning committee originally established on February 25, 1957, did not sign the March 2 Charter. Interview, Her Tasning, Jakarta, February 1, 1972. Jusuf, although he did sign the Charter, had been careful to keep in close contact with Colonel Yani at army headquarters. According to Azis Taba, Jusuf's chief of staff at RI-Hasanuddin at the time, immediately after the March 2 Proclamation Jusuf sent him to report to Yani and to request instructions from him; interview, Jakarta, February 3, 1972. Jusuf may have spoken with Yani himself prior to the proclamation when he accompanied Sumual to Jakarta on February 27, 1957.

[79] The official term is "perwira yang diper-bantu-kan"; it was known as "perwira yang diper-hantu-

The split between the Permesta officers which developed by June 1957 is sometimes described as a split between those who were "peaceful Permesta" and those who were "warlike Permesta." The split was also, however, between those who had jobs and those who did not. To a cynic it might seem less than a coincidence that those who no longer had official positions announced their determination to fight for the ideals of the Permesta Charter, while those who had such positions claimed that they valued national unity too highly to use force against the central government.

The split between the Permesta officers became a geographic one in mid-June when Sumual and most of the TT-VII officers from Minahasa (Dee Gerungan, Eddy Gagola, Lendy Tumbelaka, John Ottay) moved to Kinilow, in Minahasa. Members of Battalion 702 who were from Minahasa also went to the North at this time, and two companies in North Sulawesi which were composed largely of Buginese and Makassarese troops went south and took their place in KDM-SST.

Although the growing split within the Permesta movement was dramatized by Sumual's move to Minahasa, it was more than a division based on personal differences among the military officers involved. From the start there had been a basic difference in priority for South and North Sulawesi. For South Sulawesi internal security was the main problem, and negotiations with Qahhar Mudzakkar the main hope for solution. In North Sulawesi the last of the small rebel groups had surrendered in March, and economic development was the prime concern. Newspaper headlines tell the story: *Marhaen,* Makassar—"The Permesta Charter has no meaning for South and Southeast Sulawesi unless Security is Restored" and "The Primary Problem is Internal Security and the Second Development"; *Pikiran Rakjat,* Manado—"This is the Spirit of Permesta: Development must be Given Priority."[80]

---

kan" (hantu—ghost); interview, Bing Latumahina, Jakarta, January 19, 1972. Sumual describing such an assignment said, "It means you have no job"; interview, Jakarta, March 9, 1971.

80 *Marhaen,* June 13 and September 27, 1957; *Pikiran Rakjat,* August 3, 1957. It must, however, be noted that *Marhaen* was a PNI newspaper, which had a generally critical attitude toward Permesta.

CHAPTER FOUR
FROM CRISIS TO CONFLICT

The dissolution of TT-VII and KoDPSST in June 1957 defused the tense situation which had existed in Makassar since the proclamation of martial law on March 2. However, although most of the South Sulawesi officers were satisfied with the June agreement and the recognition of KDM-SST, there was opposition from the Minahasan officers to the division of East Indonesia into localized commands, with coordination centered in army headquarters. Officers from Minahasa had dominated TT-VII since its establishment in 1950, but it now seemed likely that they would be confined to North Sulawesi, a restricted and unpromising arena for an ambitious officer.

In North Sulawesi, Minahasa in particular, discontent with central government policies had erupted in 1956 in the takeover of the Copra Foundation and the storm of protest against the closing of Bitung Harbor (see above, p. 37). Demands for local autonomy in North Sulawesi were combined with agitation for the splitting of the island into two or more provinces. The Minahasans, the dominant political group in North Sulawesi, favored a division into two provinces, paralleling the boundaries of the colonial residencies, in which Central Sulawesi would be included with Gorontalo, Bolaang-Mongondow, Sangihe-Talaud, and Minahasa in a province whose capital would be Manado. However, press reports indicate that there was considerable sentiment in Donggala and Poso, and even Gorontalo, for a further division into separate provinces of North and Central Sulawesi.[1]

---

1 *PIA*, January 15, 1957 (a.m.), p. 6; June 30 (a.m.), p. 3; August 20 (p.m.), p. 13; November 7, 1957, pp. 8-9; *Marhaen*, June 28, August 20, and October 30, 1957; *Pikiran Rakjat*, August 31, 1957.

During the course of 1957, the split between North and South Sulawesi, symbolized by Sumual's move to Minahasa in June, deepened. Simultaneously, the possibility of reaching a solution to the regional crisis, which had been mounting in intensity since early 1956, dwindled.

Formalization of North-South Split

Soon after Sumual's move to Minahasa, he and Somba attended a Permesta working conference in Gorontalo.[2] There on June 20, 1957, the unilateral formation of a province of North Sulawesi was announced. The provincial boundaries were identical with those of the colonial Residency of Manado, thus including Central as well as North Sulawesi. The conference appointed H. D. Manoppo, Resident-coordinator of Central Sulawesi and a native of the largely Islamic kabupaten of Bolaang-Mongondow, as governor of the new province.[3] Speaking at the conference, Manoppo noted the similarity of culture and economic interest in the North, and said that the establishment of a separate province would help to overcome the difficulties caused by the centralization in Makassar of governmental control over the whole province of Sulawesi.[4] Later he explained further, "We are already fed up with the promises of the central government to help us with money and materials for the development of this area. . . . Thanks to the barter trade in copra, cloves, nutmeg, and coffee the people hope to be able to start the area's development with modern means."[5]

During the conference the heads of the six districts of North and Central Sulawesi issued a statement of support for the Permesta movement and

---

2 Also present was a Sumatran colonel, Dahlan Djambek, who had come to Sulawesi with Nasution in late May to investigate TT-VII economic and financial affairs, and who was later to join Husein and Simbolon in Padang. On the conference see *Marhaen,* June 21-27, 1957; *Pikiran Rakjat,* June 24 and 27, 1957; *PIA,* June 25, 1957 (p.m.), p. 1; Kementerian Penerangan, *Pemberontakan "Permesta,"* pp. 71-73.
3 The choice of Gorontalo as the site of the conference, and of Manoppo as governor of the new province were evidence of the desire to avoid the appearance of Minahasan domination of Permesta. Manoppo was senior to the Resident-coordinator for North Sulawesi, W. J. Ratulangie, and this, as well as a wish to broaden the base of support for Permesta, may have influenced his selection as governor; interview, H. D. Manoppo, Jakarta, May 17, 1972.
4 *Marhaen,* June 27, 1957; *Pikiran Rakjat,* June 28, 1957. One of the difficulties is sometimes said to have been the tendency of the provincial authorities to retain a large proportion of the central government subsidy for the province in the South; interview, L. N. Palar, Jakarta, March 5, 1971.
5 *PIA,* July 4, 1957 (a.m.), p. 14.

its leaders; they requested that all signers of the March 2 Proclamation remain in their positions in the area, and urged that Sumual continue to carry out his duties in accordance with the Permesta Charter and the decisions of the Bhinneka Tunggal Ika Congress.[6]

The two largest parties in North Sulawesi, Masjumi and Parkindo, welcomed the formation of a separate province as meeting the wishes of the people of the area. The PNI spokesman, E. A. Kandou, would say only that his party had fought for the establishment of a separate province for a number of years; J. A. Sondakh of the PSI noted that it would be desirable to have formal recognition from the central government of the formation of the province; the PSII and the PKI reserved comment.[7] Indeed the PKI's disapproval of the Permesta movement had been clear in a meeting of political parties in Manado with Sumual in March, and the PNI never gave active support to the movement. Both, on the other hand, supported President Sukarno's konsepsi, amidst general opposition in Manado and Minahasa to PKI participation in the cabinet.[8]

Action to silence members of the PKI, and others who might be critical of Permesta, was taken just prior to the meeting in Gorontalo. On June 19, some thirty persons, many of them PKI members, were arrested in Minahasa and interned in Gorontalo. O. F. Pua, a member of the PNI and head of the Minahasa regional assembly, was imprisoned on unspecified charges on June 21, but was held only a short time.[9]

Shortly after the conference in Gorontalo, a meeting of the Dewan Pemuda Indonesia Timur was held in Tondano, July 5-11, 1957. Delegates from South Sulawesi and from Nusa Tenggara (Bali) were present, although the chairman of the Dewan Pemuda, Nurdin Djohan, did not attend. A Permesta Youth Command (Komando Pemuda Permesta)

---

6 *Pikiran Rakjat*, June 28, 1957.
7 *Pikiran Rakjat*, June 29, 1957. In spite of Sondakh's reserved tone, he and a number of other PSI members in Minahasa later supported Permesta. One of the most prominent civilians in Permesta, A. C. J. Mantiri, was also a member of the PSI.
8 *PIA*, March 5, 1957 (p.m.), p. 3. Another PNI leader, H. R. Ticoalu, had warned in April against "dangerous excesses," and urged caution in making foreign contacts in carrying out economic activities; *Pikiran Rakjat*, April 12, 1957.
9 *Pikiran Rakjat*, July 22, September 7 and 18, 1957; *Marhaen*, July 3, 1957; *PIA*, July 22, 1957 (a.m.), p. 8; July 28 (p.m.), p. 4. Interviews: D. J. Somba, Jakarta, August 15, 1971; E. A. Kandou, Manado, March 17, 1972. As noted above, the PKI leader Karel Supit had been very critical of the operations of the Minahasa Coconut Foundation in regional assembly discussions in November 1956.

formed at the congress was given semiofficial status by Sumual.[10] Sumual, in a meeting with the delegates at his Kinilow headquarters on July 3, said that there were now only two alternatives: "to live and fight for Permesta, or to tail along behind the center." He continued, "although we will try to reach an agreement with those who are trying to block Permesta, if their actions threaten the safety of Permesta, we will be forced to exercise revolutionary judgment." Concerning his reported assignment for study in the United States, Sumual said that the timing of the offer was bad, as he liked to finish what he had started, and for the time being he planned to devote all his efforts to Permesta.[11] One of the speakers at the Congress was Professor Sumitro Djojohadikusumo, former Dean of the Economics Faculty of the University of Indonesia, who was in Minahasa as a guest of Sumual. Professor Sumitro had fled Jakarta in May 1957, in the midst of a political controversy which included allegations of corruption; he later went into exile and became a leading rebel spokesman abroad.[12]

Following the youth congress, Somba and Minahasa area head Laurens Saerang traveled extensively in North Sulawesi, where they and Permesta were warmly welcomed. In his speeches to the various mass rallies Somba said that the formation of the province of North Sulawesi was one of the results of the March 2 Proclamation, and that it was a means for fulfilling the desires of the people to develop their region.[13]

Reactions to Formation of Province of North Sulawesi

The central government was cool to the usurpation of its authority by the unilateral formation of a province of North Sulawesi, although it had

---

10 *Pikiran Rakjat,* July 13, 1957; text of declaration of Congress is in Angkatan Darat, *PRRI,* I, pp. 170-75. Interviews, Makassar: R. Amin Daud, March 9, 1972; Nurdin Djohan, March 28, 1972.
11 *Pikiran Rakjat,* July 5, 1957; PIA, July 9, 1957 (a.m.), pp. 6-7.
12 It was largely because of Sumitro's association with the rebels that the PSI was branded, together with the Masjumi, as a regionalist party. In fact, the PSI split over this issue. Party leader Sutan Sjahrir strongly urged PSI members from both South and North Sulawesi to settle their differences with the central government peacefully, and avoid an armed clash; interviews, Husain Achmad, Makassar, October 11, 1971; A. C. J. Mantiri, Airmadidi, November 26, 1971. For biographic data on Professor Sumitro see Howard Palfrey Jones, *Indonesia: The Possible Dream* (New York: Harcourt Brace Jovanovich, 1971), p. 428. Sumitro's wife is from Minahasa, and although she is not related to Sumual, the two men seem to have been friends. On Sumitro's visit to North Sulawesi see *PIA,* July 16, 1957 (a.m.), pp. 5-6.
13 *Pikiran Rakjat,* July 16 and 17, 1957; *PIA,* July 11, 1957 (a.m.), pp. 1-2; July 16 (p.m.), p. 5.

announced plans to divide Sulawesi into two provinces in January 1956. After a cabinet meeting on the question of the division of the state into autonomous regions, the Minister of Information informed the press that the government's policy on the formation of new autonomous provinces would not be determined by recent events in North Sulawesi, but by the report of the Interior Ministry's State Commission on the Division of Provinces, which had been gathering information on the matter. In fact, the Commission had visited Minahasa in March, but its recommendations had not been made public.[14]

The initial response from Makassar was reserved; the governor's office said that although they had not yet been informed about the decisions of the meeting in Gorontalo, they had long been aware of the desire of the people in North Sulawesi to have an autonomous province for their area.[15] Indeed, Andi Pangerang had spoken in February of the interest of the people of Sulawesi in having two autonomous provinces in the island, and, as noted above, had held hearings on the matter in Manado in September 1956. The original draft of the Permesta Charter, taken to the meeting on March 2, proposed that East Indonesia be divided into five autonomous provinces: South and Southeast Sulawesi, North Sulawesi, Maluku, Nusa Tenggara, and West Irian. This was changed at the meeting to the proposal that the provinces within the area of East Indonesia be given wide autonomy.[16] It is possible that it was because of Andi Pangerang's objections that the original proposal for a province of North Sulawesi was eliminated from the March 2 Proclamation. Nonetheless, in decisions made on March 20, the TT-VII military government ordered the establishment of six provinces, dividing Nusa Tenggara into East and West, and appointed governors to the newly established provinces.[17] The March decisions were not made public at the time, and it is possible that Andi Pangerang was not informed of them. Perhaps it was only the timing of the announcement of which he was unaware; when he was asked to verify the news of the proclamation of a separate province of

---

14 *PIA*, March 5, 1957 (p.m.), p. 5; June 29 (p.m.), p. 1; *Marhaen*, June 29, 1957.
15 *Marhaen*, June 22, 1957.
16 Xerox copy of typed original, in my possession.
17 Angkatan Darat, Territorium VII-Wirabuana, Surat Keputusan No. Kpts. 0139/36/ 1957 and No. Kpts. 0140/36/1957, both issued in Makassar, March 20, 1957, over Sumual's signature. (Copies stamped "Djawatan Penerangan Republik Indonesia, Propinsi Sulawesi Utara.")

North Sulawesi, he replied, "I don't know."[18] In any case, the unilateral proclamation of a separate North Sulawesi province seems to have been one of the factors increasing Andi Pangerang's distaste for the Permesta movement. By September 1957 he was reported to favor Sulawesi remaining a single province, based on his opinion that combining the two complementary economies—one a producer of copra, the other of rice—would be beneficial to social and economic development.[19]

The differences between North and South were symbolized by the different positions and attitudes of Andi Pangerang and Ventje Sumual. Andi Pangerang, considerably older than Sumual, was recognized by the central government as civilian governor of all of Sulawesi, as well as military governor of South and Southeast Sulawesi; his Permesta position was only the latter. Sumual had been military commander of all of East Indonesia as Panglima of TT-VII, and as martial law administrator for that area would have been in an even stronger position. It is not without significance that by September 1957 Andi Pangerang supported the division of the military area of East Indonesia into four commands, but opposed the establishment of a separate province of North Sulawesi; while Sumual helped to create the province of North Sulawesi, but wished at least to be head of the interregional command for East Indonesia (KADIT) since the abolition of TT-VII had eliminated his position as Panglima of East Indonesia.

Negative reactions to the formation of the province of North Sulawesi also came from nearer home. There was a rash of delegations from Central Sulawesi to the central government indicating dissatisfaction with the unilateral inclusion of the area in a province with North Sulawesi, and demanding separate provincial status. More serious discontent erupted in Central Sulawesi, near Toli-Toli, Donggala, and Poso, starting in October. In part it was a protest against the institution of monopoly control over copra trade by local military authorities (Major Palar), in part a demand for provincial autonomy for Central Sulawesi. Since the formation of the province of North Sulawesi by the Permesta leaders, the people of the area had been forbidden to communicate with Makassar. However, Manado

---

18 *Pedoman Rakjat* (Makassar), June 24, 1957.
19 *Marhaen*, September 6, 1957.

did not seem itself to be interested in looking out for the interests of the people from Central Sulawesi, and they felt themselves completely cut off from the outside world. In early December a number of government officials, including some members of the police, and a number of youths, went into the jungles, and by the end of the month they were said to control much of the interior.[20]

Permesta in North Sulawesi: Development and Copra

With an economic base in the copra barter trade that had been carried on since early 1956 by the Minahasa Coconut Foundation, North Sulawesi was in a strong position to implement the demands of the Permesta Charter for autonomy, a more favorable balance of revenue between the center and the regions, and development.

The head of the Public Works Department in Minahasa announced in August 1957 that in the five months since the proclamation of the Permesta Charter, Rp. 2,398,500 had been used to build and repair roads, bridges, and buildings, and by November 70 percent of the roads in North Sulawesi had been repaired. Virtually every day the Manado newspapers reported projects undertaken on local initiative. Drafting of a five-year development plan for North Sulawesi was begun; emphasis was to be placed on the improvement of agriculture—through improved irrigation, use of fertilizers, and organizing agricultural training courses—so that the region could become self-supporting. In the industrial field, priority would be given to construction of factories for manufacturing building materials and for processing raw materials found in the area.[21] A reported Rp. 23,000,000 was spent on improvements to the deep sea harbor at Bitung, and by the end of 1957 a reported Rp. 28,000,000 worth of copra had been exported through the new harbor. Funds from this trade in copra were used to provide equipment and supplies for use in development projects.[22] Much labor is said to have been volunteered for

---

20 *Marhaen,* October 16 and December 31, 1957; *PIA,* December 31, 1957 (a.m.), p. 5.
21 Based on an examination of *Pikiran Rakjat,* July 1957-January 1958, and occasional copies of other newspapers. See in particular: *Pikiran Rakjat,* August 5 and October 1, 1957; *PIA,* October 12, 1957 (p.m.), p. 13; October 29 (p.m.), p. 6; November 8 (p.m.), pp. 2-4.
22 *Pikiran Rakjat,* August 12, 1957, January 17, 1958. There were also reports that some of the barter proceeds found their way into personal bank accounts in Singapore and Hong Kong; see, for

such projects as widening and repairing the road between Manado and Tondano.

An estimated 20,000 to 25,000 tons of copra was exported each month from North Sulawesi, 8,000-9,000 tons from Minahasa alone. Import requirements for rice were about 2,000-3,000 tons per month for all of North Sulawesi. Copra could be bartered for rice in Singapore on a one-to-one basis; thus there was plentiful money available for other imports.[23] Because copra is a small holder, not a plantation, crop, it was easy for the Permesta authorities in North Sulawesi to deal directly with the producers and to avoid Jakarta's foreign exchange regulations. Thus, the situation was unlike that in Sumatra, a much larger earner of foreign exchange, but whose assets of oil and rubber were largely foreign owned, and whose exchange earnings were thus much less subject to local control because foreign companies continued to deal with the central government.

Little information is available on the structure of the military government established in North Sulawesi after March 1957, but it appears that a Team of Assistants was also set up there, and that the heads of its sections served as a staff to the military governor, Major Somba. The financial and economic (FINEC) section of this staff was initially headed by J. M. J. Pantouw, and seems to have taken over many of the functions of the Minahasa Coconut Foundation which he had headed since shortly after its formation in 1956. A Copra Pool, with representatives from each of the second-level regions of North Sulawesi was also set up. There also seems to have been an attempt to coordinate the copra trade throughout East Indonesia, in particular with North Maluku which produced 6,000-7,000 tons of copra per month, and with South Sulawesi which was heavily dependent economically on the transshipment of copra. Because the government in the South controlled so little of the countryside, South Sulawesi's production of copra, and of rice, was exported not by the authorities but by local DI and TNI warlords. Thus, not only did the authorities in the South not have copra to export themselves, but

---

example, *Marhaen*, July 23, 1957, and Elias H.B., *Dipalu Arus Revolusi, kissah njata* ([Jakarta]: Masjarakat Baru, n.d.), p. 19.

23 Interviews: A. C. J. Mantiri, Airmadidi, November 5, 1971; J. M. J. Pantouw, Jakarta, February 6, 1972. Between August 1957 and August 1958, 200,000 tons of copra from Sulawesi are said to have passed through Sandakan, and 30,000 tons through Tawau in British North Borneo; Mossman, *Rebels*, p. 195, and Stevenson, *Bird's Nests*, p. 205.

they had no rice to trade for copra, and were in fact by 1957 forced to import rice to meet their own requirements.[24] However, it was clear from discussions in the economic sections of the Team of Assistants and the DPP, that although the government organs of Permesta were in the South, the North was determined to control copra trade, and thus the main source of revenue independent of the central government. This potential source of division was recognized by the Permesta leaders, and in April 1957 Sumual appointed a young economist, Drs. R. A. Sual, to head the economic and finance bureau (FINEC) for the military government to insure equitable implementation of copra policy. In South Sulawesi a Copra Management Body (Badan Urusan Kopra—BUK) was established within the framework of the Team of Assistants. In April there were complaints that the head of the BUK, Drs. Baharuddin Rachman, was on his own authority selling copra abroad at a price lower than it could be sold in Java, and a few months later Drs. Baharuddin absconded to Singapore with his profits.[25]

The lack of control of the authorities in Makassar over the South Sulawesi countryside, and the channeling of the North's copra through Bitung harbor, had a damaging effect on the economic situation in Makassar, where as early as July 1957 an estimated 10,000 harbor workers in Makassar were unemployed.[26] Makassar exports, which in 1956 were an estimated 100,000,000 kilos gross weight, in 1957 were only 73,200,000 kilos, and in 1958 a mere 31,200,000.[27] Coconut oil factories in Makassar closed because of a lack of copra.[28]

In an attempt to provide employment and improve the economic situation in Makassar, Governor Andi Pangerang announced on August 14 that all export shipments and sales of copra from South and Southeast

---

24 See, for example, *Marhaen*, December 31, 1957.
25 Few documents from North Sulawesi survived the rebellion. Information in this paragraph is based on: Angkatan Darat, TT-VII/"Wirabuana" Pemerintah Militer, "Biro Finec," pp. 129-139; Dewan Pertimbangan Pusat, Pam. Mil., TT-VII/Wirabuana, "Risalah Landjutan Sidang Pleno D.P.P. ke VI" (April 14, 1957); letter from Abdul Rivai Paerai, member of BUK, to DPP and Pemerintah Militer, April 10, 1957; and on interviews in Manado: A. C. J. Mantiri, November 5, 1971; R. A. Sual, November 9, 1971; Usman Damopolii, November 15, 1971; and in Jakarta, J. M. J. Pantouw, February 6, 1972.
26 *Marhaen*, July 12, 1957.
27 Indonesia, Biro Pusat Statistik, *Statistical Pocketbook of Indonesia*, 1960, p. 110.
28 *Marhaen*, December 6, 1957, p. 2.

Sulawesi must go through Makassar harbor. Later that month an agreement was reached with Somba and Sumual to export 5,000-10,000 tons of copra from the North via Makassar each month.[29] An emergency trade bureau was established in Makassar to handle this trade. Governor Andi Pangerang explained that the barter trade would be carried on for not more than a year, and that it would be carefully regulated. Thirty percent of the proceeds would go to the central government. Such trade was not illegal, the Governor said, because Chief of Staff Nasution had given oral approval to the venture. Further, the interests of the people and the area would be given priority over those of individuals or certain groups, and the goal of the trade was to develop the community and benefit the people. The barter trade was to be carried on exclusively with the copra from the North, the first 5,000 tons of which were delivered in October. The first return shipment, cement, jeeps, tractors, etc., was not received until November, by which time the Minister of Trade had announced that the barter through the emergency trade bureau in Makassar was at least "semi-illegal."[30]

Military Aspects

Although the efforts of the Permesta leadership in North Sulawesi centered on development projects, and the copra trade which financed them, they were also concerned about the military situation in their area. It was not insurgency that was a problem in North Sulawesi, although there had been reports in December 1956 of increased activity in southern Minahasa by the rebel Defenders of Justice Army (Pasukan Pembela Keadilan—PPK), following the withdrawal of an army post in Motoling.[31] Police Mobile Brigade and army reinforcements were requested, but greater reliance was placed on negotiating with the PPK leader, Jan Timbuleng. Timbuleng's sister was married to the Minahasa area head, Laurens Saerang, and in January 1957, Saerang announced his intention to meet with the rebel

---

29 *Marhaen,* August 14 and 31, 1957; *PIA,* September 2, 1957 (a.m.), p. 1.
30 *Marhaen,* August 31, September 4 and 19, October 9, 14, 16, and 23, 1957; *PIA,* September 2, 1957 (a.m.), pp. 1-2; October 19 (a.m.), pp. 13-14.
31 *PIA,* December 10, 1956 (p.m.), p. 5; December 24 (a.m.), p. 5.

leader to convince him to "return to normal life."³² On March 7 it was announced in Manado that Saerang had met Timbuleng, and on March 8 he accompanied Timbuleng and his wife to a meeting with Major Somba, where arrangements for the surrender and rehabilitation of the 3,000 followers of the PPK were discussed.³³ The surrender of Timbuleng was cited by Sumual in his March 13 press conference as an example of the results to be expected from the policy of the Permesta military government to entrust implementation of security policy to the recently appointed military governors.³⁴

The principal concern of the military leaders in North Sulawesi was to rationalize the structure of Infantry Regiment-24, and after September 1957, its successor, the North and Central Sulawesi Command (KDM-SUT), and to strengthen the TNI presence in the area by incorporating a number of ex-KNIL soldiers into regular army units.³⁵ RI-24 formally comprised a single battalion, 714, some units of which were stationed in North Maluku. The men from Battalion 702 who came north from Makassar in June 1957, were formed into a second battalion, 717. Two TNI units in Central Sulawesi—Battalion 719 (two companies) under Major L. J. Palar (a Minahasan), and a company under the Toraja officer Frans Karangan in the Palu area—were less certainly under its jurisdiction.³⁶

Discussion of increasing the strength of the TNI in North Sulawesi and regularizing the command structure had begun prior to the proclamation of martial law on March 2, 1957. Somba, after consulting with Sumual, had proposed to army headquarters that RI-24's strength be increased to two battalions.³⁷ He received permission to form approximately two new companies from former KNIL soldiers in the area, and on March 11,

---

32 *PIA,* January 10, 1957 (p.m.), p. 4; January 12 (a.m.), p. 8; January 22 (p.m.), p. 1.
33 *Pikiran Rakjat,* March 7, 1957; *PIA,* March 12, 1957 (a.m.), p. 10; March 15 (a.m.), pp. 15-16.
34 *PIA,* March 14, 1957 (a.m.), p. 6.
35 Minahasa had been a major recruiting ground for the KNIL, and estimates of the number of KNIL veterans in the area in 1957 vary from 18,000 to 30,000. See *Pikiran Rakjat,* September 12 and 14, 1957; *PIA,* August 6, 1956 (a.m.), p. 7.
36 After TT-VII was dissolved in June 1957, and the four smaller military area commands were set up, there was some movement of units (such as part of Battalion 702) back to their areas of origin. It is not clear whether or not this was done with army headquarters authorization; neither is it clear which of the new commands had jurisdiction over some units stationed in what were now border areas.
37 Interview, D. J. Somba, Jakarta, January 22, 1972.

1957, 387 ex-KNIL men were commissioned into the TNI.[38]

Then, on June 25, 1957, the following announcement of the Information Section of the North Sulawesi Team of Assistants was published in the Manado press:

> In accordance with the intention and goals incorporated in the planned law for "universal military service," for the first time in all of Indonesia a trial militia will be established in the area of the military governor of North Sulawesi.
>
> This trial militia will be organized within a short time, and preference for training will be given to those who have in the past borne arms.[39]

This announcement, reaching Jakarta at the same time as the news of the unilateral proclamation of a province of North Sulawesi by a Permesta working conference in Gorontalo, apparently caused alarm. There were headlines in the press on the proclamation of general conscription in North Sulawesi, and accusations in Parliament that thousands (some said 15,000) of ex-KNIL soldiers were being illegally armed. In a press interview Somba denied that ex-KNIL men had been given weapons, but admitted that a proposal to incorporate 18,000 ex-KNIL into the TNI had been forwarded to army headquarters. There had been no answer to this proposal as yet, he said, nor to the request for authorization for the formation of a second infantry regiment for North Sulawesi.[40]

On September 28, 1957, the North and Central Sulawesi Military Area Command (Komando Daerah Militer Sulawesi Utara-Tengah—KDM-SUT) was officially installed by Chief of Staff Nasution, with Major Somba as commander. Sumual and Permesta Governor H. D. Manoppo were among those present at the ceremony. In his speech, Somba foreshadowed the conflict in loyalties which he and other officers were to find impossible to resolve in the months to come. "The ideology of the

---

38 *Menara* (Manado), March 12, 1957; *PIA*, March 17, 1957 (a.m.), p. 2; interview, D. J. Somba, Jakarta, August 15, 1971.
39 Text in *Pikiran Rakjat*, June 25, 1957; also reported in *Pedoman Rakjat*, June 26, 1957.
40 *PIA*, June 28, 1957 (p.m.), p. 2; September 12 (p.m.), p. 10; *Pikiran Rakjat*, September 12 and 14, 1957.

TNI," said Major Somba, "is to defend the state, and for Sulawesi Utara the ideology of the soldier must be in accordance with the wishes and desires of the people."[41]

The question of the internal reorganization of KDM-SUT, the addition of a second battalion, and the enrollment of ex-KNIL troops was discussed by Somba and Nasution a number of times during 1957 and early 1958. Apparently without formal authorization from army headquarters, KDM-SUT announced in November 1957 plans to carry out a reorganization of military units under its jurisdiction. Battalion 714 was to be split into two battalions, designated as "P" and "S," and two further battalions, "Q" and "R," were to be formed from the two companies of Battalion 719 under Major Palar and the one company under Captain Frans Karangan in Central Sulawesi, with each officer to assume command of one of the newly formed battalions.[42]

Central Government Efforts to Reach a Solution

By July 1957 the central government was expressing its concern about the problem of North Sulawesi, not the problem of Permesta. The situation in the South seemed to be well in hand, with the leadership in the hands of a respected local figure, Andi Pangerang, who often voiced his concern for the unity of the Republic, and denounced those who used the slogan of "development" to conceal separatist intentions. In the North, however, there seemed to be no local leader on whom the central government could rely. Further, Sumual was receiving enthusiastic support from his fellow Minahasans.

Jakarta decided to send to North Sulawesi a mission composed of high ranking central government officials who came from Minahasa: G. A. Maengkom, Minister of Justice; F. J. Inkiriwang, Minister of Industry; L. N. Palar, Ambassador, to Canada; and Arnold Mononutu, member of the Constituent Assembly. From July 17 to August 5, 1957 this mission traveled widely in North Sulawesi, and held discussions with Sumual, Somba, Saerang, Manoppo, and a visiting DPP delegation

---

41 *Pikiran Rakjat* and *Marhaen*, September 30, 1957.
42 *Gelora Maesa* (Manado) and *Pikiran Rakjat,* November 25, 1957. Both Palar and Karangan had reputations of being war lords; see for example, *Marhaen,* October 16, 1957.

from Makassar. During their visit the members of the mission made various complimentary comments about Permesta, and seemed to be optimistic about the possibility of reaching an agreement between the regional leaders and the central government. On July 23, after meeting with Sumual and members of his staff at Kinilow, the mission members issued a statement approving Sumual's division of East Indonesia into six autonomous provinces; supporting the establishment of a university in North Sulawesi; guaranteeing interisland air and sea communications; recommending that the province of North Sulawesi, its second level areas, and governmental offices, receive their budgets directly from the central government; and recommending that barter trade be allowed to continue until a final agreement could be reached with the central government.[43]

One of the more important recommendations of the mission to the central government was that a national conference (Musjawarah Nasional—MUNAS) be held to discuss the critical situation in the country.[44] The conference was scheduled for September 10-15, 1957, and Sumual, after talks with Prime Minister Djuanda in Jakarta in late August, announced that he would attend.[45]

Prior to the opening of MUNAS, Sumual joined the dissident Sumatran colonels Husein and Barlian for a meeting on September 8 in Palembang (which army headquarters had attempted to ban). The three signed what is known as the Palembang Charter, which expressed their doubts that the MUNAS would succeed in reaching a national settlement, set forth their main demands, and called for coordination of activities in military and financial-economic fields. The main demands were:

1) the restoration of the Sukarno-Hatta Duumvirate;
2) the replacement of the army high command, as the first step in the stabilization of the army;

---

43 Text of agreement printed in *Pikiran Rakjat*, September 30, 1957. On the mission in general see: *Pikiran Rakjat*, July 18 and 30, August 2, 3, 6, 7, and 16, 1957; *Marhaen*, July 29, August 3 and 6, 1957; *PIA*, July 17, 1957 (a.m.), p. 1; July 18 (a.m.), p. 1; July 24 (a.m.), p. 2; July 26 (a.m.), p. 1, and (p.m.), p. 6; August 6 (a.m. and p.m.), p. 1.

44 Many people claim responsibility for having originated the idea; some apparently saw the proposed MUNAS as an expanded version of the Bhinneka Tunggal Ika Congress held for East Indonesia in May 1957.

45 *Pedoman Rakjat*, September 2, 1957.

3) the decentralization of the national administration;
4) the establishment of a Senate;
5) "rejuvenation and simplification" of the state apparatus; and
6) the banning of communism, because of its essentially international nature.[46]

The Charter was not made public at the time, and the three colonels did attend MUNAS as observers. Sumual's official position at the conference was as an adviser to the delegation from North Sulawesi, which was headed by Major Somba. It included H. D. Manoppo, W. J. Ratulangie, and a number of other civilian and military members and advisers.[47] South Sulawesi had a separate delegation, headed by Governor Andi Pangerang, which included Haji Makkaraeng Daeng Mandjarungi (Chairman of the Permesta Central Advisory Council), Henk Rondonuwu (Chairman of the executive committee of the Council), Saleh Lahade, and Jusuf.[48]

The National Conference set up committees to discuss problems in four areas: (1) government and administration; (2) finance and economic development; (3) the armed forces, particularly the army; and (4) the Sukarno-Hatta Duumvirate. Detailed recommendations were presented to the conference by the first two committees; the other two committees were to continue their work after the conference to try to reach a solution. The committees on government and administration, and finance and economic development, made a number of detailed recommendations to the conference, which, in general, urged that the central government meet the requests of the regions for local control and autonomy, more

---

46 The English text of the Charter is in Indonesia, Kementerian Penerangan, *Now It Can Be Disclosed*, Special Issue no. 12 (Jakarta, 1958), pp. 20-26. The Indonesian text is in the Ministry's *Peristiwa Sumatera Barat*, I (Jakarta, 1960), pp. 52-53.
47 Ratulangie's official position was Resident-coordinator of North Sulawesi, and Manoppo's Resident-coordinator of Central Sulawesi, although he was then acting as the Permesta-appointed governor of North Sulawesi.
48 Information on the membership of both delegations is from: *Marhaen*, September 2, 7, and 18, 1957; *Pikiran Rakjat*, September 3 and 4, 1957; *PIA*, August 30, 1957 (p.m.), p. 4; September 2 (p.m.), p. 1; September 3 (p.m.), p. 1; September 9 (a.m.), p. 1. Many persons who had been, and most of those who still were, involved in Permesta seem to have attended as "advisers" to one or the other of the Sulawesi delegations. The fact that Andi Mattalatta was not included in the South Sulawesi delegation was the cause of some comment in the press; he says that he was busy with preparations for the National Games to be held in Makassar at the end of September, and with the difficult security situation in South Sulawesi; interview, Makassar, March 29, 1972.

equitable sharing of revenue, and for permission to take the initiative in development projects with financial and technical support from the central government.

At the conference Sukarno and Hatta signed a joint statement that they would cooperate with each other in the interests of the state and the people. To those present, however, the differences between the two were clear in Sukarno's idealistic invocation of the unfinished revolution, and Hatta's intellectual analysis of the economic situation facing the nation and his pragmatic insistence that thought be given to what must be done. At the conclusion of the Conference all the participants flew to Jogjakarta for a pledge of loyalty to Sukarno and Hatta—taken at the grave of the founder of the Indonesian Army, and a great hero of the revolution, General Sudirman. It was a fitting conclusion to a meeting more memorable for this ritual than for any substantive results.[49]

Despite the absence of concrete results from the MUNAS discussion, and although the dissident colonels continued the plotting they had formalized in the Palembang Charter, there was for a time an atmosphere of hope, however, superficial it appears in retrospect, that a settlement might be achieved. Sumual publicly described the results of the conference as "satisfactory," and said that the efforts of the Permesta movement to accelerate development in East Indonesia would be adapted to the decisions of MUNAS. The solution of problems within the army, said Sumual, would be left to the Seven-Man Committee appointed at the conference to deal with these matters.[50] As noted above, Somba was officially installed as military administrator of North Sulawesi and commander of KDM-SUT in September. Further, following the opening

---

49 "We returned home as wise or as foolish as before" (kami pulang sama pintar dan sama bodoh sebelumnya) was the comment of one of the participants; A. C. J. Mantiri, Airmadidi, November 26, 1971. Other interviews, Makassar: Henk Rondonuwu, June 9, 1971; Datulolo, September 13, 1971; Saleh Lahade, October 4 and 7, 1971; and Jakarta: H. N. V. Sumual, March 9, 1971; D. J. Somba, August 15, 1971; H. D. Manoppo, May 17, 1972. Press reports: *PIA*, September 15, 1957 (a.m.), pp. 17-18; September 16 (a.m.), pp. 6-9, and (p.m.), pp. 2-6; September 17 (p.m.), pp. 1-2.

50 The members of the Seven-Man Committee were: President Sukarno, former Vice President Mohammad Hatta, Prime Minister Djuanda, Third Deputy Prime Minister Dr. Leimena, former Minister of Defense Sultan Hamengkubuwono, Minister of Health Colonel Dr. Azis Saleh, and Army Chief of Staff Nasution. *PIA*, September 21, 1957 (a.m.), p. 4. In an interview in Jakarta on March 9, 1971, Sumual stated that "we" attended MUNAS because "we" really wanted to solve the regional problem, and that a solution was possible; "if the proposals of the Committee of Seven and the Fact-Finding Committee had been carried out a clash could have been prevented."

of the National Games (PON IV) in Makassar on September 27, Sukarno went to North Sulawesi for a two-day visit. In his speeches to mass rallies at Manado, Tomohon, Tondano, Gorontalo, and Palu, Sukarno received an affirmative and enthusiastic response to his appeal to national unity. Many in the audience, however, carried signs supporting Permesta, some requesting that Sumual and Saleh Lahade continue as leaders of the area, and some said, "Sorry, Bung Karno, we don't want communism." The President also spoke at the Permesta-sponsored university in Manado, where he was greeted by a banner reading "Fear of the Lord is the Beginning of All Wisdom."[51]

In early October the Permesta-designated civilian governor of North Sulawesi, H. D. Manoppo, reported on his return from Jakarta that the central government would probably agree to the formation of the province of North Sulawesi, and would supply a budget of Rp. 500,000,000. A few days later an official from the Ministry of the Interior arrived for discussions on this matter.[52]

Beneath the surface more ominous decisions were being made. Following MUNAS the Sumatran colonels met again in Palembang (September 21-22). They drew up an "annex" to the Palembang Charter entitled "Fundamental Ideas, Guiding Principles, and Joint Programme of the Regional Struggle," which Husein and Barlian brought to Makassar for Sumual's signature under cover of attending the National Games.[53] This document, like the Charter itself, was not made public at the time. There were few changes from the demand of the original Charter, but these were significant, because they indicated a belief that a settlement was virtually impossible. The inclusion of Nasution in the Seven-Man Committee that was to solve military issues was regarded as particularly unfortunate, as

---

51 *Pikiran Rakjat*, September 30, 1957; *PIA*, September 30, 1957 (a.m.), pp. 9-10; October 4 (a.m.), pp. 1-2. Interview, P. Matindas, Manado, March 16, 1972. See also report of the trip by the then U.S. Ambassador John M. Allison, who was in the group accompanying Sukarno to Sulawesi: *Ambassador from the Prairie* (Boston: Houghton-Mifflin, 1973), pp. 316-18.
52 *PIA*, October 1, 1957 (a.m.), p. 4; October 11 (p.m.), p. 13.
53 *Marhaen*, September 27 and 28, 1957; *PIA*, September 27, 1957 (p.m.), p. 8; September 29 (a.m.), p. 1; interview, H. N. V. Sumual, Jakarta, March 9, 1971. While in Makassar, Barlian and Husein joined Sumual and Saleh Lahade in addressing a meeting of Permesta youth and students; *PIA*, October 2, 1957 (a.m.), p. 3. Husein also visited RI-Hasanuddin headquarters and the military training center at Malino; he was accompanied by Major Jusuf on a call on the Rajah of Gowa, a Permesta supporter; photographs supplied by PenDam XIV/Hasanuddin, Makassar.

Nasution was himself a party to the dispute. The Duumvirate was now called a "myth," and it was agreed to strive for the election of a new president of the Republic. Further, because the colonels believed that communism was increasing its influence on the central government, they agreed to begin immediate preparations to establish an Emergency Central Government for the Republic of Indonesia (Pemerintah Pusat Darurat Republik Indonesia) outside Java. The demands for a change in the army high command, the establishment of a Senate, the banning of communism, and government decentralization were repeated essentially unchanged. It was agreed that a Joint Command would be set up and that the principle of collective defense would be adhered to.[54]

In the meantime, the Seven-Man Committee appointed by MUNAS to recommend a solution to the army's personnel problems began its work by setting up a Fact-Finding Committee of three members: Colonel Mokoginta, Colonel Sudirman, and Major Muskita. The latter committee visited Makassar and Manado in mid-October. They did not meet with Sumual, who was apparently not in Sulawesi at the time, but did talk with Saleh Lahade, who submitted to them proposals for solving the crisis which in essence reiterated the demands of the March 2 Proclamation.[55] A spokes-man told the press that the Fact-Finding Committee would forward to the Seven-Man Committee the proposal they had received in Makassar that Sumual be named commander of KADIT (Komando Antar Daerah Indonesia Timur), the coordinating command for East Indonesia. Apparently Sumual was considered seriously for a position in KADIT; he was included in a KADIT working meeting held in Bali, October 22-25. However, on October 26 it was announced that he would be posted to the army general staff in Jakarta, and that his future position would be decided by the Seven-Man Committee.[56] Saleh Lahade was assigned to attend the SSKAD in Bandung, but, although he had held no official position since the dissolution of the KoDPSST, he did not accept the offer.[57]

---

54 The English text of the document is in Kementerian Penerangan, *Now It Can Be Disclosed*, pp. 35-44; and the Indonesian text in *Peristiwa Sumatera Barat*, pp. 59-62.
55 Moh. Saleh Lahade, "Konsep Penjelesaian Persoalan Angkatan Darat" (October 15, 1957); a copy of which he kindly gave to me.
56 *Marhaen*, October 12, 23, and 30, 1957; *Pikiran Rakjat*, October 17, 1957; *PIA*, October 26, 1957 (a.m.), p. 5, and (p.m.), p. 12; October 30 (p.m.), p. 8.
57 *Marhaen*, October 14, 1957, p. 2; *PIA*, October 14, 1957 (a.m.), p. 1; interview, Saleh Lahade,

By the time the National Development Conference (Musjawarah Nasional Pembangunan) was held in Jakarta, November 25 to December 4, 1957, there was little left of the public atmosphere of hopefulness which followed MUNAS. Hatta had gone on an extended trip abroad, and there were no signs that either he or Sukarno had found it possible to give substance to their MUNAS pledge of cooperation. Debates in Parliament on a new martial law statute had provided an occasion for widespread criticism of the actions taken by the regional military commanders under the existing law, which was of colonial origin.[58] And although a campaign against high level corruption begun in July was in part a response to complaints from the regions, in early November army headquarters announced that in order to extend the investigation into corruption to the outlying areas, those in the regions responsible for solving the problem—territorial commanders, governors, and police chiefs—must first have their own personal property and wealth investigated by a committee of high ranking officers to be appointed by Chief of Staff Nasution.[59]

The regions too continued their defiance. In Manado it was announced in October that the barter trade would continue until there was a firm guarantee from the central government that the revenues from the regions would be used for the development of the regions concerned, and that the development projects which had been begun in the area would not be allowed to die for lack of funds. Further, it was said that the central government's export system (BE) was applicable only to the center, and could not be carried out in the provinces because it benefited only alien and not national enterprises.[60]

A symptom of the change in atmosphere was that the delegates to the Development Conference were much lower ranking than were those who attended MUNAS in September, although the regional commanders had been instructed to attend.[61] The one hopeful note was that the Seven-Man Committee had apparently reached agreement on a formula to grant amnesty to the various officers who had defied army authority since 1956,

---

Makassar, October 9, 1971.
58 Lev, *Transition*, pp. 67-68.
59 *PIA*, November 3, 1957 (a.m.), pp. 1-2.
60 *Pikiran Rakjat*, October 1, 1957; *PIA*, October 12, 1957 (p.m.), p. 13.
61 *Marhaen*, November 13, 1957; *PIA*, November 23, 1957 (a.m.), p. 14; November 25 (a.m.), pp. 7-8; November 28 (p.m.), pp. 2-16; December 5 (p.m.), pp. 1-6.

and to offer them an opportunity to choose between an army career or civilian life.[62]

Then, while the Development Conference was still in session, on November 30, 1957, there was an attempt to assassinate President Sukarno—the Tjikini Affair. The plot was blamed on Colonel Zulkifli Lubis, in hiding since his dispute with Nasution the year before. Because of Lubis's continued association with the dissident Sumatran colonels, the whole regional movement was accused widely in the Jakarta press of treachery. Although not announced until February 11, the recommendation of the MUNAS Seven-Man Committee on army personnel policies that there be a general amnesty for officers involved in defiance of army authority was "frozen" by the Tjikini Affair.[63]

The assassination attempt coincided with an important foreign policy defeat for the Indonesian government—the failure to obtain a two-thirds majority on a UN resolution calling on the Netherlands to negotiate with Indonesia to settle the disposition of West Irian. Reaction in Indonesia was sharp. A government-approved nationwide strike demonstrating solidarity against the Dutch position in West Irian was followed by PNI and PKI labor union takeovers of Dutch enterprises, including the KPM shipping line, banks, firms, and estates. Although the takeovers were encouraged, if not ordered by President Sukarno, neither Prime Minister Djuanda nor Army Chief of Staff Nasution fully approved of the seizures, which were disrupting banking and communications, in the short run adding greatly to the existing economic difficulties. A cabinet decision of December 5 that seized enterprises should be placed under government control proved ineffective, and on December 13 Nasution forbade further seizures and placed enterprises already taken over under army control. Following the cabinet decision, thirty-four Dutch enterprises in South

---

62 Lev, *Transition*, p. 32.
63 *PIA*, February 11, 1958 (p.m.), p. 11. The "regionalists" now blame the accusations of involvement in the Tjikini Affair on the leftist press, and say that the PKI seized an opportunity to thwart a settlement. Sumual specifically blames the Tjikini Affair for ending the possibility of a settlement; interview, Jakarta, March 9, 1971. See also Nasution's explanations of the events of this period in *Madjalah Angkatan Darat*, January 1958, pp. 6-9, and February-March 1958, pp. 4-6; and *Towards a People's Army* (Jakarta: c.v. Delegasi, 1964), pp. 7-15. Apparently arrest warrants were issued during this period for some of the officers who had been active in Permesta, although they were not served until later; interviews, Jakarta: Bing Latumahina, January 14, 1972; Dr. O. E. Engelen, February 1, 1972.

and Southeast Sulawesi were placed under the control of the provincial administration, although none had previously been taken over there by the workers. A provincial "General Supervisory Body" was established, including representatives of the civil service, the military, and the provincial Action Committee for the Liberation of West Irian, the latter being the body designated for coordinating action in opposition to the Dutch.[64]

As tension mounted in Jakarta and throughout the country, the lines of division hardened and the possibility of a negotiated settlement receded. During December a number of Masjumi leaders, harassed and threatened by accusations of lack of support for the anti-Dutch takeovers and of association with Colonel Lubis in the Tjikini assassination attempt on the President, fled Jakarta for Padang, where they made common cause with Husein and Simbolon. On December 16 the Commission of Nine established by MUNAS to reestablish cooperation between Sukarno and Hatta, announced that it had failed in its task because Hatta would "participate in administration only if he had authority as well as moral responsibility."[65]

By December the government seems to have realized that the rebellious colonels were in contact with potential foreign supporters (and suppliers).[66] The government itself had met with reluctance in its efforts to purchase arms from the United States, and in December an army purchasing mission left for Eastern Europe and the USSR.[67]

---

[64] *Marhaen*, December 4, 7, and 9, 1957; *PIA*, December 7, 1957 (a.m.), p. 11; December 11 (a.m.), p. 5. A plan for such a takeover had been produced by the economic section of the Permesta military government Team of Assistants in April 1957, but it is not known if this plan influenced the action of the provincial authorities; Badan Pengoperan Usaha2 Asing Pemerintah Militer TT-VII/Wirabuana, "Risalah Tugas/ Rentjana Kerdja, Organisasi/Susunan Personalia dan Procedure Kerdja," Makassar, March 12, 1957; approved by Seksi C, Team of Assistants, Pemerintah Militer TT-VII, April 15, 1957.

[65] *PIA*, December 17, 1957 (a.m.), pp. 14-15.

[66] Such rumors were rife in Jakarta at the time; in his questions to Sulawesi officers at a conference in early January 1958 (see below) Nasution indicated that he had information on shipment of arms from abroad to the rebels. His own writings on this period do not indicate when he first became aware of foreign contacts with and support for the rebels. According to Daniel S. Lev, Jakarta leaders were aware of the delivery of "medical and military supplies" to Central Sumatra by U.S. agents during the latter half of 1957; "America, Indonesia, and the Rebellion of 1958," *United Asia*, 17/4 (July-August 1965), p. 307.

[67] *PIA*, December 28, 1957 (p.m.), PP. 1, 11. According to Ambassador Allison, "The State Department's position about supplying arms to Indonesia ... was that it feared such arms might be used to attack separatist movements in the outer islands, or that they might be used to attack

Then on January 11, 1958 the central government issued an order declaring illegal "all regulations and decisions of either the military or civil authorities in the regions concerning foreign trade which are in deviation of the regulations instituted by the government." The recalcitrant regions were warned that if they did not comply with the order, the government would be prepared to stop its subsidy to them. The Minister of Finance explained that it was necessary to stop the barter trade in order to prevent a collapse in the state's finances.[68]

The emergency trade bureau in Makassar, which had received no more copra from the North after the initial shipment in October 1957, said that it welcomed this decision because it would be applied uniformly and all regions would be treated equally. Governor Andi Pangerang ordered that all barter trade be stopped.[69]

Major Somba said initially that barter trade in North Sulawesi would continue. However, in talks with Nasution in Jakarta in early February, he was assured that a new export-import body would be established which would meet the demands of the regions, and he then affirmed that North and Central Sulawesi would obey the instructions banning barter trade.[70]

Divisions between North and South Sulawesi also hardened during this period. There had been a last attempt to resuscitate Permesta organizations in Makassar on November 9, 1957, when a Permesta Supreme Council (Dewan Tertinggi Permesta) and a Permesta Youth Supreme Council (Dewan Tertinggi Pemuda Permesta) were inaugurated by Sumual. He himself headed the Permesta Supreme Council, with Saleh Lahade as his deputy, and Bing Latumahina as secretary. Each council had seventeen members, most, if not all, of them residents of Makassar.[71] This was indeed a small group compared to the fifty-one who had initially

---

West Irian, or, in the third place, in the event of a Communist conquest of Java, our arms would fall into Communist hands"; Allison, *Ambassador*, p. 342.

68 *PIA*, January 12, 1958 (a.m.), pp. 1-2. Nasution estimated the loss of revenue to the central government as $40,000,000 per month; *Towards a People's Army*, pp. 9-10.

69 *Marhaen*, January 14 and 22, 1958.

70 *Pikiran Rakjat*, January 14, 1958; *PIA*, February 4, 1958 (p.m.), pp. 9-10. Interview, D. J. Somba, Jakarta, August 15, 1971.

71 "Dekrit Permesta SeWirabuana," no. 001/Dok/10/1957, Makassar, Sumual/Saleh, November 9, 1957, DSM-AD, File—Peristiwa Penting Lainnja, Source—Doc SMAD TT-VII. Reported in *Pedoman Rakjat*, November 11, 1957, and in *PIA*, November 13, 1957.

signed the Permesta Charter, or the 111 who had composed the first Central Advisory Council (DPP). By the end of 1957, with the exception of Saleh Lahade, few of the original Permesta leaders from South Sulawesi remained active participants. Increasingly Permesta was identified with North Sulawesi and with a small group of ethnically mixed intellectuals in the city of Makassar.

On December 31 the Permesta governor of North Sulawesi, H. D. Manoppo, announced the ending of financial and administrative control over the North by Makassar (still recognized by the central government as the provincial capital of all Sulwesi). However, on January 13, 1958, the Minister of the Interior said that the central government subsidy for all of Sulawesi would be sent via Makassar. A spokesman for North Sulawesi said that financial matters were no problem "as we are now being flooded with money." The formation of separate vertical government services for North Sulawesi was announced by Governor Manoppo on January 7, 1958.[72]

Physical communication between North and South had also become more difficult. Interisland shipping was seriously disrupted by Jakarta's seizure of the KPM steamship line in the takeover of Dutch enterprises in December 1957. Operation of the national airline, Garuda, was also affected by the withdrawal of a number of Dutch pilots in the exodus of Dutch nationals which had followed the seizures. In January the frequency of Garuda flights to Manado was cut down, and on January 14 it was announced that Garuda connections to North Sulawesi would be halted altogether. A week later it was announced that flights to Manado would resume on a weekly basis, but would be routed via Banjermasin (Kalimantan) rather than via Makassar.[73]

The Final Stages

In the atmosphere of increased tension following the Tjikini Affair and the takeover of Dutch enterprises, the army's central leadership seems to

---

72 *PIA*, January 8, 1958 (a.m.), p. 8; January 14 (a.m.), p. 11.
73 *Marhaen*, January 11, 1958; *Bara*, January 13 and 20, 1958; *Pikiran Rakjat*, January 14, 1958; *Gelora Maesa*, January 15, 1958. There was thus no direct air service between Makassar and Manado.

have tried to obtain as much support as possible within the TNI, and to undermine sympathy for the rebel colonels. Indeed, Nasution's placement of seized Dutch enterprises under army control can be seen, at least in part, as a signal to those who had made anticommunism an increasingly prominent theme of the regional movement that he was prepared to keep communist and radical nationalist labor unions out of control of this important segment of the economy.

More direct action was taken with regard to several officers who were thought to be subject to headquarters' influence. Nasution supported Lieutenant Colonel Herman Pieters, commander of KDM-Maluku, against an attempt by Sumual to replace him in December 1957, and is also said to have authorized Pieters to continue direct barter trade.[74] Somba (commander of KDM-SUT), Jusuf (commander of RI-Hasanuddin), and Rifai (commander of RI-23) were promoted to lieutenant colonel as of January 1, 1958.[75]

A security conference of senior officers from Java and East Indonesia was held from January 7 to 9 in Tretes, East Java. Mattalatta, Her Tasning, and Jusuf attended from KDM-SST; Majors Gagola, Joseph, and Tenges represented KDM-SUT. Somba was said to be ill and did not attend. Nasution is said to have queried the North Sulawesi delegation as to Somba's absence, and to have inquired about Sumual's whereabouts (although there had been press reports that he was then in Sumatra). Both Sulawesi delegations were questioned sharply by Nasution about their involvement in barter trade, and in particular whether any weapons were being brought in to Sulawesi. He was told that the proceeds of the barter trade were food, medicine, textiles, and equipment for development—but no arms. The North Sulawesi delegation was also queried about reports of mass enlistments of former KNIL soldiers by KDM-SUT. The Minahasan officers maintained that there had been no general mobilization in North Sulawesi, and that the listing of ex-KNIL had been made to determine which were eligible for inclusion in the two additional companies which had been authorized by army headquarters.[76]

---

[74] *PIA*, February 12, 1958 (p.m.), p. 9; Justus M. van der Kroef, "Disunited Indonesia," part 2, *Far Eastern Survey*, 27/5 (May 1958), p. 73.
[75] *Bara*, February 3, 1958.
[76] Whether or not such authorization was given is unclear; possibly verbal assent may have been

Suspicions were present not only among the delegation from army headquarters but also among the group from North Sulawesi. Somba may indeed have be en ill, but it was partly fear of arrest that kept him in Manado. The members of the delegation considered his fears justified, for the plane carrying them to East Java had been ordered to land in Gorontalo by the Air Force, and was allowed to proceed only after the passengers were identified. The Permesta officers' suspicions of AURI, which with its commander Suryadarma was thought by them to have leftist leanings, were increased when they were told on the conclusion of the meeting that air connections to Manado had been closed on Suryadarma's orders. An appeal to Deputy Chief of Staff Gatot Subroto did result in the resumption of flights, but on a limited schedule.

Although Somba was not present at the Tretes meeting, he did go to Jakarta to meet Nasution on February 1. By this time it had been announced that the army was investigating press reports about the planned formation of a "Sumatra State."[77] An army spokesman had also confirmed that Sumual had recently been in Singapore, without permission of army headquarters to leave the country, and said that reports that Husein and Barlian had also been seen recently in Singapore were being checked.[78] Indeed, Somba knew before meeting Nasution that plans were under way to force a confrontation with Jakarta, and he feared that unless quick action were taken to meet the demands of the dissidents, fighting could not be averted.[79] Somba asked that the political and economic demands of the Permesta Charter be met as quickly as possible in view of the rising tension in the country; Nasution replied that these were matters which would have to be handled by Parliament. Nasution again asked for a list of weapons that had been imported; Somba told him that none had been brought in. As noted above, Somba did agree to end barter trade in North Sulawesi. He returned to Manado on February 6.[80]

---

implied, but written authorization seems never to have been issued. Reports of the meeting are in *Marhaen*, January 9, 1958; *PIA*, January 13, 1958 (p.m.), p. 12, January 17 (a.m.), p. 8. Also based on interviews with D. J. Somba, and with participants in the meeting who asked that they not be identified.

77 *PIA*, January 13, 1958 (p.m.), p. 11.
78 *PIA*, January 31, 1958 (a.m.), pp. 6-7.
79 Interview, D. J. Somba, Jakarta, August 15, 1971. See below, on cable to Somba from Sumual on decisions of Sungai Dareh meeting of January 9-13, 1958.
80 *PIA*, February 2, 1958 (a.m.), p. 2; February 4 (p.m.), pp. 9-10; February 10 (a.m.), p. 5; *Bara*,

Whatever Somba's intentions in reaching these agreements, and whatever Nasution hoped to accomplish by seeking Somba's loyalty, others were already taking actions that would determine the course of events.

Sumual had left his Kinilow headquarters just before Christmas, and from January 9 to 13 he was at Sungai Dareh in West Sumatra. There at a meeting with the dissident Sumatran officers—Simbolon, Lubis, Husein, Barlian, Dahlan Djambek—and the civilian politicians who had joined them—Dr. Sumitro Djojohadikusumo, Sjafruddin Prawiranegara, Muhammad Natsir—the decision was made to establish a rival government if Jakarta refused to accede to the rebels' demands. There was some discussion of the coordination of forces, but apparently no firm agreement on timing. Sumual says that he did expect the central government to respond with force, but that at the time of the Sungai Dareh meeting the rebels had only plans, no weapons, with which to meet an attack by Jakarta. Immediately after the meeting, Sumual left for Singapore to search for weapons.[81]

Although Sumual had informed none of his colleagues in either North or South Sulawesi in advance of the Sungai Dareh meeting, he did send a cable to Somba following it, which outlined the decisions taken and the membership of the proposed revolutionary government. Although the cable cautioned against "Jakarta provocations," it also ordered that Gerungan, aided by other staff officers, "make a plan or study for a physical attack on Jakarta, including total materiel requirements, with the operational planning to be carried out by the three rebel areas [North Sulawesi, Central, and South Sumatra]."[82]

In Singapore, according to Sumual, he met a number of people willing to sell him weapons (from the U.S., Taiwan, and Italy), but it was impossible to get an export license for a private deal. He then went on to Hong Kong, where he met Colonel Joop Warouw, his predecessor as Panglima of TT-VII, whom he had contacted at his post at the Indonesian Embassy in

---

February 5 and 7, 1958; interview, D. J. Somba, Jakarta, August 15, 1971.

81 Interviews, H. N. V. Sumual, Jakarta, March 9, 1971 and April 13, 1972; Sumual was accompanied by only two aides, Major Arie Supit and Lieutenant Tema. The Sungai Dareh meeting is mentioned in Lev, *Transition*, p. 38; *Madjalah Angkatan Darat*, February-March 1958, p. 6; *Sari Attensia*, VI/2 (1959), p. 134; Mossman, *Rebels*, p. 69.

82 "Cable diterima via S.S. 'Artemis' tg. 17/1-1958," xerox copy of typescript in my possession.

Peking. The two men then went on together to Tokyo. There, Warouw on February 5 met with President Sukarno, who had gone abroad in the hope that the mounting crisis might simmer down in his absence. Warouw had long been known as a favorite of the President; he had acted on his behalf in the aftermath of the October 17, 1952 affair, and had accompanied the President on trips to the United States, Russia, and China in 1956. Opinions vary on Warouw's attitude at this time toward the dissident officers' plans for open rebellion; he was a man known for keeping his thoughts to himself. According to some press reports Warouw met with Sukarno as an emissary of the rebel colonels, to warn the President that the rebels were prepared to establish a revolutionary government should he refuse their demand to oust communists from his government. According to Sumual, he considered the meeting between Warouw and President Sukarno as merely a ploy to gain time, while he (Sumual) sought weapons for the rebel cause. He too, however, in meetings with reporters emphasized that the proclamation of a revolutionary regime was the next step in the fight against the inclusion of communists in the Djuanda cabinet.[83]

Sumual was still abroad, in Manila, working out arrangements for obtaining arms, when an ultimatum to the President and the government was issued by Simbolon and Husein in Padang, West Sumatra, on February 10, 1958. The ultimatum, called a "Charter of Struggle for Safeguarding the State" (Piagam Perdjuangan untuk Menjelematkan Negara), demanded that the Djuanda cabinet resign, that Sukarno return to his position as "constitutional" president, and that Hatta and Sultan Hamengkubuwono be designated to form a "zaken-kabinet" (business-like cabinet) to be made up of honest, prestigious, and capable men, and to exclude "anti-religious elements."[84]

With the expiration of the deadline of the ultimatum, the establishment of a Revolutionary Government of the Republic of Indonesia (Pemerintah Revolusioner Republik Indonesia—PRRI) was announced in Padang on February 15, 1958. The list of ministers included Colonel J. F. Warouw as

---

83 *PIA*, February 4, 1958 (p.m.), p. 2; February 5 (a.m.), p. 7, and (p.m.), pp. 11-13; February 6, (a.m.), p. 8; *Marhaen*, February 4 and 5, 1958; *Sari Attensia*, VI/2 (1959), p. 134; interview, H. N. V. Sumual, Jakarta, April 13, 1972.
84 *PIA*, February 11, 1958, pp. 1, 12.

Minister of Construction and Industry, Lieutenant Colonel Saleh Lahade as Minister of Information, and Mochtar Lintang (a member of the Permesta Supreme Council) as Minister of Religion. Lieutenant Colonel H. N. V. Sumual was to be commander of PRRI ground forces.[85]

"Not Without the Americans"

Thus, in a year's time the regional movement had become a regional rebellion. Efforts at conciliation and negotiation had failed. It is possible that violence was the only exit from the impasse between the proponents of regional autonomy and the advocates of increased central authority as the solution to Indonesia's problems. However, foreign involvement made violence inevitable.

The offer of arms—and the tantalizing prospect of foreign recognition—emboldened the rebels to make demands which they must have known no government could have accepted. Foreign support made fighting a plausible alternative to the humiliation of abandoning the bold demands and bright promises of the regional councils and charters. Some of the rebels may have naively hoped that the threat of foreign involvement would frighten the government into submission; instead this threat galvanized the government into uncharacteristically decisive and speedy action. Thus the impasse was broken.

The impasse had developed in part as a consequence of the contrasting political styles of the center and the regions. The central government, hoping to avoid war, and strongly influenced by Sukarno's Javanese emphasis on consultation and consensus, seemed reluctant to comdemn the acts of defiance of the regional councils. Typically government statements were to the effect that the government understood and sympathized with the goals of the Permesta movement, and that it was only the way in which they were being carried out to which it could not agree. This was true not only of the civilian government, but of the army leadership. In spite of Nasution's prompt action in dissolving TT-VII and relieving Sumual of command, negotiations over his future assignment

---

[85] The announcement of the PRRI government was widely covered in the press; see Kementerian Penerangan, *Peristiwa Sumatra Barat*, I.

continued at least until October 1957. Somba himself says that he was surprised at the time that he was never told directly by Nasution or army headquarters that his actions were wrong. The central army leadership certainly seems to have been prepared to allow barter trade to continue in return for a guarantee of ultimate loyalty to the existing government.[86] Sukarno on his visit to North Sulawesi in October 1957 addressed the Permesta-appointed governor by that title, and seemed to give his blessing to the establishment of a "Permesta" University in Manado by speaking there.

It is of course possible that these manifestations of Javanese politeness (*halus*) were not in fact misinterpreted by their more uncouth (*kasar*) cousins on the outer fringes of the realm. In a culture which emphasizes indirection, subtlety, and politesse, there is a certain advantage to being an uncomprehending barbarian, who by ignoring the *perintah halus* (disguised command) or threatening to cause trouble and unpleasantness, gets his own way. The Minahasan political style may well be more direct and forthright than the Javanese, but those taking advantage of Javanese good manners included both sophisticated civilians and military men whose experience in Java during the revolution included such close contact with the local population that they married Javanese women.[87]

Because the national political style, heavily influenced by the dominant Javanese, emphasized consensus and unity, it was often difficult for decisions to be made—for decisions were likely to cause polarization and lead to an open split. Thus, as at MUNAS, differences of opinion were smoothed over, but were not solved.

It is impossible to say what the ultimate outcome might have been had this situation of negotiation, compromise—and impasse—been permitted to continue without outside interference. The rebels now tend to blame the Tjikini Affair for having ended the possibility of a peaceful solution to the regional crisis.[88] Yet as early as September 1957 there had been public indications of the likelihood of U.S. government support for

---

86 This is clear in a map indicating legal and illegal barter areas, in which the latter are the rebel areas; Soeripto Putera Djaja, *Kegagalan Pembrontak Husein cs* (Surabaya: Grip, 1958), p. 60. See also report that an Emergency Trade Bureau had been set up in Makassar to handle barter in accordance with MBAD instructions; *Bara*, April 2, 1958.
87 The first marriages of Sumual, Somba, and Saleh Lahade were to Javanese women.
88 Interviews: H. N. V. Sumual, Jakarta, March 9, 1971; Saleh Lahade, Makassar, October 7, 1971.

an anticommunist movement in Indonesia, and there had been private contacts between U.S. government agents and at least some of the dissident colonels.[89] U.S. support for the rebellion after it was under way has been well-documented,[90] but it is important to note that promises of such support played a role in the decisions which led to the outbreak of the rebellion.

The U.S. government did not merely take advantage of an opportunity to work against a government of which it disapproved—it worked to create that opportunity.

The U.S. Secretary of State, John Foster Dulles, had for some years been worried about the growing strength of the PKI in Indonesia, and he feared that Sukarno was allying himself with communism domestically, and Indonesia with the communist bloc internationally. The policy of support for the Outer Island rebels which he and his brother Allan, head of the U.S. Central Intelligence Agency (CIA), followed in 1957-58 was foreshadowed as early as October 1953 in his briefing of U.S. Ambassador Hugh S. Cumming, prior to his posting to Jakarta:

> ...as between a territorially united Indonesia which is leaning and progressing towards communism and a break-up of that country into racial and geographic units, I would prefer the latter as furnishing a fulcrum which the United States could work later to help them eliminate communism in one place or another, and then in the end, if they so wish, arrive back again at a united Indonesia.[91]

Dulles's instructions to Ambassador John M. Allison in early 1957 were even more to the point:

> Don't let Sukarno get tied up with the Communists. Don't let him use force against the Dutch. Don't encourage his extremism.

---

89 See the somewhat oblique reference to this in Jones, *Indonesia*, p. 74.
90 Mossman, *Rebels*, passim; David Wise and Thomas B. Ross, *The Invisible Government* (New York: Bantam, 1965), pp. 145-56; see also the *New York Times,* April 25, 1966, p. 20, and April 28, 1966, p. 28.
91 Interview of former Ambassador Hugh S. Cumming by Philip Crowl, June 22, 1967, Princeton Oral History Project. I am indebted to Goh Kian-chee for this reference.

...Above all, do what you can to make sure that Sumatra [the oil producing island] doesn't fall to the Communists.[92]

Although his later statements have received more attention, in early September 1957, Secretary of State Dulles expressed concern about the dangerous situation arising in Indonesia from the victory of communists in local elections, and it was reported from Washington that the growing communist influence in Indonesia would be discussed at an ANZUS meeting in October.[93]

Supporting these public declarations were recommendations to the U.S. Embassy in Jakarta in September 1957 from an Ad Hoc Inter-Agency Committee on Indonesia which had been established in Washington. According to Ambassador Allison, the Embassy was advised:

> ...to employ all feasible means to strengthen and encourage the determination and cohesion of the anti-Communist forces in the outer islands, particularly Sumatra and Sulawesi . . . so that they would be able to affect favorably the situation in Java and provide a rallying point if the Communists should succeed in taking over Java. . . . [And to] utilize whatever leverage was available, or might be built up by the anti-Communist forces in the outer islands, to stimulate into action the non- and anti-Communist forces in Java.[94]

Allison says that he in turn recommended that the U.S. government try to woo Sukarno by pressuring the Netherlands to discuss the West Irian question and by supporting Indonesia on this in the UN. If Washington were not prepared to follow this course, the U.S. should work for the establishment of a "satisfactory new regime," actively encouraging and providing "leverage" to those in Indonesia planning a noncommunist government by informing them of the military and economic assistance

---

92 Allison, *Ambassador*, p. 301. Both Allison and his successor, Howard P. Jones, make quite clear that Sumatran oil was a major factor in U.S. policy toward Indonesia.
93 Reported in *PIA*, September 5, 1957 (a.m.), p. 3; carried in *Pikiran Rakjat*, September 7 and 13, 1957, and in *Marhaen*, September 12, 1957.
94 Allison, *Ambassador*, p. 313.

and diplomatic support they could expect from the U.S.[95]

In this connection it is significant that the first overt rebel demand for the banning of communism was made in the Palembang Charter, signed by Sumual, Husein, and Barlian on September 8, 1957. The increasing emphasis on anticommunism in regionalist rhetoric was, however, also related to domestic events and considerations. The PKI had scored significant gains in regional elections in Java in June, July, and August 1957, and was pressing its claims to participate in government more forcefully than ever.[96] Masjumi, the party which drew most of its electoral support from Outer Indonesia and which was most sympathetic to the demands of the regions, was unalterably opposed to the inclusion of the PKI in the Cabinet. If the government were based on all four major parties, Masjumi would be the outsider, as it had been in the 1955 election campaign. Masjumi's best chances lay in pushing for a nonparty, professional cabinet (such as the zaken-kabinet of the February 10, 1958 ultimatum), headed by someone like Hatta, in which Masjumi modernist technocrats would play a dominant role. To achieve this, it was necessary for Masjumi to overthrow the ruling pro-Sukarno coalition, and by mid-1957, anticommunism was the only issue which Masjumi could exploit to gain sufficient support from parties such as the NU and the right wing of the PNI to do this.[97] Further, of all parties, the PKI had been most openly hostile to the regional councils. This was true not only at the center, but—although somewhat more circumspectly because of their greater vulnerability—in PKI branches in the dissenting regions. As noted above, a number of PKI members were arrested in Minahasa in June 1957 because of their hostility to the Permesta movement. Both Islamic and Christian leaders in Sulawesi opposed the inclusion of communists in the government. A number of people have suggested that the churches in Minahasa (influential bodies in this predominantly Christian area) were important in the inculcation of negative attitudes toward communism, and were supported in this by the Christian party, Parkindo.[98]

---

95 *Ibid.*, pp. 336-37. Allison identifies those engaged in such planning as "leaders of the Masjumi party and the right wing of the PNI."
96 Lev, *Transition*, pp. 84-101.
97 I would like to thank J. A. C. Mackie for drawing my attention to the relationship between Masjumi's interests and the increasing emphasis on anticommunism in the regional movement.
98 Interview, Dr. O. E. Engelen, Jakarta, February 1, 1972; and other interviews in Manado and

Nevertheless, however, important these domestic factors were in the increasingly anticommunist tone of the regional movement, it is certainly not insignificant that emphasis on opposition to communism coincided with U.S. overtures for an anticommunist crusade.

Permesta leaders maintain that no contact was made with foreign government agents, and that no attempts were made to obtain weapons, until after the Sungai Dareh meeting of January 9-13, 1958. It is possible that some sort of informal contact had been made earlier with potential suppliers through the Eastern Produce Agency, set up in Singapore in 1956 for the sale of Minahasan copra. Nun Pantouw, who headed the EPA, maintains that no arms were purchased until after the outbreak of the rebellion. However, during the 1945-49 revolution Pantouw had operated as a "blockade runner" for the Republic, bartering Sumatran rubber and tobacco for medicine and weapons, and it is possible that he had renewed old acquaintances in 1956 and 1957. Sumual, who with Pantouw handled most of the foreign contacts for Permesta, maintains that he had no contact with foreign agents until after the final rebel strategy meeting at Sungai Dareh, and was only offered unlimited American support after the proclamation of the revolutionary government in February 1958. Both Sumual and Pantouw say that they procured the first arms for Permesta in Manila and Taipei, and brought them to Manado on February 23, 1958, the day after the city was bombed in the opening battles of the civil war.[99]

While such lateness of contact and supply may have been true for the Sulawesi half of the rebellion, it was hardly so for Sumatra, where most of the key decisions were made. An American reporter, Keyes Beech, in an aptly titled book, *Not Without the Americans*, documents the delivery of arms to Padang in 1957:

> My first clue to what was happening in Sumatra came in 1957 during a visit to Padang. It seemed that an American freighter loaded with construction equipment also carried a cargo of arms, the latter destined for the U.S. military advisory group in Thailand.

Jakarta in 1971-72.
99 Interviews, Jakarta: H. N. V. Sumual, March 9, 1971 and April 13, 1972; J. M. J. Pantouw, January 23, 1972; confirmed by D. J. Somba, August 15, 1971.

Upon making this astonishing discovery, Lt. Col. Ahmad Hussein, commander of the Central Sumatra military district, ordered the arms unloaded for "safekeeping."

A week or so later, when I mentioned this to a CIA friend of mine in Bangkok, he was remarkably unperturbed. "You know," he said blandly, "this isn't the first time that sort of thing has happened in Sumatra."[100]

---

100 Keyes Beech, *Not Without the Americans* (Garden City, N.Y.: Doubleday, 1971), p. 270.

CHAPTER FIVE
PERMESTA AT WAR

As might be expected, the reaction to the rebel ultimatum of February 10 and the proclamation of the revolutionary government on February 15, differed in North and South Sulawesi. In South Sulawesi the decision whether or not the officers and civilians who had joined together in Permesta in March 1957 would follow Sumual and Saleh Lahade into the PRRI rebellion in February 1958, was essentially determined by a few of these officers. Support for Permesta in the South had been shrinking almost from the day of the proclamation. It was clear within a month from the signing of the March 2 declaration that Governor Andi Pangerang preferred cooperation with the central government to involvement in a movement whose economic base was in North Sulawesi and whose leadership was dominated by military officers from that area. Many of the civilian followers of Permesta had been reluctant participants from the start, and few of them anticipated that their addressing petitions for redress of grievances would lead to an armed clash. Some had distanced themselves from Permesta as early as the Bhinneka Tunggal Ika Congress in May 1957, which they thought was more show than substance. Others had become disillusioned over what they perceived to be the wasteful use of the money that had been withdrawn from the Bank Indonesia for "development" purposes. Some felt that the Permesta leadership had proved to be unable to distinguish between persons genuinely committed to the ideals of the Permesta Charter, and those who supported it for opportunistic reasons. The establishment of a Permesta Supreme Council in Makassar in November 1957 did not reverse this trend, despite the announcement on February 1, 1958 that the council had met to plan for the celebration of the first anniversary of the March 2 proclamation.[1]

The composition of the Council effectively demonstrated the extent to which support for Permesta in South Sulawesi was now essentially limited to the small multi-ethnic intellectual community of the city of Makassar, a group with few ties in the countryside. A number of the civilians were associated with the PKR and PSI, parties which had received relatively insignificant votes in the 1955 elections; some were associated with the Masjumi or Muhammadiyah, but the natural constituency of these groups was largely preempted by the Darul Islam. Many of the civilians disapproved of a resort to force. Many were afraid of being arrested.

After the withdrawal of Sumual and the Minahasan officers from the TT-VII staff to North Sulawesi in June 1957, the core of military support for Permesta in the South was narrowed to Saleh Lahade and a small group of like-minded officers. The focus of attention within the new KDM-SST was on building its own security forces and ending the existing rebellion of Qahhar Mudzakkar and the Darul Islam. With the proclamation of the PRRI, many officers felt themselves subject to conflicting pressures. Some felt that consistency in support of the unmet demands of the Permesta Charter, which they had all signed the year before, re-required that they back the PRRI. Some insisted that the original charter had not contemplated rebellion, but was only a correction of the central government. Most recognized that a decision to support the PRRI would necessitate reaching an agreement with Qahhar Mudzakkar, who still controlled most of the countryside which would provide the popular base for rebellion. This many were unwilling to contemplate. Most were cautious and afraid; they did not intend to take part in a rebellion, but they recognized that they could already be accused of insubordination, and they were fearful of the action which the central government might take against them.

The situation in North Sulawesi was quite different. There the officers who faced the same questions posed by the PRRI proclamation were under popular pressure from those aroused in support of regional defiance of the central government since the Bitung Harbor incident in June 1956. Support for the PRRI was based, perhaps, not so much on

---

1   *Bara*, February 1, 1958, p. 2.

abstract principles as on the determination to continue the profitable barter trade unless a satisfactory legal substitute was devised. In the North, the proceeds of barter trade had been used for visible projects such as road repair and improvement, and import of food, textiles, and equipment. This, combined with the earlier unhappy experience with the centrally controlled Copra Foundation, resulted in considerable popular support for Permesta and the continuation of the barter trade.

The decision of the central government on January 11, 1958 to bar barter trade was initially met with defiance in North Sulawesi. Newspaper headlines proclaimed "Permesta and Barter will Continue."[2] The Minahasa regional assembly passed a motion which urged that the central government regulate the financial balance between the center and the regions by a law which recognized the present degree of autonomy of the Minahasa region, and which reiterated the Kinilow agreement of the previous July that until there was a final settlement of problems between the central government and the regions, direct export and import would continue in North Sulawesi.[3]

Although Nasution and Somba agreed in early February 1958 that a new export-import system acceptable to the regions would be set up and barter stopped, the tide of revolt was too strong to be blocked by mere promises. Both Nasution and Somba felt at times during 1957 that agreements had been reached which would avert conflict. However, Somba himself implicitly recognized the limitations of his own ability to control the situation. "You can replace me," he told Nasution, "but another person will face the same situation."[4]

However, it was not only the civilians in North Sulawesi who were creating the situation of defiance of the central government. The barter trade, it must be remembered, was being carried out not only under military protection, but through organizations essentially under military control, in the first place, the Minahasa Coconut Foundation, headed by Nun Pantouw. When Pantouw moved to Singapore in 1957, the barter trade came under the financial and economic (FINEC) section of the Team of Assistants to the North Sulawesi military government, and

---

2 *Pikiran Rakjat*, January 14, 1958.
3 Text of motion in *Pikiran Rakjat*, January 17, 1958.
4 Interview, D. J. Somba, Jakarta, April 19, 1972.

although FINEC itself was headed by a civilian (A. C. J. Mantiri), it was part of the structure of military government.

Further, Somba was under pressure to take a strong line in opposition to the central government from a number of his staff officers. Some of them, like Lendy Tumbelaka and Dee Gerungan, had come north to Minahasa with Sumual when TT-VII was dissolved in June 1957. These two in particular were known as brilliant staff officers, whereas Somba's strength was as a troop commander. They had both, together with Eddy Gagola, been involved in the original planning of the March 2 operation in Makassar, and seem to have played key roles in the further development of the Permesta movement after it moved to North Sulawesi.

Somba's freedom of action and decision was also constrained by Sumual's presence at Kinilow after June 1957. Sumual, like Somba, was a native son of Minahasa, and as head of the Permesta military government for East Indonesia had come to symbolize the protests of the regions against excessive centralization of the government and the economy. As such he served as a rallying point for Minahasan dissatisfaction with Jakarta.

Finally, Somba's own character and personality must be considered as a factor in the situation. There is general agreement among those involved in Permesta, that whatever Somba's exploits after the fighting began, he was a most reluctant rebel. In part his reluctance was based on his assessment of the limited manpower of KDM-SUT—barely two battalions of troops. There were indeed several thousand former KNIL soldiers in Minahasa— one of the reasons the central government feared harder fighting there than in Sumatra—but they were aging. There were indeed large numbers of young men eager to carry on the military traditions of the region, but they were untrained. In part Somba's reluctance to become involved in open rebellion was a reflection of the gentleness of his own character.[5] Yet it was this same gentleness and modesty which made him subject to the influence of the more headstrong young officers around him who were far from reluctant to take on the central government. One has a sense of

---

5 The Indonesian word most often used to describe Somba is "manis." A Dutch doctor kidnapped during the rebellion described Somba as an "goedwillend sympathiek mens" (congenial man of good will); Dr. F. J. van Rootselaar, "Een Ontvoering in Noord-Celebes," *De Groene Amsterdammer*, January 16, 1960, p. 3.

a man who felt himself caught in a situation beyond his control and who hoped for decisive action from outside to extricate himself from its grasp. Yet when decisive action did occur—from the rebels and from the central government—any possibility of escape was eliminated.

Initial Reaction to PRRI in North Sulawesi

Between the issuance of the ultimatum to the central government on February 11 and the announcement of the formation of the revolutionary government in Padang on February 15, many meetings were held in North Sulawesi. With the exception of the PKI, whose leaders had been in prison since June 1957, and the PNI, which was silent, leaders of the major political parties and of leading youth groups conveyed their support for the Sumatran decisions to the military government. A mass meeting was scheduled for February 16 at Sario field in Manado. The officers of KDM-SUT met the night before.

One officer present at the meeting described the alternatives facing members of the TNI in North Sulawesi: (1) to take the side of the people and support PRRI—but this would be a violation of military discipline; or (2) be loyal to the central government and fight the people—although the demands of the people were just. Thus, the two loyalties, of which Somba had spoken at his installation as KDM-SUT commander in September 1957 were in conflict, and a choice had to be made between them.

Although it is no doubt true that many of the TNI officers did feel themselves to be in this position, it must also be noted that many civilians in North Sulawesi felt themselves to be under pressure from the TNI to support the military in defiance of the central government.

Somba himself says that he was under pressure to support PRRI and cut relations with the Djuanda cabinet not only from civilian officials and groups, but from members of his own staff. Majors Gerungan, Gagola, Runturambi, Mamesah, and Mondong were among those who strongly urged such a course. According to Somba, although he supported the Permesta program, he did not favor a break with the central government. He asked the younger officers at the meeting if they had considered the possible consequences of what they were recommending—for instance that they might find themselves fighting in the jungle. When they appeared to be adamant in their support for the PRRI, Somba instructed Gerungan,

Gagola, Mondong, and Lendy Tumbelaka to draft a statement for him to make at the rally the following day. Apparently when the officers went to the rally on February 16, Somba put the draft in his pocket, and said only that he would choose the wisest course of action. Somba was the last to speak at the rally. The civilians and political party leaders who preceded him spoke strongly in favor of the Sumatran challenge and against President Sukarno, and are said to have received an enthusiastic response from the large crowd gathered there. Somba felt he could not stand against the tide. "I stand on the side of the people," he said. "If that is your opinion, that is where I stand." On February 17 he issued an official announcement that he would cut relations with the Djuanda cabinet, and would deal only with the PRRI.[6] He and Runturambi were immediately dishonorably discharged from the TNI.[7]

Somba also issued an order of the day calling on the armed forces and people of North Sulawesi to remain calm and carry on with their work as usual. Military leaves were cancelled, and members of the armed forces in North Sulawesi were instructed to obey only those orders coming directly from KDM-SUT commander Somba.[8]

Support from local youth and civilian groups was quick in coming, particularly after it was announced that Permesta would pay salaries and pensions of officials, and that an adequate supply of foodstuffs was on hand. On February 19 the civil servants of Minahasa took a formal oath of loyalty to the Permesta leaders in their realization of the March 2 program through support for PRRI, and young people by the thousands are said to have volunteered to fight.[9]

---

[6] *Marhaen*, February 17, 1958; interviews, D. J. Somba, Jakarta, August 15, 1971, January 22 and April 19, 1972; other information from officers and civilians in Manado at the time. Officially the term Permesta was no longer used, for the rebels were part of the PRRI; in practice, however, the North Sulawesi branch of the rebellion was frequently called PRRI/Permesta, and by some continued to be called just Permesta. In order to distinguish this branch of the rebellion from that in Sumatra I have used the term Permesta throughout.

[7] *Marhaen*, February 18, 1958; *PIA*, February 18, 1958 (a.m.), p. 11. The Sumatran colonels—Simbolon, Husein, Lubis, and Dahlan Djambek—had been discharged on February 11 when the Council of Ministers rejected the Padang ultimatum; *PIA*, February 12, 1958 (a.m.), p. 1. Sumual was discharged on February 26, 1958; *Bara*, March 3, 1958.

[8] *Pikiran Rakjat*, February 19, 1958.

[9] *Pikiran Rakjat*, February 20 and 22, 1958.

Initial Reaction to PRRI in South Sulawesi

The Padang ultimatum of February 10 and the proclamation of the PRRI on February 15—in which two members of the Permesta Supreme Council, Saleh Lahade and Mochtar Lintang, were appointed ministers—brought to a head the division between pro- and anti-Permesta forces in South Sulawesi.

On the evening of February 11 a meeting was held in Makassar to determine what the response to the Padang ultimatum should be. It was apparently agreed, after considerable debate, that KDM-SST should take a neutral position, and try, if possible, to act as a mediator between the central government and the rebellious colonels. There were two reasons for this decision; first, that the Permesta movement had never intended to oppose the central government by force, and second, that the situation in South Sulawesi—where there was already one insurgency in control of the countryside and where the TNI troops were in the preliminary stages of training and consolidation—did not permit consideration of physical opposition to the central government.[10]

Neutrality, however, became more difficult after the announcement of Saleh Lahade's appointment as Minister of Information in the PRRI Cabinet. A second meeting was held in Makassar on February 15. The question was no longer just whether or not South Sulawesi should take sides in the rebellion or remain neutral, but what should be done about Saleh Lahade. The discussion was heated, and in the course of it an officer who had been a close supporter of Saleh Lahade, Major A. Lathief, decided that he would remove Saleh from the city to a safer location out of town. Some say the decision was made by the meeting as a whole to avoid an armed clash within the city. In any case, Lathief and a group of young civilians took Saleh Lahade to Barru. Mochtar Lintang was apparently

---

10 There are many different versions of what occurred in South Sulawesi in the period February-May 1958. One source reported that members of the Permesta Supreme Council (which was composed largely of civilians) attended this meeting; most other sources imply that only the senior military officers of KDM-SST met. Andi Mattalatta, commander of KDM-SST at the time, said that no meetings were held, but that he kept to his position that South Sulawesi must not be used as a base for Permesta, because if the central government reacted with force, the people would be the victims; interview, Makassar, March 29, 1972. Unless otherwise noted, the actions and opinions attributed to the persons involved in these incidents are based on interviews with them, and are not contradicted by other sources.

moved at the same time. Andi Mattalatta, commander of KDM-SST and an old friend of Saleh's, was then informed of what had been done.[11]

The following day, February 16, Chief of Staff Nasution issued an ultimatum to Warouw, Saleh Lahade, and Mochtar Lintang, giving them three days to report whether or not they accepted their positions in the PRRI cabinet. Saleh did not reply, fearing that if he did there would surely be a clash between pro- and anti-Permesta forces. On the expiration of the ultimatum Andi Mattalatta was ordered to arrest Saleh Lahade and Mochtar Lintang. This he refused to do on the grounds that Saleh had not been told in advance that he would be appointed to the PRRI cabinet, and Mattalatta personally delivered to Nasution a letter which he had had Saleh write to that effect.

No public statement was made on the whereabouts of Saleh Lahade and Mochtar Lintang, although it was reported that they had fled the city. When Deputy Chief of Staff Gatot Subroto tried to meet Saleh on February 20, he was told that Saleh had "gone north."[12] It was announced on March 3 that Saleh Lahade was dishonorably discharged from the TNI, effective February 17, 1958.[13]

On February 16 the civil and military authorities of South Sulawesi issued a carefully worded statement calling on the people to remain calm and carry out their regular duties (standard phraseology), and to be guided by the principal objective of the national struggle—safeguarding the integrity of the state and the proclamation of independence of August 17, 1945 on which it was based. The national security forces were instructed to guard against provocation and slander from any source, and to perform their duties in a calm, disciplined manner, aware of their responsibility for the safety and welfare of the Indonesian state and people. At the same time Panglima Mattalatta issued an order of the day calling on the troops in the area, and those responsible to KDM-SST in particular, to continue

---

11 Interviews, Makassar: A. Lathief and Husain Achmad, December 4, 1971; Andi Mattalatta, March 29, 1972. These three persons agree that Andi Mattalatta was informed only after Saleh Lahade had been moved to Barru. Other information from interviews with Saleh Lahade, Makassar, October 7, 1971; Bing Latumahina, Jakarta, January 14, 1972; Dr. O. E. Engelen, Jakarta, February 1, 1972.

12 *Marhaen*, February 18 and 21, 1958.

13 *Bara*, March 3, 1958.

to perform their duties calmly and efficiently.[14]

During the next three months the struggle between pro- and anti-Permesta forces continued in South Sulawesi, with each group trying to draw the respected commander of KDM-SST, Andi Mattalatta, to its side. Gatot Subroto, Nasution, and Sukarno visited Makassar in February and March, and Jusuf, Andi Pangerang, and Andi Mattalatta consulted with government and military leaders in Jakarta during this period. There were occasional press reports that Andi Mattalatta had been urged to take a firm stand against the PRRI—or that he had been arrested for failure to do so—but he retained the confidence of Nasution, and thus kept his position.

It was a difficult position in which Andi Mattalatta found himself. He and Saleh Lahade had always been a team, with Mattalatta the honest soldier and Saleh the clever political adviser. However, the options open to them now were different. Mattalatta was the first anak daerah to be commander in South Sulawesi; he was loyal to the TNI and held to military discipline. Saleh, long in an inactive status and more involved in politics than in soldiering, had no future in the TNI. Both were trapped by circumstances. Saleh realized that armed rebellion was not feasible. He had captured the desires of the people in the Permesta Charter, but he was incapable of leading them into battle in support of it. Yet, he did not publicly refuse to accept his position in the PRRI cabinet, and would indeed have gone to Sumatra had KDM-SST given Sumual permission to land a Permesta Catalina near Pare-Pare to pick up the two Ministers. Mattalatta neither supporterd PRRI nor arrested Saleh. Both seem to have hoped to maintain a neutral stance in a situation in which neutrality was impossible.

One man was prepared to take decisive action, and that man was Jusuf, commander of RI-Hasanuddin. Jusuf's opposition to Permesta had been clear to most of his fellow officers at least since June 1957. Jusuf could rely on Yani to support him at army headquarters, and he could rely on troops of RI-Hasanuddin to support him in South Sulawesi. Some troop commanders were won over with promises of promotions and a free hand in running the areas under their control; when promises failed, threats

---

14 *PIA*, February 19, 1958 (a.m.), p. 2, and (p.m.), p. 2.

were found to be effective, for Jusuf demonstrated that he was prepared to arrest those who opposed him. Equally important were Jusuf's own intelligence, cunning, and ruthlessness. Some of the targets of Jusuf's plotting might have been alerted or frightened by these qualities had they not been disarmingly cloaked by his honesty, sincerity, and charm. Jusuf seems also to have been helped by wishful thinking on the part of Saleh Lahade and Andi Mattalatta; from the record it is difficult to imagine that they could not have been aware of Jusuf's opposition to Permesta by mid-1957.

Andi Mattalatta and Saleh Lahade had been an effective team, but once that team was split by circumstance, neither was an adequate leader. Mattalatta still commanded great respect, but he was no politician, and no match for such a master of intrigue as Jusuf. Jusuf, like Mattalatta was an aristocrat, but even more than Mattalatta had the air of having been born to rule. Jusuf shared Saleh Lahade's qualities of intelligence, but his political instincts were sharper, and he was less given to philosophical analysis or self-delusion than Saleh, and more to decisive action.

While Jusuf built his support, and destroyed that of Permesta in South Sulawesi, the focus of attention was on the areas which had rebelled—Sumatra and North Sulawesi.

Central Government Reaction

Surprising both its supporters and its opponents, the central government took quick decisive action in response to the Padang proclamations. The rebel ultimatum was promptly rejected, and the officers involved in the proclamation of the PRRI were dishonorably discharged from the armed forces.

Sukarno returned to Indonesia on February 16; he met with Hatta on February 19 and again on March 3. Some have seen Sukarno's visits to Hatta as final efforts to compromise and to solve the crisis peacefully. However, the actions of the rebels themselves made such an outcome virtually impossible, whatever the possibility of restoring the duumvirate. Hatta did, apparently, favor continued efforts at a peaceful solution, and may have been supported in this by Prime Minister Djuanda, but the armed forces leadership was determined to take firm action. In this they were supported by the PNI and the PKI, and, according to Nasution and others, by Sukarno.[15]

The signal that the central government would meet the proclamation of a rebel government with force was the bombing of Padang and Manado on February 21 and 22. The decision to attack the rebel capitals was widely criticized at the time, and in later years there has been some tendency to describe it as a unilateral decision by the Indonesian air force (AURI), whose commander, Suryadarma, had strong leftist sympathies.[16] However, both Sukarno and Nasution were themselves determined to act quickly against the challenge to the central government. They were aware that time was on the side of the rebels, who were known to be in contact with foreign government agents, and to have received promises, and shipments, of arms. Nasution believed it essential to the rebels off from their overseas contacts, and to prevent their establishing a strong position which would give them credibility as an alternative government which might get foreign recognition.[17]

Granting of belligerent status to the rebels was indeed considered by the U.S. government in March; a fact made known to the Indonesian government, and one which strengthened the determination of Sukarno, Djuanda, and Nasution to take immediate action to crush the rebellion.[18]

The rebel presence near the Sumatran oil fields was also a cause for concern, as the revenue from the fields, operated by the U.S. companies Caltex and Stanvac, was a major source of foreign exchange for the

---

15 "Djawaban Tertulis Djenderal A. H. Nasution untuk (Penulisan Buku) H. P. Jones," A-72/MPRS/III/'69 (Mimeo, March 1, 1969), p. 8. A Djuanda statement of February 28 that there was no alternative to the use of force in dealing with the Padang rebellion was reported in *PIA*, March 5, 1958 (a.m.), p. 7; see also Indonesia, Ministry of Information, *Government Statement on the Current State of Affairs, by Prime Minister Djuanda, in the plenary meeting of the House of Representatives on July 4th, 1958*, Special Issue No. 14 (Jakarta, 1958), pp. 14, 25 (hereafter *Djuanda Statement*). See also Fischer, *Story of Indonesia*, p. 231; Lev, *Transition*, p. 40; Feith, *Decline*, p. 587.
16 According to Fischer, Sukarno himself ordered the bombing; *Story of Indonesia*, p. 231. The post-1965 tendency to blame all previous errors and unpopular decisions on the PKI seems to be particularly strong among the former rebels. Some people in Sulawesi seem to believe that there had been an understanding between Somba and Nasution that there would be no physical clash if North Sulawesi were not attacked by the central government, and that therefore the bombing was contrary to this agreement. The existence of such an understanding is not borne out in information received from either Somba or Nasution.
17 Nasution, *People's Army*, pp. 12-15; *Madjalah Angkatan Darat*, Feb-March 1958, pp. 4-6; interview, A. H. Nasution, Jakarta, May 17, 1972.
18 Jones, *Indonesia*, p. 116.

central government. In addition, U.S. intervention on behalf of the rebels was greatly feared (not without reason), and protection of the U.S. oil concessions and American personnel might provide the pretext.

U.S. sympathy for the rebels was scarcely disguised. The American Secretary of State, John Foster Dulles, in his press conference on February 11, 1958, made a statement which could only be interpreted as one of support for the rebel ultimatum:

> We would like to see in Indonesia a government which is constitutional and which reflects the real interest and desires of the people of Indonesia...There is a kind of a "guided democracy" trend there now which is an evolution which...apparently does not entirely satisfy large segments of the population. We doubt very much that the people of Indonesia will ever want a Communist-type or a Communist-dominated government.[19]

The supposedly secret contacts between the Sumatran colonels and American government (presumably CIA) agents were in fact well known in Jakarta, and the Indonesian government soon had solid evidence of foreign assistance in the form of captured weapons.[20]

Confirming government fears of the use of a threat to the American oil fields as a pretext for open intervention, the newly appointed American Ambassador, Howard P. Jones, on March 7, 1958 (the day following his arrival in Jakarta) called on Prime Minister Djuanda, accompanied by two senior Caltex officials, to request permission for U.S. navy vessels to evacuate American civilians from the Pakanbaru oil fields in East Sumatra. Conveniently, a U.S. navy squadron was standing by in Singapore.[21]

The government rejected the American request, promising that it could guarantee the safety of foreign nationals, and continued its swift action against the rebels. On March 12 government forces parachuted into Pakanbaru, guided by flares which had lit the runway for the

---

19 *New York Times*, February 12, 1958, p. 12.
20 See *Djuanda Statement*, pp. 25-27.
21 Jones, *Indonesia*, pp. 69-70; on general U.S. government attitudes and actions in this period see also pp. 67-85, and 113-46. For reports at the time see *PIA*, March 13, 1958 (a.m.), p. 12; March 15 (a.m.), p. 3; March 24 (a.m.), p. 4.

dropping of several crates of arms found unopened on the air field. The government was blessed not only with luck, and good timing, but with inside information on rebel plans. In more than one instance officers who had been involved in the early stages of the regional movement, decided (whether based on principle, fear, or expediency) not to follow their colleagues into open rebellion, and reinstated themselves with honor in the government's eyes by returning to the arms of the Republic bearing detailed rebel operational plans.[22]

Military operations were concentrated in Sumatra until the successful invasion of Padang on April 17 and the fall of the PRRI capital of Bukittinggi on May 4. Central government troops did make a successful landing in the Palu-Donggala area of Central Sulawesi on March 31, aided by a local TNI company under the Toraja Captain Frans Karangan, and by local Mobile Brigade troops. The landing was also no doubt made easier by the distaste of the local population for Major Palar, commander of a TNI battalion from KDM-SUT there (see above). Palar is said to have been killed during the attack.[23] With the exception of this attack and the bombing of Manado on February 22, however, Sumatra was the principal battleground until mid-May.

Reaction to Bombing of Manado—Consolidation of Support

Although the conflict had been building for over a year, it was the bombing of Manado that convinced the general population of Minahasa and North Sulawesi that this was war in earnest.[24] The initial effect of the bombing there was to solidify support behind the Permesta leadership, and to cement the alliance between the Sumatran and the Sulawesi branches of the rebellion. It was now difficult for people in North Sulawesi to say that they supported Permesta but not PRRI, as some had been inclined to do

---

22 The incident at Pakanbaru is described in *Djuanda Statement*, pp. 11-12, 25; and in Beech, *Not Without the Americans*, p. 271. Also based on interview with General Nasution, Jakarta, May 17, 1972.
23 *Pikiran Rakjat*, April 5, 1958; *PIA*, April 2, 1958 (p.m.), p. 15; June 13 (a.m.), pp. 13-14. See also, Makmun Salim, *Sedjarah Operasi2 Gabungan Terhadap PRRI-Permesta*; Seri Text-book Sedjarah ABRI (Jakarta: Departemen Pertahanan-Keamanan, Pusat Sedjarah ABRI, 1971), pp. 60-64.
24 The headline in Manado's *Pikiran Rakjat* in the issue of February 24-25, 1958, read: "Djuanda unleashes civil war . . . Djuanda's action provokes disintegration of the state."

in the period between the ultimatum/ proclamation and the bombing. The issue was now more clearly that of being on the side of the region or on the side of the center. Although some Permesta supporters who had not anticipated a physical clash were not prepared to support the demands for regional autonomy with guns, and did quietly withdraw their support, for the most part outrage over the resort to force solidified regional support for the Permesta leadership and for its decision to join in defying the central government.

One exception to this general pattern occurred in Gorontalo, where a PNI leader with impeccable revolutionary credentials, Nani Wartabone, seized control of the city from pro-Permesta authorities there on February 25. However, he and his supporters from local youth groups were in turn ousted on March 17 by pro-Permesta TNI forces, under Lieutenant Tiendas (a Sangirese).[25]

Disapproval of the bombing of Manado was an important factor in the decision of a number of Minahasan officers and civilian officials in other parts of Indonesia and overseas to join with the rebellion. Certainly the number of TNI men who fought with Permesta in North Sulawesi was greater than the number who had been assigned to KDM-SUT. Among those who returned was J. Wuisan, chief of staff of KDM-Nusa Tenggara (Bali), who was appointed to head one of the territorial commands later established in Minahasa.[26] Notably absent was Lieutenant Colonel H. V. Worang, former commander of RI-24 in North Sulawesi, who had been transferred to South Sumatra in 1956. The South Sumatra commander, Colonel Barlian, had been an active participant in the regional movement in 1956-57, and Worang is said to have supported him in this. Nevertheless, when the Padang ultimatum was rejected by Jakarta, Barlian declared his neutrality. Worang, whatever his personal inclinations, was in no position to take action in South Sumatra, an area in which he had little influence. In May 1958 there were press reports that Worang had been

---

25 Nani Wartabone had led a nationalist group in Gorontalo which seized the opportunity provided by the Japanese invasion to proclaim itself part of an independent Republic of Indonesia in January 1942. On both incidents see Indonesia, Staf Angkatan Bersenjata, *Sedjarah Singkat Perdjuangan Bersendjata Bangsa Indonesia* (Jakarta, 1964), pp. 30-32, 138-39; Makmun Salim, *Operasi2 Gabungan*, pp. 67-72. Other sources: *PIA*, February 27, 1958 (a.m.), p. 1; *Bara*, March 17, 1958; interview, Nani Wartabone, Gorontalo, November 23, 1971.

26 Letter from A. C. J. Mantiri to the author, September 14, 1974.

detained in Jakarta by army headquarters, but these reports were denied, and Worang gave public assurances of his opposition to the rebellion. He entered SSKAD in October 1958.[27]

One other senior officer from North Sulawesi did not join the rebels, Colonel Achmad Junus Mokoginta, of Bolaang-Mongondow. Mokoginta had been active in efforts to mediate the dispute in 1957; he was a member of the Fact Finding Committee established after MUNAS. His decision not to join the rebels was based on disapproval of the unconstitutional way in which they attempted to obtain recognition of their demands, and on the pragmatic view that the rebels could not successfully take on the whole army.[28]

The bombing of Manado precipitated the decision of the two most senior Minahasan TNI officers, Colonel A. E. Kawilarang, military attaché in Washington, D.C., and Colonel J. F. Warouw, military attaché in Peking, to return from abroad to join their countrymen. Warouw, who as noted above had been close to President Sukarno since the revolution, had met with the President in Tokyo in early February as a go-between for the rebellious colonels. Although he had been told in advance that he was slated for a cabinet position in the PRRI government, he was apparently not enthusiastic about participating in a rebellion. Kawilarang, named without his foreknowledge or consent to be commander-in-chief of the PRRI, refused to accept that position, although he did join the Permesta group in Minahasa.

There has been much speculation about Kawilarang's role in the rebellion, although (or because) he was the one senior officer involved who was not dishonorably discharged from the TNI and who emerged from the rebellion with his reputation untarnished. Further, the Permesta group with which he was associated regularly received army intelligence reports from friends on the central staff throughout the rebellion. Some have suggested that Kawilarang, who had been a classmate of Nasution at the KNIL academy in Bandung in 1940, was in fact acting on Nasution's behalf to negotiate an end to the rebellion. This, however, seems unlikely.

---

27 On Barlian, see *Djuanda Statement*, pp. 18-19; van der Kroef, "Disunited Indonesia," part 2, p. 76; Mossman, *Rebels*, pp. 102-3. On Worang, see *Pikiran Rakjat*, May 19, 1958; *PIA*, May 6, 1958 (a.m.), p. 4, May 9 (p.m.), p. 8; *Madjalah Angkatan Darat*, November 1958.

28 Interview, A. J. Mokoginta, Jakarta, May 6, 1972.

According to Kawilarang, he blamed the regional crisis on Jakarta's mismanagement, and telegraphed Nasution from Washington that he disapproved of what he and the government were doing.[29] Nasution says that he received several telegrams from Kawilarang, and also one from Warouw, warning against taking military action against the rebels, and that Kawilarang's final cable, sent after the bombing of Padang and Manado, was very sharp.[30] The two men had no direct contact at this time, nor did Kawilarang himself participate in negotiations when they did take place in 1960-61.[31]

Some authors suggest that Kawilarang returned to Indonesia hoping to unite the TNI against Sukarno—to whom he had been consistently opposed since the October 17, 1952 affair.[32] This is plausible, as Kawilarang was one of the most respected and admired TNI officers, and having served as commander in North Sumatra, East Indonesia, and West Java, was widely known throughout the TNI. However, Kawilarang himself maintains that he never accepted the PRRI, or a position in it, and that although he participated in discussions of military strategy and tactics in North Sulawesi, he held no formal position in the rebellion until November 1960, when he accepted the "so-called rank of Commander-in-Chief *Permesta*."[33]

---

29 Interview, A. E. Kawilarang, Jakarta, August 15, 1971.
30 Interview, A. H. Nasution, Jakarta, May 17, 1972.
31 There was some speculation in the press at the time about mediation and negotiation; see, for example, *PIA*, May 7, 1958 (p.m.), p. 6. According to General Sumitro, before leaving Washington Kawilarang informed senior TNI officers then in the U.S. that he was returning to Indonesia to act as a mediator; he was prevented from contacting either Nasution or Gatot Subroto by the then head of army intelligence, Sukendro; interview, Jakarta, May 6, 1972.
32 This is suggested in van Rootselaar, "Een Ontvoering." Manado newspapers on April 14, 1958 printed an order of the day issued in Kawilarang's name as commander-in-chief of PRRI armed forces, calling for support from state officials and the people for the struggle against Jakarta's "mismanagement" and misuse of authority; text in *Pikiran Rakjat*. Although the use of the word "mismanagement" is typical of Kawilarang's style, according to a *PIA* report (April 17, 1958 [a.m.], p. 2), Kawilarang arrived in Manila on April 13. Kawilarang himself says that he never accepted the position of commander-in-chief of PRRI forces. I have been unable to determine whether the order of the day was issued without Kawilarang's authorization, or whether the entire story lacks authenticity.
33 Letter from A. E. Kawilarang to the author, November 30, 1975 (his emphasis).

Permesta Military Strategy and Operations

Although Kawilarang and Warouw participated in discussions of military strategy after their arrival in Minahasa in late March, most of the initial planning seems to have been in Sumual's hands. Sumual, who had left Sulawesi in December 1957, returned on February 23, 1958, together with Nun Pantouw. Sumual apparently hoped that while the central government concentrated on putting down the Sumatran branch of the rebellion (which had already been supplied with arms and advisers), the Sulawesi forces could be expanded and trained. Indeed, some of the Sulawesi officers even anticipated participating in an attack on Jakarta. Having made arrangements to obtain arms, aircraft, and crews abroad, Sumual and the Permesta leaders had decided that an early objective should be to secure Morotai airfield, a still usable relic from World War II, for it was the only air base in East Indonesia large enough to take the B-29 bombers which had sufficient range to reach Jakarta. They also hoped to be able to capture the Balikpapan airfield, which was within easy flying distance of Jakarta. It was thought that an attack on Jakarta would convince sympathetic but wavering officers—in West Java particularly, as well as in places such as South Sulawesi and South Sumatra—to support the rebels; such an attack would also convince foreign suppliers that their support was being put to good use.[34]

Early planning centered on the capture of Morotai airfield, using the KDM-SUT troops stationed in North Maluku, and on retaking the Palu-Donggala area from central government forces. Contingency planning against a government invasion of Minahasa was also discussed, although reports differ on whether it was Sumual or Kawilarang who favored a frontal defense and which of them favored immediate withdrawal into positions for guerrilla warfare.

Permesta Military Forces

When relations were broken with Jakarta the Permesta leadership had available to them only three TNI battalions, and some of the troops were

---

34 Interview, H. N. V. Sumual, Jakarta, April 13, 1972.

in North Maluku, and some, under Palar and Frans Karangan, were in Central Sulawesi—and of doubtful loyalty. On February 19, 1958, Somba unilaterally carried out his long-planned division of KDM-SUT into two regiments. Major Dolf Runturambi was commissioned commander of Sector I/Regimental Battle Team "Ular Hitam," encompassing Sangihe-Talaud, Minahasa, and Bolaang-Mongondow; and Major Dee Gerungan was installed as commander of Sector II/Regimental Battle Team "Anoa," in Central Sulawesi, with headquarters in Poso.[35]

On February 24, two days after the bombing of Manado, KDM-SUT issued a call to all former KNIL trained in antiaircraft and heavy weaponry to report for service. Some 2,000 are said to have done so, including Colonel Warouw's father according to one report. Although many of the ex-KNIL were a bit elderly for combat, many volunteered to train the youths who flooded in to enlist with Permesta.[36] Some of the youth had been members of the Permesta Youth Command (Komando Pemuda Permesta), formed at the meeting of the Dewan Pemuda at Tondano in July 1957; and they presumably had some rudimentary military training in the intervening months. Some of the young volunteers had returned from universities in Java in the year since the March 2 Proclamation, and many secondary school students throughout Minahasa swelled the ranks of the student army.

In late March agreement was again reached with Jan Timbuleng to cooperate under the banner of Permesta. After his much publicized surrender in March 1957 (see above), he is said to have been dissatisfied with the treatment accorded him and his men, and had returned to the jungles of southern Minahasa later that year.[37] Toward the end of March 1958 there were reports that Timbuleng and Somba had met, and that Timbuleng and his Defenders of Justice Army (Pasukan Pembela Keadilan—PPK) would fight at the front lines and would control the jungles in the name of Permesta.[38] In April, Timbuleng and three battalions

---

35 *Pikiran Rakjat*, February 20, 1958. *Ular hitam* means black snake; the *anoa* is a species of cattle peculiar to the jungles of Sulawesi. There is an earlier report of Gerungan's installation in *PIA*, January 23, 1958 (p.m.), p. 2.
36 Text of announcement in *Pikiran Rakjat*, February 27, 1958; reports of volunteers in *Pikiran Rakjat*, February 22 and March 21, 1958, and *Bara*, March 5, 1958.
37 *Marhaen*, October 3, 1957.
38 *Pikiran Rakjat*, March 24, 25, and 27, 1958.

(about 1,000 men) from the PPK went under Somba's command to Central Sulawesi to try to recapture the Palu-Donggala area.[39]

Also in late March another rebel band joined forces with Permesta, about 300 members of a group led by Daan and Len Karamoy (the latter a former wife of Jan Timbuleng). Len Karamoy, who had a considerable reputation as a troop commander, offered to train a women's militia for Permesta, and although such a unit had been established a few days earlier, both Karamoys remained with their original band, and were incorporated into the Permesta forces.[40]

The Permesta Women's Unit (Pasukan Wanita Permesta—PWP) gained some fame during the years to come. Although its duties included administration, communications, and provision of Red Cross type services in health care and feeding the troops, its fame came from the activities of its members in intelligence and combat. The women of Minahasa lived up to their reputation for being bold and clever; it was perhaps not surprising that they were good at extricating secrets from enemy troops, but a number are said to have excelled on the battlefield. Although Mrs. Sumula, as wife of the PRRI armed forces chief of staff, was formal head of the PWP, the best known leaders were Sumual's sister, Evert, Dee Gerungan's wife Hetty Gerungan-Warouw, and the commander of the military unit of PWP, Miss S. Rotinsulu.[41]

Permesta's total armed strength by June 1958 is estimated at about 15,000 persons.[42]

Foreign Assistance

As essential to Permesta plans as the mobilization of local support and forces, was the obtaining of foreign assistance. Promises of help to the PRRI had been received from both American and British representatives. In April 1958 two of America's closest allies in Asia, Taiwan and the

---

39 Staf Angkatan Bersenjata, *Sedjarah Singkat*, p. 140. Interviews, Jakarta: D. J. Somba, January 22, 1972, H. N. V. Sumual, April 13, 1972.
40 *Pikiran Rakjat*, March 25, 1958; letter from A. C. J. Mantiri to author, September 14, 1974.
41 *Gelora Maesa*, March 21, 1958; *Pelopor* (Manado), May 21, 1958. Interviews, Manado: Annie Kalangie (also a well-known PWP leader), November 17, 1971; Hetty Sual-Rumambi, March 19, 1972.
42 The estimate was given by D. J. Somba, interview, Jakarta, January 22, 1972.

Republic of Korea, promised moral support and material aid (weapons and volunteers) to the rebels, and indicated that they were prepared to recognize the rebel government once the United States had done so.[43] Aid from these virtual American client states would only have been given with U.S. approval; indeed, it is quite likely that these countries were mere channels for getting U.S. supplies to the rebels. Manila, Hong Kong, and Singapore were frequently mentioned in press reports as meeting places, or ports of call, for the rebel leaders.

The Philippines, bordering on North Sulawesi, and the site of a major U.S. air base, Clark Field, was directly involved in support for the rebels. Yet, in the absence of any official U.S. recognition of PRRI, Manila too had to be circumspect. In March President Garcia described the rebellion as an "internal question," and Foreign Secretary Serrano called for "non-interference in the internal affairs of the Indonesian people." However, Serrano also noted that Indonesia was "free to change its form of government." The Philippine consul in Manado, who had been reported to be sympathetic to the Permesta movement, was ordered to remain at his post and to report "objectively" to Manila.[44] Later the Philippine news service reported that any arms reaching the rebels from the Philippines were the work of Sulu smugglers.[45] In May, President Garcia admitted that it was possible that some "Filipino adventurers living in Borneo were fighting with the Indonesian rebel forces," but the Foreign Secretary and Defense Minister denied that any Filipino "volunteers" had joined the rebels.[46]

As noted above (p. 91), it was from Manila and Taipei that Sumual and Pantouw obtained the first arms for the Permesta rebels; they brought them on their return to Minahasa on February 23, 1958. A major delivery of arms to North Sulawesi was made by sea in mid-May—in crates clearly marked U.S. Navy. Most of the initial shipments are said to have been

---

43 Angkatan Darat, *PRRI*, II, pp. 193-95; on South Korean support for the rebels see also Jones, *Indonesia*, p. 152. According to the Angkatan Darat volume, Kawilarang and Warouw went to Taipei and Seoul in May 1958 in search of support for the rebellion. Kawilarang says that he made no such trip, although in July 1958 he did accompany Professor Sumitro to Taipei, Hong Kong, and Singapore; letter to author, November 30, 1975.
44 *PIA*, March 15, 1958 (p.m.), p. 8; March 17 (p.m.), p. 12.
45 *PIA*, March 26, 1958 (a.m.), p. 12; *Bara*, March 25, 1958.
46 *PIA*, May 16, 1958 (a.m.), p. 1.

light arms, and this caused some problems because the KNIL veterans responsible for training the young volunteers were mostly specialists in heavy artillery.[47]

In addition to the supply of arms, foreign support included provision for training abroad of pilots and communications personnel at U.S. bases in Guam, Okinawa, and the Philippines; and foreign advisers, British as well as American, were seen in Padang and Manado.[48]

Most obvious, and probably most crucial to the rebel plans, however, was the provision of an air force—complete with planes and pilots. The Sumatran branch of the rebellion collapsed too rapidly to be able to take much advantage of this offer of U.S. generosity, but in North Sulawesi a revolutionary air force (Angkatan Udara Revolusioner—AUREV) was established in April 1958. Heading it was Air Vice Commodore Muharto, a Javanese friend of Sumual's who had been AURI base commander in Manado. By mid-April the AUREV had eight to nine planes, with American, Filipino, and Taiwanese Chinese pilots, available for its use from fields in the Philippines and in Minahasa.[49]

Military Operations

From mid-April to mid-May the rebel air force controlled the skies over East Indonesia. Reconnaissance flights had been made on behalf of the AUREV at least since late March; on March 27 an unmarked U.S. Navy photo reconnaissance plane with a gaping hole in one wing made an emergency landing in Davao, in the southern Philippines, and the evidence that the plane was acting on behalf of the PRRI/Permesta rebels

---

47 Interviews, A. C. J. Mantiri, Airmadidi, November 5 and 26, 1971; according to Mrs. Mantiri the arms were delivered on Ascension Day, which she remembered as being May 10; according to my calculations, in 1958 Ascension Day would have been May 16. Also interview with Usman Damopolii, Manado, November 15, 1971.
48 Angkatan Darat, *PRRI*, II, pp. 192-93; this source mentions the training of twelve persons, mostly from Sumatra, beginning in April 1958, as well as the presence of foreign advisers in Sumatra. Information on Manado, from interviews: A. C. J. Mantiri, November 5, 1971; Usman Damopolii, Manado, April 15, 1971. Perhaps not all the foreign advisers had originally come with the intention of remaining. One Englishman, a radio operator on a ship which delivered arms to Permesta at Inobonto harbor, is said to have stayed for two years with the rebels after his ship was bombed; interview, W. Najoan, Manado, May 9, 1971.
49 *Pikiran Rakjat*, April 11, 1958; *Angkasa*, December 1958, pp. 542-45.

seems incontrovertible.⁵⁰ The signal that more than reconnaissance flights were to come was Sumual's April order to launch a "re-offensive" against the Jakarta government.⁵¹

On April 13 the AUREV struck its first target—Makassar's Mandai airport. The bombing attack, by an obviously foreign aircraft, effectively proved government claims of foreign involvement in the PRRI/ Permesta rebellion, and in South Sulawesi certainly helped to turn sympathy against the rebels. Balikpapan was attacked three days later, and in a further attack on April 28, a British tanker was destroyed. Ambon harbor was attacked on April 27 and 29, and an Indonesian Navy corvette was sunk and a Greek freighter heavily damaged. Strafing attacks occurred against other vessels in the Makassar strait and in the waters of East Indonesia. Shipping was severely disrupted, and Manado was for the time being free of the threat of blockade or invasion.⁵²

The Permesta forces were also successful on the ground. On April 29 it was announced the Morotai airfield was in Permesta hands.⁵³ On May 8 Somba attacked government forces at Parigi, near Palu in Central Sulawesi, and within a week Parigi and Toboli were back in Permesta hands.⁵⁴

With this appearance of strength in East Indonesia, when Bukittinggi fell to government troops on May 4, the rebel capital was officially moved to Manado, and Warouw was designated to lead the PRRI government there as deputy prime minister.⁵⁵

---

50 See the detailed account of this incident, which links it clearly with U.S. support for PRRI/Permesta, by Daniel F. Doeppers, "An Incident in the PRRI/Permesta Rebellion of 1958," *Indonesia*, 14 (Oct. 1972), pp. 183-95. The incident was reported in *PIA*, March 31, 1958 (p.m.), p. 3, but I have seen no other Indonesian press comment on it. There had been a peculiar incident in July 1956 when four Americans in U.S. Navy uniforms parachuted into the Sangihe-Talaud islands, claiming engine trouble and lack of fuel, although they had been seen circling the island for some hours. The U.S. Ambassador later explained that their navigational equipment had failed, and "expressed his gratitude for the assistance given the crew members by the Indonesian citizens, and his regret that the emergency nature of the incident and the difficulty of communication with these remote islands made it impossible to give the Indonesian authorities advance notice of the entry of the American rescue plane into Indonesian territory." *PIA*, August 16, 1956 (p.m.), pp. 5-6; also mentioned in *Gaja Pergolakan* (Manado), August 25, 1956.
51 *Pikiran Rakjat*, April 15, 1958.
52 Summary of rebel raids in Doeppers, "Incident," p. 191, based on reports in the *Straits Times*; dates checked with reports in *PIA*.
53 *Pikiran Rakjat* and *Bara*, April 30, 1958; *Gelora Maesa*, May 9, 1958; *PIA*, May 5 (p.m.), p. 2.
54 Staf Angkatan Darat, *Sedjarah Singkat*, p. 140; *Bara*, June 7, 1958.
55 *Bara*, May 6, 1958; *Pikiran Rakjat*, May 7, 1958.

Military Reverses

This, however, was the high point of PRRI/Permesta success. In the week of May 15-23 the tide turned, in the air and on the ground. Permesta domination of the air was broken, first, by a series of five successful AURI raids on the Manado and Tondano airfields, in the first of which, on May 15, six AUREV planes were destroyed.[56] The second blow was the withdrawal of foreign planes and pilots following the shooting down and capture of an American pilot, Allen Pope, during a bombing raid on Ambon harbor on May 18. The capture of Pope, although described by the U.S. government as an "adventurer" (in spite of his past record as a U.S. air force and CAT pilot and his current membership in the Clark field officers' club), was an acute embarrassment to the Americans—who had just a few weeks before found it necessary to describe the U.S. weapons captured at Pakanbaru as freely available for purchase on the world market.[57]

The embarrassment over Pope's capture, combined with the disillusionment over the rapid collapse of the rebel army in Sumatra, created a situation in which John Foster Dulles's hope of granting belligerent status to the PRRI became not only ridiculous, but impossible. Further, the new American Ambassador in Jakarta, Howard P. Jones, had discovered that Nasution was as much an anticommunist as the rebels he was fighting, but would only turn his attention to the PKI when he had disposed of the immediate threat posed by the PRRI. Although the rebels in Sumatra seemed to pose little threat even with foreign assistance, the AUREV in East Indonesia was causing serious damage to shipping, and was doing so with U.S.-supplied planes and pilots. The possibility of the TNI providing a bulwark against communism had been indicated when Colonel Yani, first deputy chief of staff, and a close friend of the U.S. army

---

56 Three Mustangs and one Catalina at Manado's Mapangat airfield, and two Lockheed planes at Tondano; *Angkasa*, December 1958, pp. 542-45; *PIA*, May 24, 1958 (a.m.), p. 13; *Bara*, May 24, 1958. The planes were said to be preparing to attack the government forces approaching Gorontalo; they were usually kept in safe fields in the Philippines; interview, Usman Damopolii, Manado, November 15, 1971. According to him, the Permesta group, including Allen Pope (who was at the airfield at the time), credited the successful AURI raid to Leo Wattimena.
57 Wise and Ross, *Invisible Government*, pp. 145-56; Jones, *Indonesia*, pp. 129-31, 140-46; *PIA*, May 19, 1958 (a.m.), p. 6; May 23 (p.m.), p. 9.

attaché, Colonel George Benson, made representations to the Embassy on April 12 that U.S. aid to the rebellion "placed the pro-U.S. officers in the Indonesian Army in an intolerable position." On April 15 Jones had advised the Department of State to place "our bets squarely on the Indonesian army."[58]

Thus, when Pope fell into Indonesian government hands, there was already sentiment in favor of a shift in U.S. policy.[59] The alacrity of the response from Washington was astonishing. On May 20 Secretary of State Dulles issued a press statement in which he said that the situation in Indonesia should be dealt with without outside intervention, and the following day the Department of State granted export licenses (blocked since February) for the shipment of arms, ammunition, and other military equipment to the Indonesian government.[60]

While the U.S. government had now agreed to supply the TNI, there were no replacements for the lost and destroyed rebel aircraft. The AUREV existed only on organization charts in Permesta headquarters, and the skies over East Indonesia were now the preserve of the AURI.

Both American and British agents are said to have remained in contact with various rebel leaders for the duration of the rebellion. Supplies, whether gifts from foreign supporters, or the proceeds of private barter arrangements, continued to arrive to the end, albeit spiradically because of the increasing effectiveness of the Indonesian Navy (ALRI) blockade.[61]

---

58 Jones, *Indonesia*, pp. 124-28, 137-39. Jones does not identify the attaché to whom Yani made representations, but Benson is known to have been a close friend of Yani, and would have been the logical contact in any case because of his official position. One story current in U.S. Embassy circles in 1961 was that Benson actually helped Yani plan the invasion of Padang.

59 Jones makes a point of the Embassy's being uninformed—and claims they were unaware—of CIA support for the rebels; *Indonesia*, pp. 134-35, 143-46. His predecessor, John Allison, although he complained that Washington accepted "CIA reports in preference to those from the Embassy," leaves no doubt that the policy of both Dulles brothers, Foster as well as Allan, was to support the rebels; *Ambassador*, pp. 301, 307, 313-15, 337.

60 Jones, *Indonesia*, p. 149; *PIA*, March 21, 1958 (p.m.), p. 2; March 22 (p.m.), p. 1; *Djuanda Statement*, pp. 28-29.

61 Mossman, *Rebels*, p. 230; Stevenson, *Bird's Nests*, pp. 30-31, 202-7; interview, A. C. J. Mantiri, Airmadidi, March 20, 1972. In June 1958, the communist newspaper *Bintang Timur*, published a copy of what purported to be a letter to Kawilarang from the chief of U.S. Naval Intelligence, Admiral Laurence H. Frost, urging the rebels to continue to fight in spite of reverses and promising that U.S. aid would continue through Taiwan and the Philippines, whatever official statements might be made about nonintervention. Text of the letter is in Angkatan Darat, *PRRI*, II, pp. 195-96; Jones describes the letter as a Russian fabrication (*Indonesia*, p. 338), based on Aleksandr Kaznachev, *Inside a Soviet Embassy* (Philadelphia: J. B. Lippincott, 1962), pp. 128-29. According

Nonetheless, the level of support received by the rebels in early 1958—in particular the provision of a staffed and equipped air force—was certainly not maintained after the embarrassing capture of Allen Pope.

At the same time that Permesta lost control of the air, government forces scored a series of military victories on the ground which effectively limited Permesta control in East Indonesia to Minahasa, and the region just to the south of it, Bolaang-Mongondow. On May 20 Morotai was recaptured by government troops. Between May 14 and 20 Gorontalo was recaptured, with the aid of guerrilla units under PNI leader Nani Wartabone, who had lost the city to Permesta forces on March 17. With the loss of Gorontalo to the central government, Somba could expect no reinforcements from Minahasa; he abandoned his attempt to hold Central Sulawesi, and about May 25 began a two-month march to return to Minahasa, with heavy casualties from illness as well as attack on the way. About the same time, Dee Gerungan, who had been cut off at Poso, made the fateful decision to flee to the south, where he and his unit of about 250 men joined with Qahhar Mudzakkar's Darul Islam. To the north, central government troops under Major Magenda captured the Sangihe-Talaud islands by May 21.[62]

Finally, in this catalogue of reverses, on May 20 Saleh Lahade and Mochtar Lintang were arrested in Makassar, and the possibility that South Sulawesi might support PRRI/Permesta—or even remain neutral—was ended.

---

to Kawilarang, the story about the Frost letter is "nonsense," and photographs which appeared in Indonesian journals which were said to be of discussions with officers of the U.S. Seventh Fleet, were actually "taken in January 1948 at the end of the 1st Dutch military action in West Java during a discussion between the Dutch and Indonesian sides"; letter to author, November 30, 1975.

62 For a summary of military operations see Staf Angkatan Darat, *Sedjarah Singkat*, pp. 138-41, and Makmun Salim, *Operasi Gabungan*, pp. 60-100. Mossman was in Siau, one of the Sangihe islands, when the central government troops arrived; for his account see *Rebels*, pp. 208-24. A dispute between a Sangirese TNI officer, Major John Rahasia, and the TT-VII/Permesta leadership over copra in early 1957 may have been a factor in the anti-Minahasan sentiment in the islands; see *PIA*, January 22, 1957 (p.m.), p. 3; January 24 (a.m.), p. 5; *Marhaen*, November 4, 1957. The delegation from Sangihe to the Bhinneka Tunggal Ika Congress in Makassar in May 1957 had also raised questions about the copra trade, and there were later reports that members of the delegation were detained as they passed through Manado on their way home; Kongres Bhinneka Tunggal Ika, "Statement Delegasi Sangir Taolud pada Kongres Bhinneka Tunggal Ika," Makassar, May 12, 1957; Dewan Pertimbangan Pusat, Pem. Mil. TT.VII "Wirabuana" Badan Pekerdja, "Risalah Rapat BP-DPP ke VI jang diadakan pada tanggal 27 Mei 1957"; also mentioned in Makmun Salim, *Operasi Gabungan*, p. 73.

The End of Permesta in South Sulawesi

In the months since the proclamation of the PRRI, political maneuvering in South Sulawesi had been intense, with Jusuf actively leading the anti-Permesta forces, and the supporters of the rebellion in positions of increasing weakness and disarray.

After Saleh Lahade and Mochtar Lintang retreated to Barru in February 1958, Dr. Engelen and Captain Bing Latumahina were the most important pro-Permesta military officers still in Makassar. Both took a cautious line, and advised a youth meeting in Barru in April that it was impossible to consider fighting in South Sulawesi on behalf of PRRI/Permesta. They also helped to avoid an armed clash between pro- and anti-Permesta groups within the military. Nonetheless, action was taken against them. On April 15 they were dishonorably discharged from the TNI, and were placed under house arrest from about May 6. A number of the more vocal pemuda supporters of Permesta were arrested and imprisoned on May 9.[63]

At the same time, Jusuf moved to demonstrate his loyalty to the central government—for he, after all, had also been one of the signers of the Proclamation of March 2. Following a meeting of KDM-SST and KADIT (Inter-Regional Command for East Indonesia) officers with Nasution in March, Jusuf, apparently on his own authority, agreed to send a unit from RI-Hasanuddin (which he commanded) to participate in the planned invasion of Gorontalo. One company of men from Azis Taba's Battalion 715 and one company from KADIT, were formed into "Detachment I" which was to join Brawijaya Battalion 512 in the invasion. Forty percent of the men selected were from Gorontalo, and they were led by an officer from that area, Captain Piola Isa. Secretly, on the night of May 9-10, the two companies left from the navy-controlled

---

63 Engelen and Latumahina are said to have intervened with Sergeant-Major Pangkey (a Minahasan), who ousted the anti-Permesta commander of his artillery company and trained his six cannons on the city of Makassar; they convinced Pangkey that to open fire would bring disaster. Pangkey was arrested at the same time as Engelen and Latumahina. It was perhaps because their positions in IPRI (the officers' association) gave them an organizational base for possible resistance to the anti-Permesta forces that Engelen and Latumahina were considered sufficiently dangerous to be arrested. *Bara*, April 18, May 8 and 12, 1958. Interviews: Makassar, Husain Achmad, October 11, 1971, Abdul Muis, October 18, 1971; Jakarta, Bing Latumahina, January 14, 1972, Dr. O. E. Engelen, February 1, 1972.

area of Makassar harbor for the island of Buton, where they joined the convoy from Java.[64]

Jusuf was now ready to move against his primary target, Saleh Lahade. On May 12, Jusuf flew to Jakarta to report to Chief of Staff Nasution "on behalf of Panglima Mattalatta" on cooperation between PRRI/Permesta and the Darul Islam in South Sulawesi. Details of the agreement, signed on April 17, 1958 by Saleh Lahade and Mochtar Lintang for PRRI/Permesta and Qahhar Mudzakkar for the DI, were released to the press by army spokesman Pirngadie on May 15, and were published in Makassar newspapers on the 17th. The preamble to the agreement described it as "a joint agreement for cooperation in the common effort to wage war against the communists in Indonesia and international communism (which directly or indirectly influences and uses Sukarno and his colleagues)." In the body of the agreement the two parties pledged to reject the influence of international communism and of any foreign intervention; to renounce the sovereignty of the Sukarno government; and to face the enemy jointly.[65]

As noted above, negotiations with Qahhar had been one of the aims of the Permesta movement virtually from the start. However, in early 1957 the purpose of such negotiations was to bring the DI rebellion to an end. In 1958, with Permesta itself involved in a rebellion against the central government, negotiations with Qahhar took on quite a different aspect—that of forming a united front to continue the rebellion against the central government. This, indeed, was the essence of the draft agreement between Qahhar and Saleh Lahade, and this was treason. On this basis, Jusuf, who himself in 1957 claimed to have negotiated with Qahhar, in May 1958 prepared to arrest Saleh Lahade for having done so.[66]

---

64 M. A. Kamah, *Operasi Sapta Marga II* (Makassar: n.p., 1959), pp. 12, 16-23.
65 *PIA*, May 16, 1958 (p.m.), pp. 5-7; *Bara* and *Marhaen*, May 17, 1958; interview, Saleh Lahade, Makassar, October 7, 1971.
66 According to Andi Mattalatta, after the, PRRI proclamation, because the situation was confused, he ordered Saleh Lahade and Her Tasning, then chief of staff of KDM-SST, to contact Qahhar to ask him not to attack KDM-SST, and thus to avoid a civil war; interview, Makassar, March 29, 1972. If this was Saleh Lahade's mandate, he obviously went beyond it. Sometime after Saleh Lahade's meeting with Qahhar, Her Tasning and Azis Taba (chief of staff of RI-Hasanuddin) met with Qahhar to assure him that the anti-Permesta group was not pro-*pusat* (neither could remember the date of the meeting); interviews, Jakarta: Her Tasning, February 1, 1972; Azis Taba, February 3 and 8, 1972.

Jusuf returned to Makassar on May 18, apparently having met not only with Nasution but with Sukarno, and, according to a number of sources, having been empowered by the President to assume command of KDM-SST and ordered by him to carry out the arrest of Saleh Lahade which Andi Mattalatta had refused to do. Mattalatta had been in poor health for some months, and this provided a pretext for Jusuf's assumption of command. On May 19 the chief of staff of KDM-SST, Major Her Tasning, issued a press communiqué stating that Panglima Andi Mattalatta had been granted a month's sick leave from the 17th of May, and that for the period he was unable to carry on his functions, he had designated Lieutenant Colonel M. Jusuf to represent him.[67]

On the same day, Andi Pangerang as head of the Regional War Administration for South and Southeast Sulawesi announced the banning of the so-called "revolutionary government" of the Republic of Indonesia (PRRI), and the "freezing" of the Permesta organization, including all its branches and sections. In discussing the order with a newspaper reporter, the chief of staff of the Regional War Administration, Major Her Tasning, mentioned that several persons had been arrested as a concrete step to implement the order, but he did not identify them.[68]

Although the May 19 announcement had said that Andi Mattalatta would be on leave for a month, on May 21 an announcement was issued, signed by Jusuf as "deputy panglima," stating that Andi Mattalatta would resume his duties the following day.[69] The reasons for Mattalatta's unexpectedly rapid recovery became clear when it was revealed that one of those arrested while he was in the hospital was Saleh Lahade. However, Andi Mattalatta's resumption of command on May 22 could not save his old friend, and on May 28 he again took sick leave and reentered the hospital. Once again Jusuf was named acting commander.[70]

Arrested with Saleh Lahade were Mochtar Lintang, and three of their associates who had participated in the negotiations with Qahhar

---

67 *Bara* and *Marhaen*, May 19, 1958. Additional information from officers who were in Makassar at the time.
68 *Marhaen*, May 21, 1958.
69 *Marhaen*, May 21, 1958; *Bara*, May 22, 1958. From this time on Jusuf was referred to in the press as "deputy panglima."
70 Mattalatta was reported to have resumed his duties on July 14, 1958; *Bara*, May 31 and July 15, 1958.

Mudzakkar which had precipitated the arrests—Captain W. G. J. Kaligis, who had been in the secretariat of the Team of Assistants of the military government and was close to Sumual; Captain Anwar Bey, a member of the KADIT Chaplains' Corps; and Naziruddin Rachmat from the Religious Education Inspectorate (which Mochtar Lintang had headed).[71] Explaining the arrests on May 27, Her Tasning said that they had been made in accordance with an order from the Army Chief of Staff in his capacity as Central War Administrator, and were based on a decision of KDM-SST and the Panglima. No mention was made of the fact that at the time the arrests were made it was Jusuf who was acting panglima of KDM-SST.[72]

Saleh Lahade and Mochtar Lintang were held in Makassar until November 1958, when they were sent first to Den Pasar, and then to Madiun where they were interned until 1962. The three men arrested with them (Kaligis, Anwar Bey, and Naziruddin Rachmat), Dr. Engelen, Bing Latumahina, and Sergeant-Major Pangkey were sent to Jakarta on May 29, and were interned there and in Madiun until 1962.

Fighting in North Sulawesi

Thus in one week, May 15-23, 1958, Permesta lost all hope of support from South Sulawesi; was driven out of Central Sulawesi, Gorontalo, Sangihe, and Morotai; and was left without an air force. And, as a result of the capture of Allen Pope, there had been a significant reversal in U.S. policy, and any further American aid was likely to be on a much diminished scale. The hopes and plans for an attack on Jakarta crumbled as rapidly as the Sumatran rebels had disappeared into the jungle.

---

71 *Marhaen*, May 22, 1958.
72 *Marhaen*, May 27, 1958. According to Andi Mattalatta, he was sick in the hospital when Jusuf carried out the arrests; he denies a widely circulated story that he fell ill during a tense discussion on May 18, in which Andi Pangerang and his father-in-law, H. M. Junus Daeng Mile (former Mayor of Makassar), at Jusuf's initiative urged him not to go to Barru to meet with Saleh Lahade; interview, Makassar, March 29, 1972.

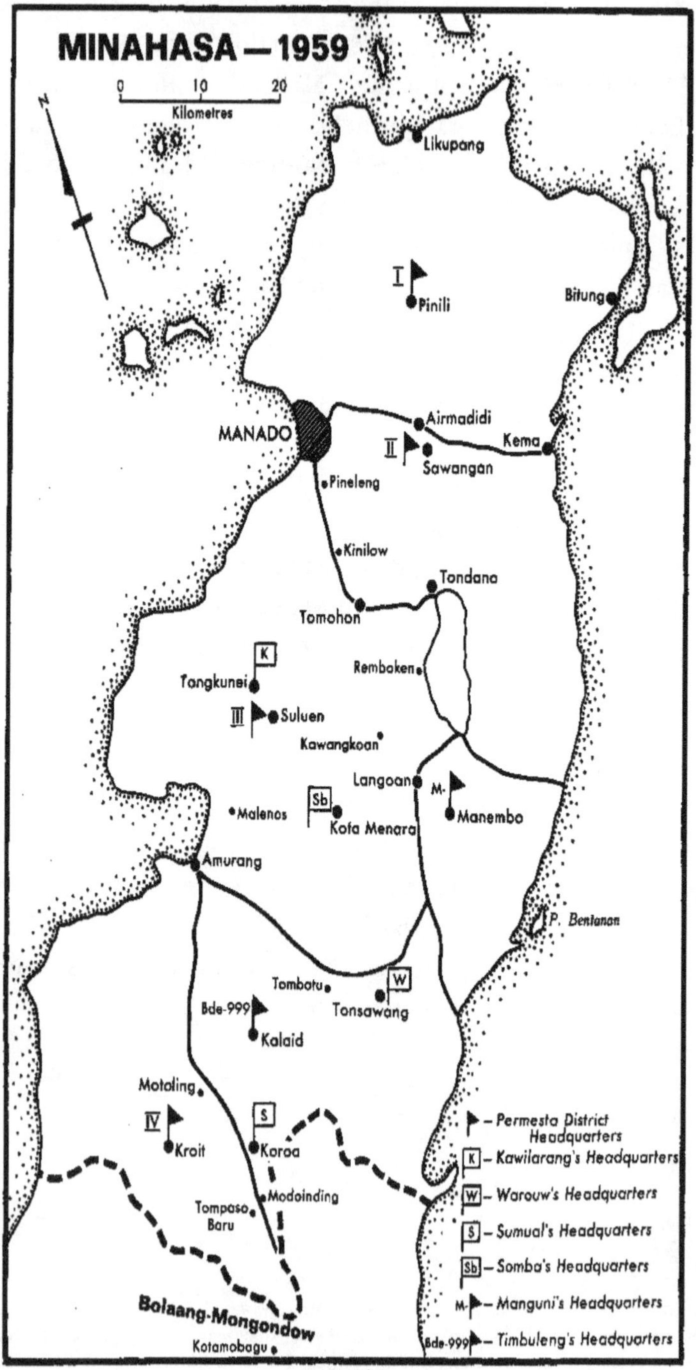
MINAHASA — 1959
0
10
20
Kilometres
N
Likupang
I
Pinili
Bitung
MANADO
Airmadidi
II
Sawangan
Kema
Pineleng
Kinilow
Tondano
Tomohon
K
Tangkunei
Remboken
III
Suluen
Kawangkoan
Langoan
M-
Manembo
Sb
Kota Menara
Malenos
Amurang
P. Bentenan
Tombatu
W
Tonsawang
Bde-999
Kalaid
Motoling
IV
Kroit
S
Koroa
Modoinding
Tompaso Baru
Bolaang-Mongondow
Kotamobagu
– Permesta District Headquarters
K – Kawilarang's Headquarters
W – Warouw's Headquarters
S – Sumual's Headquarters
Sb – Somba's Headquarters
M- – Manguni's Headquarters
Bde-999 – Timbuleng's Headquarters

MAP III

By the end of that fateful week there were newspaper and radio reports that Sumual, as chief of staff of the PRRI armed forces, had requested negotiations with Jakarta to reach a "reasonable solution" to the present situation. The Army Information Department issued a communique stating that negotiations would be considered only after the unconditional surrender of the rebels, and the Ministry of Information stated that government policy was to crush the rebels, not to negotiate with them.[73] A U.S. Embassy effort to promote a cease-fire on May 15 had been similarly rejected by Djuanda and Sukarno.[74]

Sumual and Warouw replied in interviews in Manado newspapers that the offer to negotiate had been made not out of weakness, but out of humanitarian feelings on seeing the consequences of a civil war, and out of a desire to convince Jakarta that such a war could only harm the entire Indonesian nation. Warouw added that the Permesta position was strong, and that there were no grounds for speculating that PRRI/ Permesta might surrender—or even negotiate—unconditionally.[75]

Whatever the brave words of Sumual and Warouw, with Permesta control of the skies broken, and its geographic base narrowed, the way was now open for government forces to invade Minahasa. Navy shelling of Manado began on June 8, and the air force joined in attacks on Manado's Mapangat airfield, Tondano and Tomohon on the 11th and 13th. Government troops, spearheaded by the RPKAD (army paratroop regiment) and the KKo (marine corps), began to land north of Manado on June 13, and on the 16th there were large-scale landings at Kema, south of Bitung. Permesta forces, largely youths from the Komando Pemuda Permesta, put up strong resistance, and it took government troops ten days to fight their way the 25 kilometers, along a good road, from Kema to Manado. Additional troops were landed north of the city on June 21 and 24, and Warouw, as PRRI Deputy Prime Minister, ordered that the city be evacuated. By June 26 it was occupied by government troops of the Merdeka Command, under Lieutenant Colonel Rukminto Hendraningrat.[76] The troops came primarily from the Brawijaya Division,

---

73 *PIA*, May 23, 1958 (a.m.), p. 1, and (p.m.), p. 4.
74 Jones, *Indonesia*, pp. 148-49.
75 *Gelora Maesa* and *Pikiran Rakjat*, May 23/24, 1958.
76 Makmun Salim, *Operasi2 Gabungan*, pp. 75-85; KODAM XIII/Merdeka, Staf Koord. Artileri,

although some Diponegoro, Siliwangi, and later Hasanuddin, units were also involved.[77]

On July 1, 1958 an interim civilian government for Manado and Minahasa was established under Captain Bert Supit; and on July 19 E. A. (Nus) Kandou, a PNI leader, was made secretary to the military government. On September 23 Kandou was made acting area head of Minahasa, and J. P. Mongula was appointed acting mayor of Manado. Both had been active in Minahasa politics for some years, Kandou in the PNI, and Mongula in the left wing of the Christian party, Parkindo. Mongula had served as Minahasa area head in 1953-54, and Kandou had been runner-up to Saerang in the election to this position in 1956.[78]

After the February bombing of Manado, Permesta headquarters had moved to Pineleng, on the southern outskirts of the city. Before the landing of government forces, the Permesta civil and military administration was moved further inland to Tomohon. Most of the civil government officials and their families followed Permesta, first to Tomohon, then to southern Minahasa. Of the eight district officers in Minahasa in 1958, only one, caught in Bitung when the government troops landed, remained in the area under central government control. Indeed, there was widespread support for the rebellion. The government-appointed area head of Minahasa, E. A. Kandou, says that the ruling public opinion was pro-Permesta, and that it was difficult to change the way of thinking of the people.[79]

Sedjarah Artileri Dam XIII Merdeka (Manado, April 1961), pp. 7-10; *PIA*, June 16, 1958 (a.m.), p. 1, and (p.m.), p. 1; June 18 (a.m.), p. 10; June 21 (p.m.), p. 9; June 25 (a.m.), p. 1; June 27 (a.m.), pp. 1 and 7; "Pengumuman: Wakil Perdana Menteri Merangkap Menteri Pertahanan ad interim Pemerintah Revolutioner Republic Indonesia," Manado, Colonel J. F. Warouw, June 27, 1958 (photocopy in my possession). Interviews, particularly, H. N. V. Sumual, Jakarta, April 13, 1972.

77 Diponegoro units were involved in the capture of Tomohon, and Siliwangi in the capture of Kotamobagu (see below). A Hasanuddin infantry battalion was in North Sulawesi from January through May 1960, although it is said not to have engaged in much fighting; the Hasanuddin men say that their old friends in Permesta avoided battle. See "Operasi: Pemberangkatan B.T.P. I/ Hasanuddin Kedaerah Operasi KODAM XIII/ Merdeka" (January 28, 1960); and "BTP I/HN Tiba Kembali di Makassar (May 3, 1960); DSM-AD, File—PUL & PAN, T, III, no. 334; Source—DOC SEM DAM XIV/HN. Interviews with A. R. Malaka, Makassar, March 2, 1972; and H. Andi Unru, Sengkang-Makassar, July 6, 1971.

78 Djawatan Penerangan Kotapradja Manado and Daerah Minahasa, in cooperation with Penerangan Komando Operasi "Merdeka," *Berita Penerangan: Berkala Mingguan*, I/1 (November 3, 1958), p. 38 (hereafter cited as *Berita Penerangan*); list of area heads in Manado and Minahasa provided by Governor's Office, North Sulawesi, November 11, 1971; interview, E. A. Kandou, Manado, March 17, 1972.

79 Interviews, Manado, P. Matindas and B. Lengkong, May 12, 1971; E. A. Kandou, March 17, 1972.

At the time of the government landings Warouw was the senior civilian representative of PRRI in Sulawesi. Effective military command was in Sumual's hands. Sumual was in direct command of the Permesta forces during the Kema landing, and was in fact wounded there. Somba was designated commander of Minahasa, but did not arrive back from Central Sulawesi until July 25. Kawilarang, the most senior of the Minahasan officers, was still abroad, and did not return until August.

The fall of Manado had greater political and psychological than military effect, for Permesta military strength was not broken, and plans had already been made for withdrawal to guerrilla bases. The fighting on the road to Manado had demonstrated, however, that whatever the bravery of the youths fighting under the Permesta banner, they were scarcely trained soldiers, and if they continued to be used in frontal battles casualties would be high and supplies of ammunition would soon be exhausted. The Permesta forces withdrew to Tomohon, where it was planned to make a further stand against the advance of central government troops. Many of the units composed largely of young boys returned to their home villages to prepare for guerrilla fighting. Not all initiative was in the hands of the government forces, however, for on August 14, Permesta troops attacked Pineleng, their former headquarters, on the outskirts of Manado.[80]

It was nearly a month after the fall of Manado when government troops captured Tondano on July 21, after a week of heavy fighting. Tondano, Minahasa's second largest city, together with the town of Tomohon dominated the plateau around Lake Tondano which was the principal rice growing area of Minahasa. Control of the two towns was thus important to control of the food supply for the area. With the fall of Tondano to the central government, both sides knew that the next target would be Tomohon, and both prepared for heavy fighting.[81]

The commander of the Tomohon sector was Major Eddy Mondong, one of the officers who had pressed most strongly in February for breaking relations with the central government and supporting PRRI. By August, however, he had begun to question that decision. He came to Somba's

---

80 KODAM XIII/Merdeka, *Artileri*, pp. 9-12; *Bara*, August 20, 1958. Interviews with people in the area at the time, particularly with H. N. V. Sumual, Jakarta, April 13, 1972.
81 KODAM XIII/Merdeka, *Artileri*, p. 12; Makmun Salim, *Operasi2 Gabungan*, pp. 90-91.

headquarters near Tomohon to ask if the policy could be changed. When Somba asked why he wanted now to change the policy, Mondong replied that the situation was difficult, with Minahasa being shelled from the sea on both sides, and that the war was already lost. Somba replied that it was a bit late to realize that Minahasa was a narrow peninsula and that two battalions contained only 2,000 men, and that it was too late to change the policy of breaking with the central government. When Mondong then asked if Somba would turn over command to him, Somba realized that Mondong intended to surrender. He refused to do so, saying that such a decision would be unacceptable to the other officers. However, Somba seems to have made no move to replace Mondong in spite of his suspicions as to his intentions.[82]

It is likely that at the time Mondong spoke with Somba he was already in contact with central government forces. On August 6 he sent a courier to the Diponegoro troops in Tondano who were preparing for the attack on Tomohon, to inform them that he and the 1,500 men in his sector were prepared to surrender to the government forces. Final arrangements for the surrender were worked out on August 14-15, as preparations for the final attack were under way, and on August 16 government troops entered Tomohon, thanks to Mondong meeting scarcely any resistance.[83]

From Tomohon-Tondano the government troops moved quickly to take Langoan on August 20, then Kawangkoan, and by the end of September, Amurang. The front seems to have stabilized along that line for nearly a year. The Permesta civil government, under Warouw's direction, but including Governor Manoppo and other civilians, moved in August from Kawangkoan further south to Tompaso Baru, then to Modoinding. It continued to function there, along the border with Bolaang-Mongondow, until the fall of Kotamobagu, capital of Bolaang-Mongondow, in September 1959.[84]

---

[82] Interview, D. J. Somba, Jakarta, April 19, 1972; he said that Mondong came to see him one or two days before the fall of Tomohon.

[83] Kapt. Soewondo, "Kisah Penggabungan Pasukan Mondong dan Direbutnja Kota Tomohon," *Madjalah Angkatan Darat*, 9/7 (July 1959), pp. 24-30.

[84] KODAM XIII/Merdeka, *Artileri*, p. 12. Interviews, Manado: G. M. A. Inkiriwang, April 28, 1971; J. A. Sondakh, November 4, 1971, and March 18, 1972; R. A. Sual, November 9, 1971; Jakarta: H. D. Manoppo, May 17, 1972.

With the stabilization of the front along the Amurang-Langoan line, the area under open Permesta control was limited to southern Minahasa and Bolaang-Mongondow. It was in this area, at Tombatu, that Sumual had his headquarters. His staff officers, and the commander of Bolaang-Mongondow, Dolf Runturambi, were also located there. The area north of the Amurang-Langoan line was contested territory, with central government troops controlling the towns and main roads, but with Permesta forces controlling the countryside. When Somba returned from Central Sulawesi in late July 1958, he assumed command of Minahasa. Prior to the Kema landings of the central government troops Sumual had divided Minahasa into four military districts (*wehrkreise*—WK), and these divisions were retained for the duration of the rebellion. (See Map 3 and Appendix V.) Somba, and the district commanders, established headquarters in mountainous or isolated areas within their commands, suitable as bases for guerrilla warfare.

The period of withdrawal was the most difficult one for the Permesta forces, for the initiative lay with the government troops. However, once the Permesta units had withdrawn to bases in the mountains, it was they who decided when to fight and when to sleep. Government forces then had always to be on the alert against sudden attack from the hills, and traveled only in convoy along the main roads.

The worst of the fighting, however, was not over by September 1958. Indeed it is estimated that casualties in 1959 were greater than in the initial year of fighting.[85] Although much of the fighting after September 1958 was in the form of small scale guerrilla raids and attacks, there were several major battles. On February 17-19, 1959, Permesta forces launched a general attack against Amurang, Kawangkoan, Langoan, and Tondano. They nearly succeeded in capturing Kawangkoan, and did force back government troops all along the line. Casualties were heavy on both sides,

---

85 An army doctor who served in Manado December 1958 to April 1959 says that casualties were high because there were many all-day battles; it was sometimes necessary to fly some of the wounded to Surabaya immediately because there were too many to be treated locally; Dr. Majoedin, Bandung, August 8, 1971. Estimates of casualties for the total period of the rebellion vary; some say as few as 3,000 persons, military and civilian, on the Permesta side died; others place the civilian figure at 7,000-8,000 dead from illness or war, about 2,000 Permesta military (mostly among irregular troops), and about 4,000 TNI; interviews, Manado: Annie Kalangie, November 17, 1971; J. A. Sondakh, March 18, 1972; A.C.J. Mantiri, March 20, 1972.

with Permesta losing more than a hundred men. Some have suggested that the attack was made to strengthen Permesta's bargaining position in anticipated negotiations with the central government. Sumual says that the aim of the attack was to boost the morale of the PRRI in Sumatra and to strike a blow at that of the government troops. The attack failed, according to Sumual, because of difficulties in coordinating the Permesta troops, and because they had not been trained for frontal fighting or occupying towns.[86]

Although the February 1959 offensive by the Permesta forces failed to dislodge the government troops, it demonstrated that the rebels were far from defeated. In an analysis of the situation in mid-1959, the army central intelligence staff noted that although government troops occupied all the important strategic points, Permesta activities were on the increase. This was attributed to the following factors:

1) Permesta forces still controlled guerrilla base areas;
2) leaks in TNI security, which were a result of close family ties among the people of Minahasa, almost all of whom had relatives with Permesta, and the lack of caution among government troops and officials in selecting laborers to help in operations or in discussing military matters with (or in the presence of) Minahasan girls;
3) the mountainous terrain of Minahasa, which was an advantage to the Permesta guerrillas;
4) difficult logistics—bad roads, and guerrilla ambushes;
5) bad physical condition of government troops, half of whom were sick;
6) lack of cooperation from the local population in giving information on the location or activities of Permesta troops.[87]

The situation, however, soon began to change. In May 1959 the government for the first time began to use North Sulawesi as a testing ground for its new Czech rockets, and it became more difficult for the

---

86 KODAM XIII/Merdeka, *Artileri*, pp. 16-17. Interviews, Manado: Annie Kalangie, November 17, 1971; E. A. Kandou, March 17, 1972; Jakarta: H. N. V. Sumual, April 13, 1972.
87 *Sari Attensia*, VI/7 (1959), pp. 497-506.

Permesta forces to concentrate for an attack.[88] Nonetheless, in May 1959 Permesta troops repulsed an attack on Bolaang-Mongondow, launched by government forces in Gorontalo. A return attack on Gorontalo by Permesta forces is said to have been planned for December 1959; it was thought that sufficient time would have elapsed by then that popular resentment would have developed against the occupying Brawijaya troops there. Events, however, intervened, and on September 18, 1959, Kotamobagu, capital of Bolaang-Mongondow, fell to government troops.

The Fall of Kotamobagu[89]

The fall of Kotamobagu was a major turning point in the rebellion, and marked the beginning of the final phase of the war; thus, it is worth examining the situation surrounding it in some detail.

Bolaang-Mongondow was under the command of Dolf Runturambi, who had been appointed by Somba to head the northern sector of KDM-SUT on February 19, 1958, and who was given command over Bolaang-Mongondow in the division of Minahasa and North Sulawesi into military districts by Sumual in June 1958. Most of the plans for the defense of Kotamobagu, however, are said to have been made by one of Sumual's staff officers, Lendy Tumbelaka. There were only two roads into the city, and both were controlled by Permesta units. Based on the tactics of the TNI in Minahasa, it was expected that in Bolaang-Mongondow too they would use heavy weaponry and thus would be forced to travel along main roads. However, while Permesta troops stood off two Brawijaya battalions along the road from Inobonto harbor, a Siliwangi battalion marched through the jungle from the south and took the city on September 18, 1958, after several days of sharp fighting.

Permesta defenses were weakened not only by bad intelligence, but by policies which had lost them the sympathy of the people of Bolaang-

---

88 KODAM XIII/Merdeka, *Artileri*, pp. 18-21.
89 The account which follows is based on the following sources: KODAM VI/Siliwangi, *Sejarah Militer, Siliwangi Dari Masa Kemasa* (Jakarta: Fakta Mahyuma, 1968), pp. 464-75; KODAM XIII/Merdeka, *Artileri*, pp. 19-20; interviews, Manado: Usman Damopolii, November 15, 1971; Annie Kalangie, November 17, 1971; P. Matindas and J. A. Sondakh, March 18, 1972; Jakarta: H. N. V. Sumual, April 13, 1972.

Mongondow. Against the advice of Permesta officers from the area, Runturambi ordered the carrying out of a scorched earth policy. On September 14, as TNI troops neared, Kotamobagu, capital of Bolaang-Mongondow was set alight. The hospital was almost the only building left standing. Then, as the Permesta troops retreated toward Minahasa, they set fire to the countryside. An estimated 60 percent of the houses of Bolaang-Mongondow were burned. A similar policy had been followed in southern Minahasa,[90] but with less disastrous results. Although there was resentment of the policy there too, the burning was carried out by local troops, sometimes sons of the inhabitants. The promises of future rehabilitation were more readily believed there than in Bolaang-Mongondow, where relations between the Permesta troops, largely Christian Minahasans, and the Moslem local population were far from close.[91]

The burning of Bolaang-Mongondow so aroused feeling against the Minahasans who had ordered it, that Minahasan settlers at the Dumoga transmigration center were forced to flee north to Minahasa, a number of them dying on the way. One of those who was present in the area at the time commented, "After the burning of Kotamobagu, we had not only to face the enemy, the TNI, but had also to look over our shoulder to see whether the people had a knife ready to stick in our back."

With the fall of Kotamobagu there was no secure base area for Permesta, and the military staff, civilian government, and Permesta Woman's Corps scattered to various pockets in the mountains along the Minahasa-Bolaang-Mongondow border. Some staff officers, including Lendy Tumbelaka, Arie Supit, and Joseph, moved north to District III, commanded by Wim Tenges, where both Kawilarang and Somba had their headquarters. The Permesta units in Northern Minahasa had been

---

90 See, for example, report in *Berita Penerangan*, 1/36-37 (July 6-13, 1959), p. 22; the burning of Kotamobagu is also mentioned in Van Rootselaar, "Een Ontvoering." The scars of abandoned house foundations were still visible in both areas in 1971.

91 91There had been one Permesta battalion composed largely of students and some former TNI from Bolaang-Mongondow, and commanded by two young officers from the area, Captain Gonibala and Usman Damopolii. However, on August 16, 1959 Gonibala was arrested on suspicion that he intended to surrender to the central government. Damopolii succeeded his briefly as commander, but was removed from the battalion and ordered to form a new unit just a few days before the Siliwangi attack. Gonibala was killed, presumably on Runturambi's orders; Damopolii was captured by the Siliwangi troops and imprisoned in Manado for a year.

fighting a guerrilla war since September 1958. Now all of Permesta was confined to isolated guerrilla pockets within the boundaries of Minahasa.

CHAPTER SIX
THE END OF THE REBELLION

The fall of Kotamobagu in September 1959 was a serious blow to the Permesta rebellion, for although the Permesta forces did retain considerable ability to continue a protracted guerrilla war, their position was significantly weakened. Internal strains in the rebel forces—between leaders, between units, and between the rebels and the people were exacerbated. The rebels now lost their secure base area in southern Minahasa and Bolaang-Mongondow, and all were now scattered in isolated pockets in mountainous or jungle areas, as, indeed, had been the case with those units remaining north of the Amurang-Langoan line after September 1958. Many of the commanders had lost their communications equipment, and contact between them became more difficult. Except for those few located in coastal areas, supply became more of a problem. Although barter trade of copra for food, medicine, and weapons continued through to the end of the rebellion, in many areas arms and ammunition became scarce.

In this situation, more than ever, military factors were dominant. The civilian government had never been of more than limited significance. While still compact and based in Modoinding it did issue money and stamps (printed abroad, probably in Hong Kong), cabinets met and were reshuffled, and political advisers wrote speeches for Warouw to give to rouse the spirit of the people to support the struggle.[1] The civilians in Permesta, unlike those who had joined the PRRI in Sumatra, were men of only local influence, they were not national political figures. The military

---

1 Interviews, Manado: G. M. A. Inkiriwang, April 28, 1971; J. A. Sondakh, November 4, 1971 and March 18, 1972; R. A. Sual, November 9, 1971; Jakarta: H. D. Manoppo, May 17, 1972.

leaders of Permesta, however—Kawilarang, Warouw, and Sumual—were senior TNI officers with national reputations. It is not surprising that they dominated the scene. Further, in a situation of guerrilla warfare, each sector was relatively autonomous, and it was the military commander of the sector who was in effective control. As one of the senior civilian officials described the situation:

> It was a guerrilla state; each area had its own authority. The regional government's authority was no longer strong. Juridically the regional government still existed, but in practice it was the commander of the military district who controlled the area. The regional government head was more a symbol; he was very much respected, but it was military power which was the determining factor.
>
> In a situation of guerrilla warfare each commander felt himself strong—and autonomous. In guerrilla warfare, in the jungle, he who rules is he who first draws his gun.[2]

There was competition for weapons both between and within rebel units, for, as one observer commented, "A soldier without a gun has zero value." The shortage seems to have been particularly severe in those units composed largely of youth and students rather than of former TNI soldiers. In Laurens Saerang's Mangune Brigade, for example, it is estimated that by early 1961 the number of soldiers without weapons was two to three times that of armed men. Many of the soldiers were very young men and boys who had recently been secondary school students, and fights between them over weapons are said to have been frequent.

Not all the conflicts, however, were within the Permesta ranks. Although at the outset the rebels had been strongly supported by the people of Minahasa, the years of war began to erode that support. The burning of southern Minahasa and much of Bolaang-Mongondow turned many people against the rebellion. A number of the Permesta commanders became known for their cruelty; some are said to have been killed by their own men for this reason. Some say that this problem was

---

2 Interview, J. A. Sondakh, Manado, March 18, 1972.

greatest among the generally undisciplined youths who had received little military training. As the rebellion wore on, for many of the people life was difficult, not least when they faced a youth with a gun.

However, it was not so much the shrinking of the base area or the lessening of popular support for Permesta—or even the success of the central government troops—which brought the rebellion to an end, but the failures of the Permesta leadership. This failure was not due to any lack of military ability, but to the fatal splits which developed among the Permesta officers. Differences among them had been muted during the early months of the rebellion when morale was high, but as the fighting dragged on inconclusively, and as communication between them became more difficult, suspicion and tension increased. The splits revolved around a number of substantive issues: disposition of military units; attitude toward the Sumatran half of the rebellion—particularly after the proclamation of the Republik Persatuan Indonesia (RPI—Indonesian Federal Republic) in February 1960;[3] and negotiations with the central government. However, the divisions also involved personalities, and as these were important in the reactions to the substantive issues, it may be well to begin with a look at some of the leading figures in Permesta.

The Permesta Leaders[4]

Alex Kawilarang had been the most senior Minahasan officer in the TNI, and was a widely respected professional soldier of unquestioned ability. Although he had been appointed commander-in-chief of the PRRI/

---

3 The difference in opinion in North Sulawesi about the RPI, in which PRRI became formally linked with the Darul Islam rebellion, centered on the question of whether PRRI should adhere to its initial goal of setting up an alternative government for the Republic of Indonesia, or move to the establishment of a rival state. Opposition to the RPI in North Sulawesi was not based on fears of possible domination of the new government by Moslem groups, according to interviews with many of the Permesta leaders. Although the military leaders of Permesta were all Minahasan Christians, and some, Kawilarang in particular, were suspicious of the Masjumi politicians associated with the PRRI, the Permesta-appointed civilian governor of North Sulawesi, H. D. Manoppo, was a Moslem.
4 For basic biographic data see Appendix I. All the principal leaders were Minahasan, although they came from different language groups within Minahasa. This, however, was no barrier to communication, as all spoke Dutch, and almost certainly also spoke Manadonese Malay (bahasa Melayu Manado), a form of Malay very similar to the official Indonesian language, and in wide use in eastern Indonesia. All the military leaders of Permesta, and most of the civilians, were Christian.

Permesta forces, he refused to accept the position. He did, however, leave his post and return to Indonesia, where he joined the Permesta forces. Kawilarang made no secret of his disapproval of the PRRI, which he regarded as a barely disguised separatist movement. The prominent role of Masjumi leaders in the PRRI was also undoubtedly a factor in Kawilarang's attitude, for he had spent much of his military career fighting Darul Islam rebels, and he blamed Masjumi politicians for influencing successive cabinets to negotiate with the rebels rather than to exterminate them.

Kawilarang was himself a rather unlikely rebel, and he was suspected by some of the Permesta officers of being an agent of his old classmate Nasution, sent to Minahasa to try to negotiate an end to the rebellion. Some even implied, apparently without basis, that he had encouraged Mondong's surrender in Tomohon in August 1958, which had so disrupted Permesta military plans. It is true that alone among the TNI officers involved in the rebellion Kawilarang was not dishonorably discharged; he was, however, officially suspended from the army on May 6, 1958. The group of Permesta officers with which he was associated received army intelligence reports regularly from friends at army headquarters, but these were shared by the entire leadership group until mid-1959, when communications between them were disrupted.

During the Permesta rebellion Kawilarang commanded no troops of his own. His main activity seems to have been visiting units in the guerrilla areas, coordinating and, it is said, inspiring them. His influence was felt throughout the Permesta ranks, and among the people of Minahasa. An unpretentious man, despite his height and bearing, Kawilarang dressed not in military uniform, but in short trousers and rubber thong sandals. Although this simplicity of manner was one of the things which endeared him to the ordinary people, some of the Permesta troops felt it was conduct inappropriate for the "Panglima Besar."[5] Neither Kawilarang's morale nor his morals was affected by the jungle rot which was a threat to which many succumbed in the situation of guerrilla warfare.

---

5   Although Kawilarang refused to accept the position of commander-in-chief, he was acknowledged to be the most senior among the Permesta officers. In part because of his informal dress Kawilarang was not always recognized by the troops as he traveled about Minahasa, and the story is often told that he was once relieved of his watch as he passed a Permesta guard post.

Joop Warouw was three years older than Kawilarang, but junior to him in rank. During the revolution Warouw had been associated with ALRI and Brigade XVI, and had closer ties with the "pejuang" (fighter) group in the army than the Siliwangi professional Kawilarang. At the time of the revolution he had been thought to have vaguely leftist sympathies, in particular with the nationalist communist Murba party. By early 1958 these sympathies had dissipated; Warouw also abandoned his previously close relationship with President Sukarno. After the bombing of Manado, Warouw joined the rebellion, and was not only suspended, but dishonorably discharged, from the TNI on May 6, 1958.

Like Kawilarang, Warouw commanded no troops in the Permesta rebellion. His designation as deputy prime minister and head of the PRRI civilian government in Sulawesi was more a symbol than a position of real power. However, Warouw was a man to whom all the other leaders would speak, and he seems to have had an important role in keeping communications open among them. A rather quiet and serious man, but not much given to deep thought, Warouw was widely liked among the troops and among the people. It was his death in October 1960 that brought the leadership crisis to a head.

Ventje Sumual was, like Warouw, from Remboken, a village on the shores of Lake Tondano. Of the Permesta leadership, Sumual, whose official position was as chief of staff of PRRI/Permesta, was the one whose name had been associated with Permesta from the night of the Proclamation on March 2, 1957. Yet in a curious way, he had not initially seemed deeply involved in the movement. Other officers took the initiative in drafting the Charter and making the operational plans. And although Sumual busied himself with building links to his rebellious colleagues in Sumatra and with obtaining support for them all from abroad, he seems to have spent little time building a base of support in Minahasa. Although he was in overall command of Permesta forces, Sumual had few troops of his own. Somewhat isolated with his staff in southern Minahasa, he seems to have become dependent on troops from Jan Timbuleng's Brigade 999, particularly on the first and second battalions commanded by Lisangan and Goan, who were also from Sumual's home village, Remboken. Brave—some might say reckless—and intelligent, Sumual seemed to some to be more interested in protecting his own reputation and position than in safeguarding the lives of the young men who were only too willing to sacrifice them for Permesta.

Daniel Julius Somba was the most junior of the four top Permesta officers. He was known not as a staff officer, but as a good troop commander. In character rather like Warouw, he was a quiet and gentle man. Of the Permesta leaders it was Somba who commanded the most troops. Although he had only been commander in North Sulawesi since December 1956, he held the loyalty of the members of the TNI who had pushed him into rebellion a little more than a year later. As Permesta commander of Minahasa, he had under him the commanders of the four military districts into which it had been divided, who together controlled some 15,000 troops. Somba's headquarters were in District III, commanded by Lieutenant Colonel Wim Tenges, whose troops were the best trained and disciplined, and had the highest morale and most impressive fighting record of any Permesta unit.[6]

Two others who played important roles in Permesta leadership positions did not join the rebellion directly from the TNI, although both had at one time served in it. Laurens Saerang, dapper and wealthy, had been elected Minahasa area head in 1956, and during Permesta led his own unit, Brigade Manguni. Many of the civilian officials of the Minahasa region, as well as of the Permesta civil government, stayed at his headquarters in his home area in or near Langoan and Mount Soputan after September 1959, and most surrendered with him in February 1961.

More important in the conflicts which developed among the senior Permesta leaders was Saerang's brother-in-law, Jan Timbuleng, one-time leader of the rebel Defenders of Justice Army (PPK). As noted above, after talks with Saerang in late 1956 and early 1957, Timbuleng had surrendered with some 2,000 followers in March 1957. Although this initial settlement lasted only a few months, Timbuleng again joined forces with Permesta in March 1958, after the proclamation of PRRI. Three battalions from the PPK, and Timbuleng himself, went with Somba to Central Sulawesi in April-May 1958, earning a reputation for toughness and loyalty to the Permesta cause. From his long years as a rebel, Timbuleng had

---

6   Tenges had fought with Brigade XVI in East Java during the revolution, and then with the TNI in South Sulawesi and South Maluku. He had joined KDM-SUT in August 1957, after attending SSKAD. Tenges was noted for his deafness, which had a certain willful quality about it. Some have said that although he was totally incapable of hearing orders he did not wish to carry out, yet he seemed to have no difficulty hearing those he found agreeable.

acquired a reputation for invulnerability. Bullets were said to bounce off him because of the strength of his magic powers. It was widely believed that so long as he was in contact with the earth he could not be killed. Timbuleng's reputation for bravado and invulnerability may have been one of the reasons why many of the youth who fought with Permesta were attracted to join his Brigade 999. Estimates of the strength of Triple Nine vary widely, but according to official sources its formation included only five to six, not nine, battalions, and its total strength was only about 2,000 men, although 1,200 of them were armed.[7]

The reputation of Timbuleng and his Triple Nine was tarnished somewhat during the period of withdrawal to guerrilla bases in 1958 and 1959, for they became famous not for their bravery in battle but for their skill in disarming any who passed through their area. Timbuleng's strength in Permesta, however, was not based on the number of men or weapons he controlled, but on the area he dominated. Triple Nine had not been given a territorial command in Sumual's original division of Minahasa into military districts, but they occupied a strategic position in southern Minahasa, in much the same area where they had earlier operated as the PPK. Sumual and Warouw, and the civilian government, had their headquarters in the southern part of this area; Somba and Kawilarang were located to the north of it. In order to contact each other it was necessary that they cross Timbuleng's territory.

Differences between these men and their units, which may have been muted during the first year of fighting, came to the surface in October 1959 with the loss of Kotamobagu. The Permesta units in northern Minahasa had been fighting a guerrilla war since September 1958. However, now with the base area in Bolaang-Mongondow lost, all the Permesta forces were scattered into guerrilla pockets.

---

7 *Sari Attensia,* VII/9 (1960), p. 584, and VIII/1 (1961), p. 33; *Berita Penerangan* (November 24, 1958), p. 20. Timbuleng's deputy, Gerson Sankaeng (Goan), estimated that Brigade 999 contained 16,000-18,000 men in 28 battalions; interviews, Manado, November 20, 1971 and March 16, 1972. Some claim that Timbuleng's motives in joining Permesta, and in acquiring a large stock of arms, were to gain eventual acceptance into the TNI when the inevitable negotiations were held. Earlier negotiations with the PPK had apparently always foundered, among other reasons, because of the great disparity between Timbuleng's claims of numbers of followers, and the number of weapons in hand. In various negotiations with rebel groups in Indonesia, the TNI had always been reluctant to consider unarmed followers as rebel soldiers worthy of possible membership in the TNI.

Divisive Issues: Military Reorganization

There was bitterness among the Permesta officers over the fall of Kotamobagu, and an apparent readiness to spread—but not share—the blame for the defeat. As noted above, several officers who had served on Sumual's staff, including Lendy Tumbelaka, Arie Supit, and Joseph, moved north to District III, where both Kawilarang and Somba had their headquarters. From this time on, Sumual seems to have been quite isolated from the other leaders, and some of the difficulties which ensued can be attributed to this fact.

On October 11, 1959 Sumual, as chief of staff of PRRI/Permesta, issued order number 004, which reassigned territorial command responsibilities.[8] According to Sumual, he felt it was necessary to disperse the Permesta troops, for if all were concentrated in a small area it would be difficult to have contacts abroad or to maintain communications with Dee Gerungan in South Sulawesi, from whom a courier had recently arrived. Not all troops could remain in Minahasa, said Sumual, some should go to the Gorontalo area.

Timbuleng had been urging that he be given a territorial command. Sumual, unaware that Timbuleng was already in contact with representatives of the central government, believed that as a long-time rebel Timbuleng would never surrender. Therefore, he could safely be given command of the area near Manado where it was inevitable that Permesta units would have contact with central government troops, and might be persuaded to surrender. The then commanders of the four military districts in Minahasa were all former TNI men, and Tenges and Ottay in particular were known to have many old friends among their present enemies, the central government forces. Timbuleng also apparently convinced Sumual that Tenges and his troops were avoiding battle with the TNI, and should be replaced for that reason.[9] One other

---

8 Sources for this section: *Sari Attensia*, VII/9 (1960), pp. 579-583, and VIII/1 (1961), p. 34; also chart "Schema-Organisasi-Bajangan; sesuai Kpts. no. 004/Kpts/DAS/ 1010/59, 10-11-59" (a copy of which was lent to me by Mr. H. M. Taulu); interviews, Jakarta: H. N. V. Sumual, April 13, 1972; J.M.J. Pantouw, February 6, 1972; D. J. Somba, January 22, 1972; Airmadidi: A. C. J. Mantiri, November 5, 1971.

9 There is said to have been a long history of personal animosity between Timbuleng and Tenges, PPK headquarters had been in Tenges's home village, and Tenges is said to have held Timbuleng

consideration was that Timbuleng had become very difficult to control, and Sumual thought it preferable to have him nearby in Minahasa, rather than send him to Gorontalo where he could not be watched. Some of the other Permesta leaders believed that Sumual acted only because of intimidation from Timbuleng.

Sumual's original plan was apparently to assign Timbuleng the territorial command over southern Minahasa (a portion of which was already under his de facto control), and to divide northern Minahasa between Tenges and Ottay. Somba was to retain his position as overall commander of the Minahasa region, and in addition would be made deputy chief of staff to Sumual. The original plan for the redivision of Minahasa was changed, however, and in Order 004 southern Minahasa was assigned to Timbuleng, and northern Minahasa to Ottay. Tenges and his troops were ordered to assume a combat role in the Gorontalo/Bolaang-Mongondow area, which was now totally under the control of central government troops. Tenges, with the support of his troops, and of the other Permesta units and leaders in northern Minahasa, refused to carry out the order. This area had been in a state of guerrilla warfare for more than a year, and the men stationed there had succeeded in consolidating their position and building good relations with the local population. They claimed that Timbuleng and his Brigade 999 had notoriously bad relations with the population in the area under their control, and extending that area could only damage the Permesta cause. Of undoubted importance was the fact that the four established commands in Minahasa contained a high proportion of the former TNI troops, whereas Timbuleng's Brigade 999 consisted of the former PPK rebel band plus recently added youths. Professional jealousy and personal rivalry, as well as seemingly well based opposition to Timbuleng's operational methods, were involved in the opposition to Order 004. The Permesta commanders and their troops in northern Minahasa refused to carry out the order. In November and December fighting broke out between units from District III, Tenges's

---

responsible for a number of terror killings in the village. It is possible that Tenges, although his troops were the most compact and disciplined, did not often do battle with his old TNI comrades. Although avoidance of battle with old friends was more common in "the very civil war" in Sumatra (as Mossman termed it) than in Sulawesi, it has been said that commanders who knew each other tried to keep fighting to a minimum. This was sometimes justified in terms of reducing civilian casualties.

command, and those from Timbuleng's Brigade 999.

Divisive Issues: The Republik Persatuan Indonesia[10]

Order 004 was the most serious of the issues that brought dissension among the Permesta leadership to a head. The second issue, which had begun some months before, concerned the plans devised by PRRI and DI leaders in Sumatra to combine these rebellions into a united front against the central government through the formation of an Indonesian Federal Republic (Republik Persatuan Indonesia—RPI). Discussions had begun in Sumatra in early 1959, and by August that year proposals for the new structure were apparently forwarded to Sulawesi.

There was no contact between Permesta in the North and Qahhar Mudzakkar's Darul Islam in the South concerning the RPI. After Gerungan went South in mid-1958, he contacted Qahhar, and signed a formal agreement for military cooperation with the DI/TII in May 1959. There had been no discussion of the possibility of working together with Qahhar and the DI in the Permesta planning of military operations in North Sulawesi, according to both Sumual and Somba. However, in 1957 Gerungan had been a member of the security section of the Team of Assistants to the Permesta military government; he would have been aware of the discussions concerning negotiations with Qahhar Mudzakkar, and if any meetings with Qahhar took place in 1957 he may well have taken part in them. After Gerungan joined Qahhar the only contact with the Permesta leaders in the North was via couriers who arrived with a request for more weapons in the first half of 1959. Couriers sent by Sumual in response apparently never arrived. Gerungan had lost his telecommunications equipment, and there was no further contact between Permesta in the North and Gerungan and Qahhar in the South.[11]

---

10 On the RPI see Mossman, *Rebels*, pp. 226-30; Herbert Feith and Daniel S. Lev, "The End of the Indonesian Rebellion," *Pacific Affairs*, 36/1 (Spring 1963), pp. 39-40; *Sari Attensia*, VII/4 (April 1960), pp. 202-5, and VIII/1 (1961), pp. 102-17. Information on reactions in North Sulawesi based on interviews, particularly with A.C.J. Mantiri, Arimadidi, November 5, 1971; G. M. A. Inkiriwang, Manado, April 28, 1971; and in Jakarta with: H. N. V. Sumual, April 13, 1972; J.M.J. Pantouw, February 6, 1972; and D. J. Somba, January 22, 1972.

11 *Sari Attensia*, VII/4 (April 1960), pp. 197-99; see also Harvey, "Rebellion," pp. 404-7, 411-13.

In August 1959 Warouw chaired a meeting in Sinsingon, on the northern outskirts of Kotamobagu, to discuss the Sumatran RPI proposals. He had received a cable from PRRI President Sjafruddin Prawiranegara which outlined the proposal to establish a federal government, in which each component state would determine its own state religion or philosophy. The meeting was attended by members of the civil government and by senior military officers with the exception of Kawilarang and Somba. There was apparently some reluctance to make a decision until there had been an opportunity to examine the proposed constitution, but in general the meeting was favorable to the proposal. Warouw, however, was opposed. PRRI had been an attempt to establish an alternative central government for the Republic of Indonesia; the RPI was an attempt to establish a separate state. Panca Sila would be abandoned as the state philosophy, and the red and white flag of the Republic of Indonesia would be replaced by a star-studded banner. The central symbols of the revolution and the Republic would thus be discarded. Warouw refused to make a decision, being opposed to the consensus of the meeting, and cabled Kawilarang to join them. When Kawilarang arrived four days later (on foot), he supported Warouw's position. He is quoted by one of those present as saying:

> Many of our comrades have died defending this red and white flag; we have as much right to it as does Sukarno. It is our possession; we will not abandon it or the Panca Sila.[12]

On November 18, 1959 a document entitled "Struggle Program—Revolutionary Government of the Republic of Indonesia" was issued in Minahasa over Warouw's signature. In this document the goals of the struggle in which the PRRI was engaged were said to include the defense of the Proclamation of August 17, 1945 and the Panca Sila, the reunification of the Indonesian people, the implementation of regional autonomy, the peaceful settlement of the West Irian crisis through the United Nations, the ending of the regime of Sukarno, and the elimination of international communism from Indonesia. Attached to this document

---

12 Interview, A. C. J. Mantiri, Airmadidi, November 5, 1971.

was a "work program" which outlined the responsibilities of the various ministries in the civil government. Each minister was given authority to act on his own, and to carry on the civil government if anything to happen to the others.[13] Except for this latter provision, the discussion of the organization of the civilian government seems quite unrelated to the actual situation by November 1959, when the government was scattered, and power more than ever was in the hands of the guerrilla military commanders. The documents do indicate, however, that Warouw was not prepared to abandon the original goals of the rebellion or the most sacred symbols of the Indonesian nation.

There was apparently an attempt to consult with the Sumatran leaders on the proposed Federal Republic, but after it was proclaimed in Sumatra on February 8, 1960, Sumual and Pantouw felt that it must be accepted, and ordered that the new flag be flown in Minahasa. Kawilarang and Somba, however, never considered themselves to be part of RPI, and now that it had replaced the PRRI, they described themselves simply as Permesta.

Warouw Attempts to Heal the Divisions

It was partly to attempt to resolve the differences over the RPI, and partly to try to put an end to the fighting between the troops of Timbuleng and Tenges that Warouw in January 1960 went north from his headquarters in Tonsawang to meet with Kawilarang, Somba, and the officers in that area.

While in his home village of Remboken, he was visited by Ds. A. L. R. Wenas, head of the Synod of the Protestant Evangelical Church of Minahasa (Gereja Masehi Injili Minahasa). Pastor Wenas brought a letter from Sukarno suggesting negotiations to end the rebellion. According to Drs. R. A. Ventje Sual, who was present at the meeting, Warouw put forward a number of conditions that would have to be met before he would consider negotiations, among them that all central government troops must first be withdrawn. Sual concluded that in view of Warouw's

---

13 Documents (mimeographed), which I was permitted to read and make notes on in Manado, April 1971.

uncompromising attitude, Jakarta would probably try to get rid of him. Such a move would also be in the interest of the central government, according to Sual, because Warouw was the one person who was able to overcome the divisions in the Permesta leadership. Only he could talk with both Kawilarang and Sumual. The division between them weakened the rebellion, and thus it would be to the advantage of Jakarta to exacerbate it, rather than to see it healed.[14]

A somewhat different picture of Warouw's attitude toward negotiations is given by Somba and Abe Mantiri. According to Somba, Warouw had advised from the start of the rebellion (which he had joined with reluctance) that "the back door be kept open" in case there were an approach from the government to negotiate. Mantiri, together with Kawilarang (and possibly Somba), met with Warouw at Tangkunei in early 1960, shortly after the meeting between Warouw and Pastor Wenas. As Mantiri describes the meeting, Warouw seemed to feel that the time had come to make peace. Warouw said that the letter from Sukarno would have to be kept secret, and that he would go first to talk to Sumual and try to convince him to consider opening negotiations. He added that if anything should happen to him and he did not return, the others should follow through on the offer.[15]

Warouw did then return to the south and met with Sumual, although they apparently talked more about trying to settle the clash between Tenges and Timbuleng than about negotiations.[16] Warouw then set off either to return to his own headquarters in Tonsawang, or to return to the north for further discussions with Kawilarang and Somba. Whether Warouw intended to go to District III or to his own headquarters, he would have to pass through the area controlled by Brigade 999.

Not only were the headquarters of both Sumual and Warouw within the area under Timbuleng's control, but many civil government officials, and members of the families of both the civilian and military officers were caught in the area controlled by Triple Nine. Timbuleng was

---

14 Interview, R. A. Sual, Manado, November 9, 1971. Sumual and Kawilarang had been at odds from the start over Kawilarang's lack of enthusiasm for PRRI, and this was reinforced by Kawilarang's opposition to the RPI.
15 Interviews: A. C. J. Mantiri, Airmadidi, November 5, 1971, and March 20, 1972; D. J. Somba, Jakarta, January 22, 1972.
16 Interview, H. N. V. Sumual, Jakarta, April 13, 1972.

thus in an excellent position to exert pressure on and to intimidate the other leaders. Further, as Timbuleng had been operating in southern Minahasa for some five years as a guerrilla prior to Permesta, he and his battalion commanders knew the terrain and were familiar with the type of operations required. Finally, the troops of Brigade 999, although among the best armed, as former "bandits" and schoolboys were among the worst trained and disciplined of the Permesta troops.

The events which followed, Timbuleng's arrest of Warouw, and the eventual deaths of both men, are difficult to reconstruct. They are still matters of controversy and a source of bitterness among the surviving Permesta leaders. However, because these events were crucial in determining the further course of the rebellion and its conclusion, they will be recounted in some detail.

The Deaths of Warouw and Timbuleng[17]

While Warouw was still in the Brigade 999 area, one of his couriers who was carrying a letter to Somba critical of Timbuleng, was captured by one of Timbuleng's units. With this incident intimidation of families and civil officials began. On March 23, 1960 one of Warouw's close political advisers, Professor G. M. A. Inkiriwang, was detained by the third Battalion of Brigade 999, under Major Korua.[18]

Warouw and Nun Pantouw, Sumual's intelligence officer, then met with Goan, commander of the second battalion of Brigade 999, a man trusted by Sumual and Pantouw. They decided that Warouw should leave the Triple Nine area as soon as possible.[19] Warouw asked Pantouw for an additional squad of men to strengthen his own unit of about forty persons for the journey to District III. However, when Pantouw sent

---

17 In general, I have relied on the description of events given by J. M. J. Pantouw in an interview in Jakarta on February 6, 1972, partly because his was the most complete account, and partly because his account is substantiated in several important details in the only written report of the deaths of Warouw and Timbuleng which I have seen, that in *Sari Attensia,* VIII/1 (1961), pp. 22-23, 33-35.

18 Interview, G. M. A. Inkiriwang, Manado, April 28, 1971.

19 Goan (Gerson Sankaeng) describes a meeting between himself, Warouw, and Sumual to discuss the problems which had arisen, after which Warouw was to go north to propose solutions to the leaders there. He says that he accompanied Warouw on the first part of his journey. Interview, Manado, November 20, 1971.

the requested squad, a unit loyal to Timbuleng prevented their joining Warouw.

Sumual, aware of the mounting danger, called Timbuleng to a meeting at his headquarters. Timbuleng replied by asking that Warouw also go to Sumual's headquarters, and requested that Sumual write a letter to that effect. This Sumual did—and that letter was used by Timbuleng to stop Warouw from leaving his area.[20]

When Warouw was detained by Timbuleng he was shot in the knees, so that he would be unable to escape. Those with Warouw, including the area head of Gorontalo, Sambia, were also arrested and held.[21]

The news of Warouw's detention, and condition, reached Pantouw and Sumual within a few days. Sumual asked the commander of Triple Nine's first battalion, Lisangan (who like Goan and Sumual was from Remboken, and had quietly shifted allegiance from Timbuleng to Sumual), to confirm the truth of the news of Warouw's arrest. Lisangan reported back that Warouw and a number of cabinet ministers had been detained, but that according to Timbuleng they were in good condition. Timbuleng himself later told Sumual that he had taken action against Warouw because Warouw was favoring the troops in the north.[22]

To avoid further incidents, Sumual then ordered that the rest of the civilians, government officials, and family members, in the Triple Nine territory be moved to Kotabunan in northern Bolaang-Mongondow, outside Timbuleng's grasp. This Lisangan and Pantouw succeeded only with difficult in doing over the next few months.

According to Goan, two months after Warouw's arrest, Sumual himself was placed under guard by Timbuleng, and for a period of three months was not permitted to leave his own area.[23] During this period attacks

---

20 Warouw is said to have sent a letter to Kawilarang accusing Sumual of having ordered (or authorized) his arrest; both Sumual and Pantouw deny this, and Pantouw's explanation of how a letter which might be interpreted as an arrest order came to be written sounds reasonable. According to army intelligence sources, Warouw was arrested on April 5, 1960 by Captain Robby Parenkuan, commander of Battalion 7 of Brigade 999, based on a verbal order from Jan Timbuleng and a note from Sumual; *Sari Attensia*, VIII/1 (1961), pp. 33-34.
21 The arrests and the shooting of Warouw in the knees were mentioned in a number of interviews: Jakarta, J. M. J. Pantouw, February 6, 1972, H. N. V. Sumual, April 13, 1972; Manado: G. M. A. Inkiriwang, April 28, 1971, Annie Kalangie, November 17, 1971, Gerson Sankaeng (Goan), November 20, 1971.
22 Interview, H. N. V. Sumual, Jakarta, April 13, 1972.
23 Interview, Gerson Sankaeng (Goan), Manado, November 20, 1971.

from central government troops continued, and this also was a factor in the difficulty with which action was taken against Timbuleng.

It is widely believed in North Sulawesi that Timbuleng wanted to capture all the Permesta leaders—and in fact had been paid a large sum of money, and promised a commission in the TNI, by the central government via the Mayor of Manado, J. P. Mongula, to do just that. It is true that during the period when Warouw was detained he was forced to write letters to the senior military commanders saying that he was now in good health and requesting that they come to meet him. Kawilarang, Sumual, Somba, Pantouw, and Tenges are said to have received such letters. All believed the letters to have been written under duress, and all interpreted the writing of them as a tactic of Timbuleng's to lure then to his area where he could arrest, and probably kill them.[24]

An opportunity to act against Timbuleng arose when Sumual was able to call a meeting of Triple Nine battalion commanders at his headquarters in early October. Timbuleng came with his third and fourth battalions, commanded by H. Korua and B. Pandairoth, and several of his senior officers. Lisangan and Goan, commanders of the first and second battalions of Brigade 999, were also present. Timbuleng and those with him seem not to have been aware of the shift in allegiance of these two men. Timbuleng apparently felt his position sufficiently strong that he made no objection to complying with Sumual's rule that no weapons be brought into his headquarters. Then, while Timbuleng and his senior officers were meeting with Sumual, Goan's unit easily disarmed the troops waiting outside, for they still trusted him as one of them. When Goan signalled (by firing a 50-point machine gun) that the task of disarming Timbuleng's men was completed, Sumual called the meeting to a close. As Timbuleng and his men passed the headquarters guard post they were arrested.[25]

---

24 Some attribute Mongula's role to his leftist sympathies and desire to destroy the anticommunist Permesta rebellion; others say personal revenge against Warouw was involved. Interviews, Manado: A. C. J. Mantiri, November 5, 1971 and March 20, 1972, R. A. Sual, November 9, 1971, Gerson Sankaeng (Goan), March 16, 1972; Jakarta: D. J. Somba, January 22, 1972, J.M.J. Pantouw, February 6, 1972, H.N. V. Sumual, April 13, 1972.

25 The *Sari Attensia* account suggests that Lisangan assisted in disarming battalions 3, 4, and 7 (Parenkuan). Sumual mentioned two battalions (three companies each) disarmed by Goan at his headquarters. Goan says that he had been ordered by Timbuleng to kill Sumual, but used the ruse of telling Timbuleng that they would first have to meet before the order could be carried out, and that when Timbuleng arrived for the meeting, he (Goan) captured Timbuleng and disarmed his unit.

Sumual planned to court martial Timbuleng and the arrested officers of Brigade 999. However, some time after his arrest (accounts vary from eight hours to two days), when guards came to move Timbuleng to another place of detention, he panicked, thinking he was going to be shot, and tried to escape. He was being held in the upper story of a traditional village house, and as the guards approached, he grabbed a gun from one of the guards and jumped out the window, yelling for help. Another guard shot him in mid-air. Pantouw and Sumual rushed to the scene, and found Timbuleng's body on the ground. In his pockets were a ring and a watch belonging to Warouw, and photographs of Warouw's family, as well as letters from Mongula.[26]

According to the official army account of the incident, Korua, Pandairoth, and another officer were then shot to prevent their escaping. However, others of Timbuleng's men apparently did escape, and returned to the place where Warouw was being held to carry out an earlier order from Timbuleng that Warouw be killed. Sumual had also sent troops to try to rescue Warouw. However, as these men approached, a member of Parengkuan's seventh battalion of Brigade 999 shot and killed Warouw on October 15, 1960. The marksman, Hermanus Jus, Parengkuan, and some 1,000 members and families of the battalion then surrendered to government troops.[27]

Everyone involved in Permesta was shocked by Warouw's death, although few knew the precise circumstances which surrounded it. His

---

[26] The date of Timbuleng's death is given in *Sari Attensia* as October 9, 1960; Goan in one interview said that Timbuleng was arrested on October 8 and shot on the 10th (November 20, 1971); when questioned again, Goan said that Timbuleng was killed on October 8 (March 21, 1972). According to Pantouw, the letters from Mongula offered Timbuleng a commission in the TNI if he would capture the Permesta leaders, and himself surrender to the government through Mongula. Contact between Timbuleng and Mongula is mentioned in *Sari Attensia*, VIII/1 (1961), p. 34. Some suggest that Goan and Lisangan, knowing the secret of Timbuleng's invulnerability, threw him out the window so that they could shoot him in mid-air.

[27] These details are from the army's account, *Sari Attensia*, VIII/1 (1961), pp. 34-35. Parengkuan is widely mentioned as having been involved in the shooting of Warouw. Pantouw and Sumual both believe that Warouw was still alive at the time Timbuleng was shot, although both say it is not certain when or where Warouw was killed. Sumual says that Timbuleng was found to be carrying a recent letter from Warouw to him (Sumual) when Timbuleng's body was examined. Professor Inkiriwang, who was freed soom after Timbuleng's death, also believes that Warouw was killed first. However, according to Goan, Timbuleng told him that he had ordered that Warouw be shot, and then himself killed the members of the squad who did it so that no one would know when Warouw was killed, or where he was buried.

arrest and death brought to a head the tension that had been mounting since the Sinsingon meeting in August 1959. Many of the northern Permesta group blamed Sumual for Warouw's death. Some believed that Sumual had ordered Timbuleng to arrest Warouw; many believed that because Timbuleng was located near Sumual's headquarters and Sumual had close relationships with Brigade 999, that Sumual was inevitably responsible for Timbuleng's actions, including Warouw's detention and death.[28] This intensified their earlier reaction against his Order 004 giving Timbuleng command over Minahasa, and his support for the separatist RPI. In November 1960, at the request of the Permesta officers in the north, Kawilarang assumed overall command. Sumual's authority was no longer acknowledged. North-south communications, difficult in any case, became strained and infrequent.

The Permesta group in northern Minahasa, who had already embarked on a course of negotiations to end the rebellion were strengthened in their determination to do so by the horror which they felt at the death of someone who was so much one of them. "If we have begun to kill each other, it is time to end it," was a common view.

Negotiations[29]

Even before the meeting of Pastor Wenas and Warouw in January 1960, another attempt to open negotiations had been initiated. It was, however, to be several months before any meetings were held, and more than a year before an agreement was reached which did effectively end the Permesta rebellion.

In October 1959, F. J. "Broer" Tumbelaka, a former senior staff officer of TT-VII, who had been working as a civilian contractor in East Java

---

[28] Mentioned in a number of interviews; Kawilarang, in particular, holds Sumual responsible for Warouw's death, interview, Jakarta, August 15, 1971. Sumual and Pantouw are aware of these accusations; interviews, Jakarta, J.M.J. Pantouw, February 6, 1972, H. N. V. Sumual, April 13, 1972. Their explanation of the circumstances is indicated in the text, and footnote 20.

[29] Unless otherwise noted, information in this section is based on discussions with F. J. "Broer" Tumbelaka, in Jakarta, April 15-21, 1972, and on documents in his possession which he generously permitted me to read. Tumbelaka's account of the negotiations was confirmed in a discussion with D. J. Somba, Jakarta, April 19, 1972. A brief published account, Radik Djarwadi, *Kisah Ambruknja Permesta* (Surabaya: GRIP, n.d.), contains some of the same information, and may be based on material provided by Tumbelaka, as he and the author are old TNI comrades.

for some two years, contacted Colonel Surachman, commander of the Brawijaya Division. This division was supplying the bulk of the troops for the military operations against the rebels in North Sulawesi, and the commanders of Operation (later KODAM) Merdeka had been Brawijaya officers. Tumbelaka, although a Minahasan, had grown up in East Java, and had fought there during the revolution in a battalion that later came under the East Java Division. Tumbelaka was not the only Minahasan to have fought in East Java in 1945-49, Warouw and Somba had fought in Surabaya and the Malang area, and they too had developed close ties with Brawijaya officers.

Tumbelaka and Surachman talked about the situation in North Sulawesi, where their erstwhile comrades were now in rebellion. Surachman also spoke of his concern about the growing strength of the PKI in East Java. Both seem to have agreed that the rebellion drained the strength of the TNI, and that its continuation could only work to the advantage of the PKI. Tumbelaka suggested that he would be willing to try to reach a settlement with the Permesta rebels, but said that adequate preparations would first have to be made. Surachman suggested that they meet again after he had spoken with his staff.

During November, Tumbelaka met twice with Surachman and senior Brawijaya officers, Lieutenant Colonel Sigit Sutarti (First Assistant/Intelligence), and Chief of Staff Lieutenant Colonel Soenarjadi, who had just been appointed to take over the Merdeka Command in North Sulawesi. In the course of these discussions it was agreed that Tumbelaka should go to Minahasa to investigate possibilities for reaching an agreement with the Permesta rebels. As it was important not to create friction with leaders in the area who had remained loyal to the central government, it was thought that such an inquiry could best be handled by someone from the area, sensitive to the local situation and to local feelings.

On January 5, 1960, Broer Tumbelaka went to Manado. He met first with a few selected members of the KODAM XIII/Merdeka staff, particularly with the assistant for intelligence, Captain Aris Mukadar, who was to be of particular help to him in his mission. He also renewed old acquaintances, and discussed the local situation with civilians in Manado. During this period he decided that the Permesta leader he would try to contact was Somba. Both Somba and Warouw were old friends, but it was Somba who had issued the declaration of support for PRRI and broken relations with the Sukarno government. Further, it was Somba who had the most and best armed troops, and most of those who like himself had been in the TNI. Although Warouw was the senior civilian representative of the PRRI in North Sulawesi, it was Somba as troop commander who was thought to be in a decisive position to determine whether or not the rebellion would continue. Tumbelaka knew Kawilarang and Sumual less well, therefore he could be less sure of their reaction should he choose to initiate contact through one of them. Further, he was well aware of the ambiguity of Kawilarang's position in the rebellion: he had refused to accept the position of commander-in-chief of PRRI forces, and was already suspected in some quarters of being an agent of Nasution. At that time Kawilarang had no operational control over any troops in North Sulawesi. As for Sumual, aside from the fact that he had been in the Jogjakarta area during the revolution and was thus less well known either to Tumbelaka or to the Brawijaya officers, it was Sumual who had the closest ties with Sumatra and the PRRI (and RPI), and he was therefore thought less likely to be amenable to a partial settlement involving only North Sulawesi. Sumual controlled fewer troops than did Somba, and these were mostly irregulars—rebels and school boys—not former TNI.

Thus, it was decided that Somba was the logical choice for the target of the approach. A courier, Tjame (Samuel Hein Ticoalu) was obtained with the aid of KODAM XIII, and on February 3, 1960, Broer Tumbelaka wrote a note to Somba suggesting that they meet. He explained his intentions:

> I have come here not because I have been forced to do so by anyone, but because of the urging of my own heart. I sincerely want to contribute my strength and my thoughts to an effort to seek a good solution to this dispute which still continues.[30]

Tjame was able to enter the Permesta-held areas on the pretext of contacting his son, who was a radio operator at District I headquarters in Pinili. It was there, indeed, that Tjame finally met Somba on February 23, 1960, at a dance party to welcome the visiting commander. Somba

---

30 Letter, Broer Tumbelaka (using alias "Dr. Brundsted" so that Somba would know it was authentic) to Joes (D. J. Somba), February 3, 1960. Aliases were used throughout the negotiations which followed to maintain their secrecy.

was surprised to see Tjame, an old acquaintance, but was startled when Tjame said, "Broer sends greetings." Somba pocketed the letter to be read after the dance, but neither a rebellion nor the prospect of ending it can be allowed to interfere with this favorite Minahasan pastime.[31]

Somba's reply was brief. He agreed to meet, "the sooner the better."[32] Kawilarang was with Somba when the letter from Broer Tumbelaka was received. They agreed to send a cable to Warouw, who had gone to the south in January to discuss the Wenas overture and other matters with Sumual. Warouw cabled back that the contact should be maintained, so long as it was not disadvantageous to do so.[33]

The first meeting of the negotiations was between Somba and Broer Tumbelaka, and was held on March 15, 1960 in the village of Matungkas, near Airmadidi. Broer reiterated that he had come as an old friend, although with the knowledge of Colonel Soerachman and Colonel Soenarjadi, hoping to be able to assist in restoring peace to the area. Somba replied that Warouw had always advised that a door be kept open for a settlement of the rebellion, and that Warouw, Kawilarang, Sumual, and he himself were in agreement on this. They had not yet determined whether a settlement could be reached locally, or would have also to include Sumatra, Somba added, but in his opinion the problems everywhere were essentially the same. Somba then reviewed the issues which had led to the rebellion, emphasizing the questions of provincial autonomy, regional development, financial balance between the center and the regions, and allocation of foreign exchange earnings.[34] If accommodation could be reached on these matters, for which the rebellion had been fought, the question of what would be done with the rebels themselves would be left up to the Jakarta government. Somba indicated that a number would want to be accepted back into the TNI, some (including Kawilarang) had indicated an interest in going abroad. The question of what would be done

---

31 Interview, D. J. Somba, Jakarta, April 19, 1972. The incident is also mentioned in Radik Djarwadi, *Ambruknja Permesta*, pp. 22-23.
32 Copy of note, D. J. Somba to Broer Tumbelaka, original dated February 23, 1960.
33 Interview, D. J. Somba, Jakarta, January 22, 1972.
34 Interestingly, the question of communism was not raised at this initial meeting, although it later became a principal issue. This meeting is mentioned briefly in Radik Djarwadi, *Ambruknja Permesta*, pp. 28-29; details of this and other meetings are from discussions with F. J. Tumbelaka (as noted above).

with the "real" rebels, the groups of Jan Timbuleng and Daan Karamoy, was raised, and Somba indicated that they would follow whoever gave them the best offer. Tumbelaka said that the TNI was certain not to accept the proposal of Warouw for a return to the situation prior to February 17, 1958, or of Kawilarang for a cease-fire while negotiations were under way. He could, however, guarantee a safe place for further meetings. They parted, agreeing to meet again on May 1.

However, it was not until August that the second meeting was held. In the interval Broer Tumbelaka met with Chief of Staff Nasution on April 14, and received full backing from him to continue with the effort to reach a settlement. On March 31, 1960, a Presidential Instruction was issued by which Sulawesi was divided into two provinces, with Manado the capital of North and Central Sulawesi.[35] Arnold Baramuli[36] was appointed governor, and on May 25, 1960, Broer Tumbelaka was made deputy governor, with special responsibility for the restoration of security in the area. Military operations continued, with particularly strong Permesta attacks in July and August on Tomohon, Sonder, and several other towns.[37]

On August 9, 1960, Tumbelaka met again with Somba, who was accompanied by Wim Tenges, commander of District III (in whose area, near Amurang, the meeting was held), and by Abe Mantiri, who was to play a major role in further negotiations.[38] The Permesta team began by welcoming the establishment of a separate province of North and Central Sulawesi, and by congratulating Tumbelaka on his appointment as deputy

---

35 Peraturan Presiden No. 5, 1960 (Lembaran Negara RI, No. 38, 1960).
36 Baramuli had been military and provincial attorney-general for Sulawesi. His father was Sangirese, his mother from Pinrang, in South Sulawesi. He is said to have been recommended for the position of governor by Yani and Jusuf; he had worked closely with Jusuf in 1957-58. Interview, Arnold Baramuli, Jakarta, January 14, 1972. He was replaced as governor by Tumbelaka in June 1962.
37 *Sari Attensia*, VII/9 (1960), p. 577; Benno R. "Tewasnja djagoan Permesta dipagi buta," *Sketsiana*, 7 (January 25, 1961), pp. 4-6, 22, 24.
38 Tenges had also known Tumbelaka before; Mantiri and Tumbelaka seen not to have been acquainted prior to this meeting. Mantiri, a civilian, had been commissioned a lieutenant colonel by Permesta, and his official position was as secretary general of the Ministry of Defense and fourth assistant (logistics) on Sumual's staff. Mrs. Mantiri is a full cousin of Alex Kawilarang. Both Mr. and Mrs. Mantiri were active in obtaining the agreement of the various Permesta units in northern Minahasa to the negotiation of a settlement. Mantiri's influence seems to have been based on his ability and intelligence, and on the fact that he was somewhat senior to the young officers with whom he was now associated. The meeting is mentioned in Radik Djarwadi, *Ambruknja Permesta*, pp. 30-34; other information from cited discussions with F. J. Tumbelaka, and interviews with A. C. J. Mantiri, Airmadidi, November 5 and 26, 1971.

governor. They noted, however, that the province was an administrative division and not an autonomous first-level region, and that thus there was no guarantee of a fair financial balance or division of foreign exchange between the center and the regions. Tumbelaka replied that these matters would have to be resolved gradually, and should be handled through the Parliament. Discussion then turned to what was to become a central theme in the negotiations—the growing strength of communism in the Republic of Indonesia. Tumbelaka assured the Permesta group that the TNI as a whole was firmly opposed to communism, and held to the Panca Sila as the basis of the state.[39] The tragedy, he said, was that those who were of the same opinion concerning communism were now fighting against each other, rather than against it.

Somewhat to Tumbelaka's surprise, Somba abruptly asked, "Have you made plans for taking care of our troops?" Tumbelaka replied that he could only do that after discussions with the army leadership, and that it would first be necessary for the Permesta leaders to withdraw their political demands. To his even greater surprise, Somba immediately agreed to do so. This meant that a settlement was virtually assured. The working out of arrangements for the return of the rebels to the Republic and their subsequent treatment could be handled within the TNI, without involving the civilian government in any substantial way, as would have been necessary had the Permesta leaders insisted on political conditions for ceasing their rebellion.

Although Somba's withdrawal of political demands at the August meeting with Tumbelaka seemed to clear the way for a settlement, negotiations continued for another eight months and eight meetings. In part the delay was occasioned by the need to resolve differences of opinion among the Permesta leaders, and in part by the need to convince subordinate units and commanders of the wisdom of ending the rebellion. Not all were as ready to abandon political demands as was Somba. The additional meetings were not held without difficulties, for they had to be conducted in secret, and while military operations continued. There was opposition to a negotiated settlement from some on both sides. Sumual,

---

39 This was a time when Panca Sila was often used as a code word to indicate opposition to communism.

who maintains that he was never contacted about the negotiations, sent a telegram on December 15, 1960 to Permesta district and battalion commanders, ordering that if the reports of meeting of certain RPI army leaders with the enemy were true, such action should be considered treachery, and efforts should be made to prevent it.[40] Nonetheless, the efforts to reach a settlement initiated by Tumbelaka and Somba continued.

Following the August meeting, Tumbelaka discussed proposals for the treatment to be accorded to the returning rebels with Nasution, who was in Manado at the time, and with Yani and Brawijaya officers in East Java in early October. Proposals worked out in these discussions were put to the Permesta negotiators in a meeting in Lahendong (near Tomohon) on October 13, 1960, attended by Somba, Mantiri, and Broer's cousin, Lendy Tumbelaka.[41] Following the meeting the TNI proposals were discussed with Permesta commanders and senior civilians in the guerrilla area; amendments based on these discussions were submitted to Tumbelaka by Mantiri and Arie Supit at a meeting in Malenos/Maliku on December 17.

During the course of the negotiations the Permesta leaders stressed that they were not delaying the reaching of a settlement in order to have a breathing space (*adempauze*), as had been done by such "real" bandits as Qahhar Mudzakkar and Jan Timbuleng. They emphasized that they were themselves negotiating with their subordinate commanders to ensure that when an agreement was reached between the Permesta leadership and the TNI, the Permesta troops would follow their leaders back to the fold, and armed groups would not remain in the countryside, terrorizing the people. Somba and Mantiri personally briefed not only the four district commanders, but leaders of autonomous units, while the settlement was being negotiated. It was initially contemplated that the negotiations, and any settlement reached, would include everyone involved in PRRI/Permesta in North Sulawesi.[42] As noted above, Warouw, and through him Sumual, are said to have been informed when the initial contact

---

40 Xerox of typed copy, "Berita sadapan, Eo. 52 Plm. Op 1217=0700." Since the proclamation of the RPI in February 1960, Sumual considered that the PRRI no longer existed.
41 Broer Tumbelaka was accompanied by Warouw's father, who was hoping to obtain information about his son. Mentioned in Radik Djarwadi, *Ambruknja Permesta*, p. 35.
42 A. C. J. Mantiri, letter to author dated September 14, 1974.

was made by Tumbelaka. Certainly in the first meeting between Somba and Tumbelaka in April 1960, the question of the status of Timbuleng and Karamoy, and the members of their units, were among those raised. However, after the death of Warouw in October 1960, there was little further contact between Sumual and those remaining with him in the south, and the bulk of the Permesta leadership in the north.

The civilians consulted by the Permesta leadership, while acknowledging that military considerations would be the determining factors in the negotiations, noted four areas of concern: (1) treatment of military participants in the rebellion; (2) treatment of civilian participants in the rebellion; (3) provincial autonomy (including questions of government, finance, economy, education, and development); and (4) Panca Sila must be the basic philosophy of the state.[43] Thus, although Somba had agreed to withdraw all political demands in the August meeting, the question of provincial autonomy, and the question of the influence of communism in Indonesia, continued to be of importance in the negotiations. It is interesting that although copra played such a large part in inspiring the rebellion, it seems not to have been discussed in the negotiations which concluded it, although satisfactory national trade and export arrangements had yet to be worked out.[44]

Primary attention in the negotiations, in spite of the continuing concern with autonomy and communism, was focused on the treatment to be accorded to those who had participated in the rebellion on their return to the Republic. Leaders and men alike were concerned that they be treated not as bandits or renegades, but as rebels who had fought—however mistakenly—for worthy ideals.

Thus, in their discussions with Tumbelaka the Permesta leadership refused to accept a simple granting of amnesty and abolition of charges (the usual treatment of surrendering rebels), but insisted on an agreement which gave them a defined legal status as a guarantee that the undertakings reached would be carried out. It seems to have been agreed

---

43 "Working-paper *Pusat dan Kita* untuk dasar perundingan," R. C. L. Lasut, November 14, 1960.
44 A Central Copra Cooperative (Induk Koperasi Kopra Indonesia) had been established in July 1957, but as late as October 1958 an instruction was issued that the IKKI was to replace the defunct Copra Foundation, and in February 1959 it was noted that purchase and export of copra had not yet been regularized; *Berita Penerangan*, I/1 (November 3, 1958), pp. 12-17; and I/14-15 (February 2-9, 1959), p. 47. The organization of copra export was still being debated in 1972.

from the outset on both sides that some provision would be made for those among the rebels who wished to return to school or to positions in the civil government, or to join the TNI, to be able to do so. The Permesta leadership opposed any obvious discrimination in treatment between those who had and those who had not been members of the TNI before the rebellion, for this would cause dissension within their own ranks. However, they did agree to the stipulation that the number of Permesta members to be accepted into the TNI was to be in a one-to-one ratio with the number of weapons held by the rebels, and most of their armed men were indeed former members of the TNI. A University of North and Central Sulawesi had been established in Manado with the support of KODAM XIII/Merdeka on March 21, 1959, and it was apparently contemplated that many of the young rebels would be accommodated as students in this institution.[45]

Tumbelaka and the TNI, for their part, were concerned about the psychological effect on those, both military and civilian, who had remained loyal to the government, should the Permesta rebels receive too generous treatment.[46] In late November and early December, Tumbelaka met with groups of prominent ministers and with intellectuals in Manado to enlist their support in the effort to end the rebellion.

The details of the treatment to be accorded the returning rebels was not the only matter slowing the reaching of an agreement. Although the Permesta leaders shared Tumbelaka's opinion that the TNI was the best defense against communist domination of Indonesia, they continued to raise questions about the TNI's commitment to an anticommunist policy. Somba, in a letter to Tumbelaka on September 11 asked for an explanation of the fact that although the TNI disapproved of communism, it approved of a government which was in league with communists. (He added that Sumual and Warouw shared this concern.)

Tumbelaka raised this question with Nasution in a letter dated December 4, 1960. There remained three difficult problems in the

---

45 *Berita Penerangan,* I/26-27 (April 27-May 4, 1959), pp. 26-27; I/34-35 (June 22-29, 1959), pp. 21-22.

46 The decision as to what was to be done with Kawilarang seems to have been particularly difficult, for he was both so senior and so respected that should he remain in the TNI he would of necessity have to be given a quite senior post. At this time it was apparently planned that he would be sent abroad, possibly to a study assignment. This was later vetoed, and he was pensioned instead.

negotiations, he wrote: anticommunism, regional autonomy, and the treatment of the returning rebels in a way that would not cause them to lose prestige. The latter two could be resolved, said Tumbelaka, but he himself feared that the Indonesian socialism of NASAKOM might be the prelude to a state based on communism rather than on the Panca Sila. He suggested that for himself, and for many others, Nasution was the one person who could clarify the situation. He concluded by urging that Nasution publicly provide strong assurances concerning Panca Sila as the basis of the state, not only in the interest of restoring security in the area, but in facing the future of Indonesia.

Nasution assured Tumbelaka privately that he would resist "pulls from the left or from the right,"[47] and in a speech over RRI Manado on December 17, 1960 he discussed this and other matters at issue in the negotiations. He announced the passage of a law granting autonomy to the province of North and Central Sulawesi effective in January 1961. He then noted that at a recent conference of Christian ministers of North Sulawesi he had explained that the importance of the return to the constitution of 1945 was that the constitution itself clearly stipulates that the State of Indonesia is based on belief in One Almighty God.[48] The return to the constitution of 1945, he added, "must also be interpreted as a return to the spirit of 1945, at which time our nation was united to defend the Republic of Indonesia, which is based on Panca Sila." He spoke of the suffering of the people of the region as a result of the armed clash which had not yet ended, and promised efforts to rehabilitate the area. He closed by calling for increased devotion to the state, nation, and people; and for renewed efforts to improve attitudes and actions in order to be one again with the community in striving to restore peace and rehabilitate the region.[49]

The conference of ministers which Nasution mentioned in his speech ended on December 18 with a call for a cease-fire and the establishment of a liaison committee to arrange it. There was a sharp response from the North and Central Sulawesi committee of the PKI. In a statement issued on December 19, 1960, the committee denounced the decision of

---

47 Xerox copy of note, dated December 17, 1960, from A. H. Nasution to F. J. Tumbelaka.
48 The implication that it could not then be a communist state would have been clear to his audience.
49 Xerox copy of text in my possession.

the ministers as being contrary to Manipol, which clearly affirmed that the government could not negotiate or compromise with rebels. The only acceptable settlement was for the rebels to surrender unconditionally, and be brought to trial. The security policy of Manipol was not to achieve a national peace in which counterrevolutionary elements would be left free at any moment that suited them to put Indonesia under the foot of the imperialists.[50]

By this time, however, negotiations were far advanced. Although some details remained to be worked out, at the December 17 meeting between Tumbelaka, Mantiri, and Arie Supit, agreement was reached on the procedure that would be followed in bringing the rebellion to an end. The steps to be taken were as follows:

1) an appeal by the Minister of Defense/Chief of Staff (Nasution) to the rebels to return to the fold;
2) an official statement on the part of Permesta that they had returned to the "arms of the motherland";[51]
3) a cease fire;
4) a formal meeting to discuss technical military matters such as questions of supply and the disposition of the Permesta troops in designated areas;
5) an inspection of the ex-Permesta troops by Minister of Defense/Chief of Staff Nasution.

The Permesta negotiators were concerned that the ceasing of the rebellion be handled in such a manner that it did not appear to be an outright surrender. Thus, it was agreed that although the rebels would have to register their weapons, and their arms would then become the possession

---

50 Typed copy of "Keterangan Comite PKI Sulawesi Utara Tengah: - PATAHKAN USAHA2 MEMPERALAT AGAMA KRISTEN UNTUK BERKOMPROMI DENGAN GEROMBOLAN PEMBRONTAK PERMESTA !!! -LAKSANAKAN DENGAN KONSEKWEN GARIS2 KEAMANAN MANIFESTO POLITIK !!!," Manado, December 19, 1960, signed by J. Suak, secretary.

51 According to F. J. Tumbelaka, the decision was made to use this formula (*kembali kepangkuan Ibu Pertiwi*) without mentioning the Republic of Indonesia, because this enabled formal negotiations to take place between the two sides without implying a government-to-government relationship. Thus, the central government was not placed in a position of seeming to accord recognition to the rebel government, and Permesta was effectively disassociated from the PRRI or RPI.

of the central government, they would be allowed physically to retain them during the time the Permesta troops remained in designated areas (*rayon*) pending implementation of the agreement.

One other matter was discussed at the meeting—that of other contacts being made on behalf of the central government with other rebel leaders. As noted above, it was widely believed in Minahasa that Jan Timbuleng had been in contact with Piet Mongula, the mayor of Manado, and that through Mongula, Timbuleng had received a large bribe to kill the leaders of the rebellion. It was apparently believed by the Permesta group that contacts between Mongula and Brigade 999 were continuing. They asked that these be stopped.[52] Initially they also asked that contacts be discontinued between the Minahasa area head, E. A. Kandou, and his predecessor, Laurens Saerang, now head of the Manguni Brigade. However, recognizing that the situation in the Manguni area, where many of the civilian government people were located, was very difficult because of shortages of food and medicine, the Permesta group then suggested that a settlement be reached first with Saerang, and that they would resume negotiations with Tumbelaka following the reaching of an agreement with Manguni. In the period February 11-15, 1961, 11,343 persons from the Manguni Brigade, members of the Permesta Women's Unit (PWP), and civilians from five guerrilla bases in the Langoan-Kakas area, under the leadership of Laurens Saerang surrendered to the Republic. They were received by Major General Yani, deputy army chief of staff, and head of the East Indonesia Regional Command since January 1960, in a formal ceremony on February 15, 1961.[53]

Following the settlement with Saerang, meetings between Tumbelaka and the Permesta leaders were resumed. In the meantime Tumbelaka had

---

52 Mongula's past pro-Dutch record was described in a Permesta briefing paper as "unacceptable" to the ex-TNI group in Permesta, and the background of Brigade 999 (the former Pasukan Pembela Keadilan) "we all know." This could have referred to their background as a "bandit" group, their responsibility for the capture and death of Warouw, or possibly to the belief that Triple Nine was heavily infiltrated by communists. Although one must be wary of post-1965 attributions of earlier communist affiliation, Timbuleng is widely described in Minahasa as at least a sympathizer, if not a cadre, of the PKI.

53 Reports in *PIA*, February 10, 1961 (p.m.), p. 10, and February 15 (p.m.), p. 12. The latter report states that 6,000 troops, 2,000 followers, and 1,003 weapons surrendered at this time. Also interviews, Manado: Annie Kalangie, November 17, 1971; Hetty Sual-Rumambi, March 19, 1972.

met with General Nasution and Yani, Brawijaya commander Soerachman, and with Colonel Sunandar, commander of KODAM XIII/Merdeka, and officers on his staff, to discuss the changes Permesta had requested at the December meeting in the proposals for the treatment of the surrendering rebels. Tumbelaka, and Minahasa officers such as Bert Supit, argued that it was necessary to consider the psychological factors which were so important to the Permesta rebels in the working out of the peace settlement. The rebellion was not merely a matter of personal clashes and ambitions, but had been based on real social forces. The forces and ideals to which it had responded must be dealt with if any settlement reached was to have meaning. The desire for regional development, for example, could be guided by the government into proper channels through using those who had joined Permesta in constructive social and economic programs.[54]

Tumbelaka, who is acknowledged by both sides to have performed an extraordinary service in bringing about agreement between them,[55] also turned his considerable persuasive powers on the Permesta leaders. In a long letter to Somba on February 5, 1961, and again at a meeting with Somba, Lendy Tumbelaka, and Mantiri at Malenos on February 12, Broer urged that a final decision be made quickly. He feared that the chance to conclude an agreement might be lost if the negotiations were not soon concluded. He summarized the changes that had been made in the nation in the past three years which met many of the original demands of Permesta for provincial autonomy, a stronger voice for the regions in the national government, and greater attention to economic development and planning. The original goal of Permesta had been to champion the interests and development of the region, but with the turning to armed rebellion in support of these aims, the people of the region had suffered greatly for nearly three years, and instead of the region being developed, it was being destroyed. Tumbelaka reiterated that the return to the Constitution of 1945 ensured that the state ideology would remain Panca

---

54 Xerox copies of "Pendjelasan," Broer Tumbelaka to Panglima Soenandar, February 12, 1961; and "Beberapa 'Pemikiran Sumbangan' dalam Menghadapi Penjelesaian Persoalan Keamanan di Daerah ini," Bert Supit, Manado, February 17, 1961.
55 Interviews: A. C. J. Mantiri, Airmadidi, November 5, 1971; Jakarta: D. J. Somba, August 15, 1971; A. H. Nasution, May 17, 1972; mentioned in Makmun Salim, *Operasi2 Gabungan*, pp. 107-9.

Sila, and that it was a tragic mistake that the supporters of Panca Sila were fighting each other rather than uniting to fight its enemies.

Finally, concerning the treatment to be accorded the members of Permesta, he said that although what the TNI and the government were prepared to offer might not be all that they hoped for, they must recognize their error in breaking relations with the central government and recognizing the PRRI and be prepared to accept the consequences of that act. Once again, Broer was surprised by the speed with which Somba agreed. The time was ripe to make a decision, said Somba, only minor problems remained, and they could be settled later.[56]

Why did Somba, and the Permesta leaders, agree to concede so readily? Indeed, why had Somba earlier agreed to negotiations and to give up all political demands? In part it was because Tumbelaka was an old friend and comrade, someone Somba trusted, and a man whose intelligence and good will all Permesta leaders acknowledged. In part it was, as Somba later admitted, that he realized they had lost the war.[57] By November 1960 both sides knew of Warouw's death,[58] and the resolve of the Permesta group to end the rebellion had been strengthened by their horror at the fratricide.

In an analysis of their situation made in January 1961 as the negotiations neared completion, the Permesta leaders acknowledged the problems they faced: internal divisions within the rebellion, hostility between battalions, lack of authority of commanders over their subordinates; shortages of ammunition, medicine, and in some areas food; illness—in some districts as many as 30 percent of the troops suffered from malaria; and war weariness among both troops and the population, which had resulted in passivity in the conduct of the war, with the Permesta units more often responding to rather than initiating attacks. Further, since May 1959 the TNI had been using its new Czech rockets in Minahasa with considerable

---

56 Xerox of typed copy, letter from "Broer" to "Joes," Amurang, February 5, 1961; discussions with F. J. Tumbelaka, and D. J. Somba, Jakarta, April 19, 1972.
57 Somba described his initial reaction to Broer's first note as "That's it; we've lost, we'll just surrender." He said it was Mantiri and Lendy Tumbelaka who did the talking, and who haggled over this and that in the negotiations. Discussion with Somba and Broer Tumbelaka, Jakarta, April 19, 1972.
58 Broer Tumbelaka queried Somba about Warouw in a note of November 15. On December 4, 1960, Kawilarang, who had assumed command in Minahasa the previous month, ordered seven days of mourning for Warouw; see *Sari Attensia*, VIII/1 (1961), p. 23.

destructive effect, and the Permesta leaders were aware of the possibility (indicated in reports received from friends at army headquarters) that Minahasa would be the testing ground for other new weapons.[59]

The Permesta leaders also realized that they could not attain their original objectives by continuing to prolong the fighting. The original motif of Permesta was regional development; the continuing warfare was causing only death and destruction. The economic difficulties, regional and national, which the rebellion was exacerbating, would work to the advantage of the PKI. Yet opposition to the growing influence of communism had been an important motivation in Permesta as it developed from a movement for regional autonomy into a rebellion. The Permesta leaders now realized that the continuation of the rebellion could only weaken the anticommunist forces in Indonesia.

One of those involved in the negotiations, Abe Mantiri, summarized the reasons for the decision to negotiate, and for doing so with Tumbelaka, acting on behalf of the TNI, rather than pursuing overtures from the civilian government, such as that Warouw had received from President Sukarno via Pastor Wenas:

> We felt that the only guarantee against the increasing strength of the PKI was the TNI. Yet if the rebellion continued, more than half of the government's budget would be used for military operations; the government's programs to provide food and clothing for the people would suffer, inflation would continue, the people daily would become poorer and the PKI stronger.
>
> Further, in the region itself, guerrilla and antiguerrilla warfare was causing much suffering and difficulties for the people, and they were daily more easily influenced by the PKI.
>
> The longer this situation continued, the more unpopular the TNI would become, and they would be blamed for all the wrongs occurring.
>
> Although the TNI was also infiltrated [by communists], we felt that it was the only force on which we could rely. Nasution and

---

59 Interviews, A. C. J. Mantiri, Airmadidi, November 5, 1971 and March 20, 1972. On the use of rockets see KODAM XIII/Merdeka, *Artileri*, pp. 18-20.

Yani had made clear their opposition to political influence in the army.

If Permesta wanted to negotiate, it had to do so with the army. In the first place, the army had power; and second, we had many friends and comrades in the army, we could understand each other. This was not true of the politicians.

These were the arguments which the Permesta leaders used to convince their subordinate commanders to accept the wisdom of the decision to end the rebellion, and to agree to the government's proposals for screening and reeducation of the rebels prior to their acceptance into the TNI. Mantiri continued his meetings with civilian and military Permesta followers in central and northern Minahasa in January and February 1961, and following the February meeting with Tumbelaka, Somba made a final effort to contact Sumual. He went to southern Minahasa, and sent a courier to Sumual requesting a meeting. According to Somba, Sumual replied that he appreciated Somba's offer, and suggested that Somba come to his headquarters at Karoa. Somba says that he was prepared to go, but that his courier advised against it, warning that all the troops there were from Brigade 999, and that should Somba enter their area he would never return alive.[60]

It was the end of March before Somba returned to the north. In the meantime, General Nasution, as Minister of Defense and Chief of Staff of the army, on March 3, 1961 issued an appeal to the rebels to return to the arms of the motherland.[61] This was the first step in the procedure for settlement which had been agreed to in December. The second step, the announcement by Somba of the Permesta decision to return to the fold, could only be scheduled when it was known when he would return from the south. As the weeks went by, Broer Tumbelaka began to fear that the atmosphere favorable to a settlement might dissipate. He met with Lendy

---

60 Interview, D. J. Somba, Jakarta, January 22, 1972. According to Sumual, the commanders in the north did not report to him about the negotiations, but he knew of them through decoding messages; interview, Jakarta, April 13, 1972.
61 Periodic appeals had been made by KODAM XIII/Merdeka between November 27, 1959 and May 11, 1960. Copies of ten such appeals, several of which specifically tried to isolate Sumual and Dolf Runturambi from the rest of the rebels, were given to me by the Military History office of KODAM XIII/Merdeka in November 1971.

and Mantiri on March 20 to urge that a way be found out of the impasse created by Somba's absence. At their suggestion, Kawilarang, who had assumed overall command of Permesta forces in November 1960, and who was at the time in a nearby village, was contacted. Although he had not previously been involved in the negotiations, Kawilarang agreed to authorize the initialing of a statement of return on Somba's behalf, as well as that of other documents necessary to proceed with the final arrangements.[62]

By this time it was realized that Sumual would not agree to a settlement, and it was feared that he would try to use his position as chief of staff of the rebel armed forces to countermand orders issued by Somba that the Permesta units should return to the Republic.[63] Not only had he denounced negotiations as treachery in his December 15 telegram, but it is said that a courier whom he sent to those who had surrendered with the Manguni group in February, had easily influenced many of them to return to their guerrilla bases.[64] Thus, both sides believed it essential to conclude the settlement as quickly as possible.

On March 25, Mantiri informed Tumbelaka that Somba was expected by the end of the month. Tumbelaka and Colonel Sunandar then agreed that the pamphlets containing Nasution's appeal would be distributed from March 31, that the ceremony for the formal signing of Somba's statement of return would be held on April 4, and that the cease-fire would go into effect on April 11.

Final arrangements for the April 4 ceremony were made after Somba's return from the south, at meetings on April 1 and 3 between Broer Tumbelaka for the TNI, and Somba, Abe Mantiri, and Lendy Tumbelaka for Permesta. The ceremony was to follow standard military procedures. It was agreed that KODAM XIII/Merdeka commander, Colonel Sunandar, would act as inspector of the ceremony, in which two Permesta companies would participate. The ceremony itself would be followed by a meeting between Somba and Sunandar and their staffs, in which would be discussed the designation of the areas in which the Permesta troops

---

62 Radik Djarwadi, *Ambruknja Permesta*, p. 40, and discussion with F. J. Tumbelaka.
63 Letter from F. J. Tumbelaka to Panglima KODAM XIII/Merdeka (Soenandar), Manado, March 24, 1961.
64 Interview, Annie Kalangie, Manado, November 17, 1971.

would be grouped, the registration of weapons, the implementation of the cease-fire, communications, etc. According to Broer Tumbelaka, in closing the meeting he asked whether the Permesta leaders would come by themselves to the place where the ceremony was to be held, or whether they wished to be escorted there. Lendy replied, "It is your moral obligation to meet and escort us, Broer. Don't at this last moment order us to walk alone. These last steps, Broer, are the hardest."

At the April 4 ceremony Colonel Sunandar was accompanied by the North and Central Sulawesi chief of police, Drs. Moerhadi Danuwilogo, the commander of the second Regimental Battle Team, Lieutenant Colonel Sampoerno, and several other officers from KODAM XIII. In addition to Somba, Permesta was represented by Lendy Tumbelaka, Wim Tenges, and Abe Mantiri. Sunandar and Somba, who had been classmates at SSKAD, embraced when they met. The ceremony began with the inspection of the troops, both Permesta and TNI, by Sunandar, accompanied by Somba, Sampoerno, and two other TNI officers. Then the statement that Permesta had returned to the lap of the motherland was read. Somba signed the statement, then he and Sunandar signed the agreements that had been reached on the treatment to be accorded to the rebels. Significantly, Somba signed these documents as commander of KDM-SUT, although it had been officially dissolved on August 23, 1958; this accorded him recognition as a former member of the TNI, and emphasized the common bond between the rebels and the government troops. The ceremony closed with a march past of Permesta troops, who, although shoeless, were fully armed.[65]

Within a week there was a cease-fire, and the Permesta troops were gathered in their designated areas waiting the final step in the settlement procedures—inspection by Chief of Staff Nasution.

---

65 Text of Sunandar-Somba statement is in Radik Djarwadi, *Ambruknja Permesta*, pp. 40-41; and Makmun Salim, *Operasi² Gabungan*, pp. 109-10. Report of the ceremony, *PIA*, April 5, 1961 (p.m.), p. 7. In principle, all those covered by the agreement were to be permitted to join the TNI, return to government service, school or the community; however, a statement of clarification attached to the agreement indicates that it was made easier for former members of the TNI to become full members of the army (at their old rank) than those Permesta members who had not been in the TNI before the rebellion. It was further stipulated that those wishing to join the TNI would be screened individually in accordance with army regulations, and the number to be accepted would be in proportion to the number of armed men among the rebels. "Ketentuan2 Mengenai Penjaluran ex-Anggauta Permesta," April 4, 1961.

There was, however, one matter which still awaited resolution—what to do about Kawilarang. Because of his seniority, and his prestige, his return could not be handled locally, but required the attention of the central army leadership. It was decided that a further ceremony would be inserted into the agreed procedure, prior to the final inspection by Nasution. One of the most senior army generals, Major General Hidajat, Deputy Minister of Defense, was designated to act together with Kawilarang as inspector of a parade of Permesta and TNI troops near Tomohon in a ceremony on April 14. General Yani, and foreign military attachés, among them Colonel George Benson, the U.S. Army attaché, were present. Although Benson was a great friend of Yani, his presence was more significant for the symbol it provided of the reversal in official U.S. sympathies toward the rebellion.[66]

The final step in the procedure outlined in December took place on May 12, 1961, when General Nasution observed a parade of Permesta troops in a ceremony near Tomohon. He also met privately with Kawilarang.[67]

On June 22, 1961, a Presidential decree was issued granting amnesty to the followers of Kawilarang, Somba, and Saerang who had answered the appeal to return to the fold. A ceremony in Manado on July 29, 1961 confirmed the granting of amnesty and the abolition of legal charges against the former rebels.[68]

As a result of the settlement with Kawilarang and Somba, an estimated 27,055 persons, 25,176 of them military men, 8,000 of them armed, ended their rebellion.[69] Of this number an estimated 5,000 were former

---

[66] General Hidajat was older than Kawilarang, and it may have been thought more appropriate for Kawilarang to meet and discuss his future with Hidajat than with his former classmate and contemporary, Nasution. General Hidajat's wife, Ratu Aminah Hidajat, head of IP-KI (a minor party but one with close army connections), is said by some to have played a role in the negotiations. The ceremony was reported (as a separate surrender by Kawilarang) in *PIA*, April 15, 1961 (a.m.), p. 4. Other information from A.C.J. Mantiri, interview, March 20, 1972; letter, September 14, 1974. The last ship bearing supplies for the rebels arrived at the time of this ceremony, which Permesta called "Appel of Heroes." After the ceremony, Muharto, who had headed the rebel air force, left for abroad on this ship; he is said to have returned to Indonesia only after 1966.

[67] Kawilarang was sick with malaria at the time, and there had been some worry that the meeting could not take place. However, although Kawilarang did not participate in the ceremony, Nasution met with him before attending it himself. This ceremony was reported in *PIA*, May 15, 1961 (a.m.), pp. 1-2.

[68] *Sari Attensia*, VIII/6 (1961), pp. 458-63.

[69] List dated April 6, 1961, signed by Lendy R. Tumbelaka, as head of the KDM-SUT liaison team; nearly half of those included, 13,673, were in District III; there were 3,000-4,000 in the other

members of the TNI. After screening, some 8,000 men were sent to East Java for political quarantine and reindoctrination before being accepted (or reaccepted) into the TNI.[70] Some 11,000 persons, military and civilian, had surrendered with Manguni and Saerang, and a number of other Permesta units had surrendered to local TNI troops. There remained the group in southern Minahasa—Sumual, Pantouw, and the two 999 battalions under Goan and Lisangan: an estimated total of 1,500 persons, 900 of them armed.[71]

The return of the bulk of the Permesta troops with Somba and Kawilarang not only made difficult the position of those remaining in rebellion in North Sulawesi, but was disheartening to the much demoralized rebels in Sumatra. Splits had developed there too in the course of the rebellion, partly, as in Sulawesi, over the proclamation of the RPI. After the virtual ending of the Sulawesi half of the rebellion in April 1961, Simbolon and Husein disassociated themselves from the RPI, formed an Emergency Military Government (Pemerintah Darurat Militer), resumed negotiations with the TNI, and in June and July 1961 surrendered with a total of 24,500 men.[72]

On August 17, 1961, RPI President Sjafruddin Prawiranegara announced the end of hostilities, and ordered the ending of all acts of opposition to the government of the Republic of Indonesia and its armed forces.[73]

By the time of this announcement a copy of which was sent to him as chief of staff of the RPI armed forces, Sumual's position was extremely

---

three Districts. There were about 3,000 weapons registered in each of Districts two and three. In February 1961, Somba had estimated Permesta's total strength at 43,000 men, of whom 5,000 were from the old KDM-SUT (probably to be interpreted as former TNI from whatever unit), and 9,000 were formed KNIL members (1,000 of them already pensioned). The number of members of the Pasukan Wanita Permesta who surrendered at this time was between 1,413 (Annie Kalangie's figure) and 1,502 (in cited list).

70 Feith, "Dynamics of Guided Democracy," p. 346; there is a report in the Diponegoro commander, Colonel Pranoto, welcoming ex-Permesta rebels to Central Java, in *PIA,* April 7, 1961 (a.m.), p. 9.

71 *PIA,* May 15, 1961 (p.m.), p. 5; citing Lieutenant Colonel Batubara, commander of Brawijaya's First Regimental Combat Team.

72 Earlier negotiations in 1958 and 1959, in Singapore, Hong Kong, and Geneva, had been unsuccessful; Feith and Lev, "End of the Indonesian Rebellion," pp. 39, 43.

73 Xerox copies of "Pengumuman Pemerintah," Republik Persatuan Indonesia, Sjafruddin Prawira Negara, Sumatera, August 17, 1961; and letter to Minister of National Defense/KSAD Nasution from Sjafruddin Prawira Negara, President RPI, dated August 28, 1961.

difficult. Fewer than 200 troops remained with him. Family members, other civilians, and the sick and injured, had been allowed to surrender in May.[74] In July, Nun Pantouw, whom Sumual had appointed to replace Somba as commander of Minahasa, and Sumual's younger sister Evert (active in the PWP), were captured by one of the units under Somba which had already gone over to the TNI. Broer Tumbelaka came to meet Pantouw and Evert Sumual on July 10, 1961, and turned them over to Colonel Sunandar at their request. They were taken to Java, and Pantouw was detained, first under house arrest and then in prison, until July 1966.[75]

Treatment of the surrendering rebels was now much harsher than it had been for those who returned with Somba and Kawilarang in April; this was one of the effects of the reaction of the civilian government to the leniency with which the earlier rebels had been received. It was no longer left to the TNI to work out the conditions of the agreement on a brotherly basis, and many of those who surrendered later found themselves in prison, or at least detained, rather than being welcomed back into the TNI.

The President's amnesty offer to the rebels, repeated in his Independence Day address on August 17, 1961, was to expire on October 5, 1961. The deadline was, however, stretched in both North and South Sulawesi to include rebels who made contact with the TNI within the amnesty period.

Members of the Brawijaya First Regimental Battle Team, stationed in Amurang, had apparently been trying to contact Sumual for some time. After an exchange of letters, Sumual surrendered unconditionally on October 20, 1961, his formal statement of surrender, addressed to Army Chief of Staff Nasution being backdated to October 4. About 50 persons surrendered with him; very few remained in the jungles after that. Sumual too was taken to Jakarta, where he was held under house arrest in Cipayung until the ending of martial law in 1963, then imprisoned until July 1966.[76]

---

74 There is a "belated" report of the surrender in *PIA*, June 21, 1961 (p.m.), p. 12. Mrs. Sumual, Mrs. Gerungan, Mrs. Pantouw, and Governor H. D. Manoppo were in the group.
75 *Sari Attensia*, VIII/6 (1961), pp. 456, 463-65; interview J. M. J. Pantouw, Jakarta, January 23, 1972.
76 Radik Djarwadi, *Ambruknja Permesta*, pp. 46-49 (text of October 4 statement on pp. 48-49); interview, H. N. V. Sumual, Jakarta, April 13, 1972.

Also in October 1961 negotiations were opened in South Sulawesi between Qahhar Mudzakkar, officially a part of the RPI since February 1960, and the KODAM XIV/Hasanuddin commander, Colonel M. Jusuf (who had succeeded Andi Mattalatta one year earlier). Gerungan, who by this time was one of Qahhar's trusted staff officers, participated in the negotiations. Although a preliminary agreement to end the rebellion in South Sulawesi was reached in November, a final settlement was never concluded. Within a year, Qahhar, Gerungan, and many of those who had surrendered with them, had resumed their rebellion. It ended when Qahhar Mudzakkar was shot on February 3, 1965; Gerungan was captured on July 19, 1965, tried by a summary court, and executed.[77]

---

77 Harvey, "Rebellion," pp. 416-21. Some say that Gerungan returned to the jungle with Qahhar Mudzakkar in 1962 because he feared retaliation if he did not do so. Others say that Gerungan felt that his career was already at an end, his marriage destroyed (his wife, who had been a leading figure in the Permesta Women's Corps, had become involved with Sumual during the rebellion, and later married him)—and he surrendered to his fate.

CONCLUSION

The PRRI/Permesta rebellion ended nearly two years after a new era in Indonesian political history, Guided Democracy, was formally inaugurated in July 1959 with the return to the 1945 constitution. The rebellion had begun partly as a protest against Sukarno's vision of a "guided democracy," but the effect of the rebellion was to strengthen precisely those trends its leaders had hoped to forestall. Central authority was enhanced at the expense of local autonomy; radical nationalism supplanted pragmatic moderation; the influence of Sukarno and the PKI were augmented at the expense of Hatta and the Masjumi.

The high point of central government concessions to demands for regional autonomy had been reached prior to the outbreak of the rebellion, with the proclamation in January 1957 of Law One on local government which provided for the election of regional assemblies and regional heads. The implementation of the law was obstructed virtually from the outset because of the declaration of nationwide martial law in March 1957, and the key provisions for the election of regional heads were reversed by presidential decree in September 1959.[1] Thus, although in January 1961 the central government granted autonomous status to the recently created province of North Sulawesi, central control continued to be exercised through the appointed regional head, who was simultaneously governor of the province.

Even before the proclamation of the PRRI in February 1958 the focus of rebel protest had begun to shift from Nasution and the army leadership to President Sukarno and his leftist supporters. Anticommunism had become an increasingly important motif of the regional movement as early

---

1 Legge, *Central Authority*, especially pp. 21, 123-30, 201-17.

as 1957, both as a genuine response to signs of growing PKI strength in Java, and as an opportunistic ploy to attract foreign support. In the course of the fighting, anticommunism came to be a primary justification for the rebellion, as it became necessary to rationalize a war that was destroying so much of what it had set out to save. In the end, the rebels found it expedient to come to terms with the very leaders of the army whose ouster they had initially sought. This was not only because the rebels realized that they lacked the power to attain this and their other goals, but because it had become clear that they could not oppose Nasution without abandoning chances of a negotiated settlement. Further, by 1960 the rebels acknowledged that the army represented the most effective bulwark against further communist advance. For its part, the army leadership was vulnerable to leftist charges that its security policies were failing as long as the rebellion dragged on. Both the rebels and the army leaders recognized their mutual interest in curbing the growing influence of the PKI, and both believed that this could only be done after the rebellion was ended. This recognition of mutual interest provided the basis for the settlement of the Permesta rebellion as an internal army affair. The terms granted the Sulawesi rebels in April 1961 by the TNI were quite generous, particularly in comparison with the harsher provisions insisted upon by civilian leaders who subsequently became involved in surrender arrangements.[2]

The central army leadership was greatly strengthened by the victory over the rebels, and since 1957 the army as a whole had come to play a more active political role throughout the country as martial law

---

2 Mentioned by General A. H. Nasution in an interview in Jakarta, May 17, 1972. Many of the former TNI officers who returned with Somba's Permesta group were given positions in army intelligence (Bakin), the Strategic Command (KOSTRAD), or the North Sulawesi military command (KODAM XIII/Merdeka). Sumual, and a number of the Sumatran PRRI leaders, established a Development Consultants firm in Jakarta after their release from prison in July 1966; this group seems to have a special relationship with Lieutenant General Ali Murtopo, who was head of special operations (Opsus) and a private assistant to President Suharto until January 1974. It is noteworthy that the release of the last of the PRRI/Permesta rebels from prison came immediately after the parliamentary confirmation of the transfer of power from President Sukarno to General Suharto formally instituted the New Order in Indonesia. Because the brutal murder of six senior army generals on September 30, 1965, which was the beginning of the end of the Old Order, was blamed on the PKI, anticommunism became the official ideology of the new regime. The PRRI/Permesta rebels could now be seen as having acted in defense of the nation against the threat of communism, and their defiance of the legitimate government of the day was forgiven.

administrators. The principal antagonist of the regionalists, the PKI, had grown in influence not only at the center, where it had become one of the chief props of Sukarno's position, but in the rebellious regions themselves.[3] Sukarno dominated the political stage after 1959; Hatta was completely in the shadows. Sukarno, the army, and the PKI—these were to be the principal actors in Guided Democracy. Parliamentary institutions, and the parties which had flourished in them, were ineffectual survivors of the earlier age of Liberal Democracy.

By pressing their claims outside the institutions of government the regionalists had helped to destroy representative institutions. Their resort to violence had discredited political groups associated with the rebellion. The Masjumi and the PSI, the two parties most strongly opposed to the communists, had been banned in August 1960 for failing to condemn the rebellion, in which a number of their members participated.[4]

Thus, the rebellion was crucially important in precipitating the transition from Liberal to Guided Democracy, and was by no means an insignificant episode in Indonesian political history. However, quite apart from its effect on national politics, the rebellion is of intrinsic interest for the light it sheds on the character of fissiparous tendencies in Indonesia. As noted at the outset, because of the regional basis of socio-economic differences in Indonesia, questions of national policy inevitably have a regional dimension. One of the significant features of the PRRI/Permesta rebellion was that it was essentially a movement for the change of national policy, not for separation from the Indonesian state. The PRRI was an

---

3 A number of scholars had concluded even before 1966 that the strength of the PKI was more apparent than real; for a judicious assessment of these arguments see Feith, "Dynamics of Guided Democracy" pp. 338-42. On balance, Feith seems to accept the arguments of Donald Hindley's "President Sukarno and the Communists: The Politics of Domestication," *American Political Science Review*, 56 (1962), pp. 915-26, presented at greater length in his dissertation, which was published as *The Communist Party of Indonesia, 1951-1963* (Berkeley and Los Angeles: University of California Press, 1964). It is clear in the briefing papers of the Permesta negotiators (as well as in interviews with many of the Permesta leaders in 1971-72) that they believed that the PKI was gaining strength in Minahasa. In the briefing papers the increasing poverty of the people as the rebellion continued is given as the principal reason for the growing attraction of the PKI. In interviews, the influence of leftist members of TNI in Minahasa was also mentioned as a reason for the increase in the PKI's following. As no elections were held between 1961 and 1966 (when the PKI was banned), there is no way of proving, or disproving, these assessments.

4 Although only one national PSI leader, Professor Sumitro, was actively involved in the rebellion, in both North and South Sulawesi PSI members were prominent among civilian supporters of Permesta.

alternative government, not an alternative state. When the rebellion moved away from this position in the proclamation of an Indonesian Federal Republic (the RPI) in 1960, its disintegration was rapid. For most of the rebels, the Republic for which they had fought during the revolution, and the flag under which they had defended the nation against other threats, held their loyalty despite their disappointment with the unfulfilled promises of independence. Thus, although it was a regional rebellion, in that its base was in the Outer Islands, it was not an attempt to set up a separate state.

In part the very diversity of Indonesia inhibits its disintegration as a national entity. Regionalism and ethnicity, although overlapping, are not synonymous. An attempt to redraw boundaries along ethnic lines carries with it the danger of further fragmentation. The gradual shrinking of the geographic base of the Permesta rebellion is instructive in this regard. The initial demand for local autonomy was soon followed by demands for a separate province in North and then in Central Sulawesi. Further, and more dramatically, although popular support for Permesta in East Indonesia was initially based on the economic interests of the copra producers of the region, as well as on religious and ideological opposition to communism, the principal basis of support after the fighting began seems to have been that of kinship and ethnic ties. These primary loyalties provided a solid basis of support for the rebellion in Minahasa itself, the area from which many of the leaders came, and induced other anak daerah such as Kawilarang and Warouw to join in a rebellion of which they disapproved. However, the importance of Minihasan ethnic solidarity in support for the rebellion seems certainly to have been one of the reasons for the falling away of support for the rebellion in other areas of East Indonesia. The people of Minahasa, Christian and well-educated, were not only a religious minority, but were an elite group in colonial and independent civil and military services. As such they had perhaps more often incurred the resentment and envy than the affection and respect of their less privileged neighbors. This was important when the central government made available rewards for loyalty or a change of heart.

This shrinking of the area of support for Permesta is one of the reasons it can be described as "half a rebellion," for it was fought in only a small part of the area originally encompassed in the Charter of Inclusive Struggle proclaimed in Makassar on March 2, 1957. Much of the initial impetus for the March 2 proclamation came from officers from South Sulawesi. However, there were conflicting objectives among these officers, and basic differences of interest between North and South Sulawesi, which led to the withdrawal of effective Permesta activity to North Sulawesi by mid-1957. The lack of unity within the regional movement was at least as great as that the rebels criticized in the national government, and was a fundamental factor in the rebellion's ultimate defeat.

There were also sharp divisions among Permesta leaders in Minahasa, divisions which by 1959 had engendered fighting between Permesta units as fierce as that between the rebels and the TNI. The Permesta label was used by only some of those in Minahasa who participated in the rebellion; in this sense, too, Permesta was only half a rebellion. Kawilarang considered himself part only of Permesta, he never accepted the PRRI or the separatist RPI; Sumual abandoned the use of the term Permesta when the PRRI was proclaimed in February 1958, and as the principal link with the Sumatran branch of the rebellion, he followed his colleagues there in moving on to the proclamation of the RPI in February 1960.

More obviously, Permesta was only half of the Sumatra-based PRRI rebellion. Although nationally important political figures were found only at the Sumatran headquarters of the PRRI, and most of the political decisions affecting the proclamation of the rebel governments were made there, the heaviest fighting of the civil war occurred in the Permesta stronghold of Minahasa. It was also in the Permesta area that the first agreements to end the fighting, as well as the last surrenders, took place.

Indeed, the rebellion as a whole, the PRRI/Sumatra branch as well as the Permesta/Sulawesi branch, might be described as little more than half a rebellion. This description might be deserved on the basis of the half-hearted nature of the rebellion—the reluctance of many of the participants to fight, and the failure of many of the participants to foresee the consequences of their actions, or to make adequate preparations for likely contingencies. The rebel leaders made a serious miscalculation in thinking that their challenge to the central government would receive wide backing throughout the country, including Java itself, and in believing that the central government would not be prepared to assert its authority by force of arms. Many rebel leaders did not expect their bluff to be called, and were unprepared to back up their threats with force. The assurance of foreign assistance which had emboldened them to make these threats, however, also compelled the central government to take action against them, and both military and civilian leaders in Jakarta were prepared to meet the challenge of the regionalists with rapid military action.

The half-hearted quality of the rebellion is also a reflection of the limited nature of the goals of its leaders and those who participated in it. The rebels were motivated by a desire to change national policies, not to create a totally new society. Popular support for the rebellion was based more on ethnic and regional sentiment than on any broadly based commitment to abstract principles. Thus, although the Permesta rebellion received sufficient support in Minahasa to sustain nearly three years of guerrilla warfare, it did not generate any large scale mobilization of the mass of the population of those areas on the basis of ideological appeals. One of the consequences has been that the bitter legacy of destruction and division it engendered has thus far proved stronger than memories of shared struggle for common ideals.

APPENDIX ONE
BIOGRAPHIC NOTES

Dr. O. E. ENGELEN, a Minahasan, is a graduate of the Jakarta Medical School, where he was active in the Student Christian Movement. He completed his studies during the revolution, in which he fought in West Java and with the Brawijaya Division in East Java. Following the transfer of sovereignty he served with TT-VII in Maluku and South Sulawesi. In 1957 he was Chairman of the Officers' Association (IPRI) of East Indonesia, and had the rank of lieutenant colonel in the TNI. He was instrumental in bringing together the military participants in the planning for the March 2 proclamation, and headed the Education and Culture/Social and Health section of the Team of Assistants to the Permesta military government. In November 1957 he was named a member of the Permesta Supreme Council. On April 15, 1958, he was dishonorably discharged from the TNI; he was arrested in May of that year, and was imprisoned in Jakarta and Madiun until 1962. In 1972 he was treasurer of the Indonesian Council of Churches. *PIA,* January 7, 1957 (p.m.), p. 3; and November 13, 1957, p. 6. Interview, O. E. Engelen, Jakarta, February 1, 1972.

J. W. "Dee" GERUNGAN was Minahasan, his wife was Hetty Warouw. In 1953 he returned from the Netherlands War College (*Hogere Krijgschool*) in Breda, and was assigned to SSKAD, Bandung, as an instructor, with the rank of captain. In 1954 he was sent to TT-VII, East Indonesia, as a battalion commander, and by 1957 had been promoted to major, and assigned as Fourth Assistant (Logistics) on the TT-VII staff. He was a member of the committee which planned the March 2 Proclamation, and was a member of the Security Section of the Team of Assistants to the Permesta military government. He moved to Minahasa in June 1957, and following the break with the central government, was installed on February 19, 1958 as commander of Regimental Battle Team Anoa, with headquarters at Poso, Central Sulawesi. After the landing of central government troops in Palu and Donggala in March and April 1958, he went south with 200 men, and in May 1959 signed a formal agreement for military cooperation with the DI/TII. After an abortive attempt to flee in April 1960, he converted to Islam, and became a trusted aide of Qahhar Mudzakkar. He participated in negotiations between the DI and TNI in October 1961, but remained with Qahhar when the rebellion was resumed in 1962. On July 19, 1965 he was captured, tried, and executed. *Madjalah Angkatan Darat,* III/34 and 35 (September and October 1953); *Pikiran Rakjat,* February 20, 1958; *Sari Attensia,* VII/4 (April 1960), pp. 197-99. Supplemented by interviews.

Andi Muhammad JUSUF Amir was born in Kajuara, Bone, South Sulawesi, on June 23, 1928. His father was the rajah of Kajuara; during the revolution he married a member of the Jogjakarta aristocracy; he later married Elly Saelan, Makassar-born of Javanese-Madurese parents. He was educated at the HIS (Dutch Native School) in Watampone. During the revolution he was with Sulawesi units in Jogjakarta, and served as an aide to Qahhar Mudzakkar. In December 1949, as a captain in the military police (CPM), he was appointed to the staff of the Military Commission for East Indonesia, and then served as an aide to Colonel Kawilarang when TT-VII was established in April 1950. He attended SSKAD, Bandung, in 1952-53, and then returned to TT-VII, first as chief of staff to RI-24 in Manado, and then as Second Assistant (Operations) on the TT-VII staff. In 1955-56 he attended the U.S. Army Infantry Officers' Advanced Course at Fort Benning, Georgia. He was appointed to head the newly formed KRU- (later RI-) Hasanuddin in October 1956; he was then a major. He participated in the planning of the March 2 Proclamation, but never served as head of the Security Section of the Permesta military government to which he was appointed. In January 1958 he was promoted to lieutenant colonel, and in February 1959 he was made chief of staff, and in October 1959, commander of KDM-SST. In July 1960 he was promoted to colonel, and in August 1964 to brigadier general. In July 1965 he was named Minister of Basic and Light Industry, and has served in successive cabinets as Minister of Trade Affairs and Minister of Industry with the rank of lieutenant general. O. G. Roeder, *Who's Who in Indonesia* (Jakarta: Gunung Agung, 1971), p. 165; *Indonesia Timoer,* January 18, 1950; KODAM XIV/Hasanuddin, Sejarah Militer,

Sulselra Bangkit (Makassar, 1964). Supplemented by interviews.

Alex Evert KAWILARANG was born in Jatinegara, West Java, on February 23, 1920. His father, a major in the KNIL, was from Tondano, and his mother from Remboken, both in the Toulour language area of Minahasa; both parents were from families prominent in the civil service. His first wife was Nelly van Amden; they were divorced sometime after 1958 and he later married Henny Lie Sumual (the former wife of H. N. V. Sumual). He was educated at a Dutch commercial high school (HBS), and the KNIL Academy, Bandung, where he was a member of the class of 1940. At the start of the revolution he was a member of KRIS in Krawang, Jakarta, then became a staff officer in the West Java army corps headquarters from 1946 to 1948. In 1948 he was appointed commander of the First Siliwangi Brigade, and then subterritorial commander in Tapanuli, North Sumatra. He remained in North Sumatra as commander of TT-I from December 1949 to April 1950, when he was appointed commander of TT-VII, serving simultaneously as commander of the Expeditionary Force sent to East Indonesia. From November 1951 to August 1956 he was commander of TT-III/Siliwangi, West Java. He was then assigned as military attaché in Washington, D.C., a post which he left in March 1958 when he was named commander-in-chief of PRRI. Although he did not accept this position, he did join the Permesta rebels, and assumed command of Permesta forces in northern Minahasa in November 1960. Following the conclusion of Permesta negotiations with the TNI in April 1961 he was placed in inactive status. In 1972 he was deputy general manager of Jakarta Racing Management, at Pulo Mas in Jakarta. Marpaung, *Almanak Angkatan Perang*, p. 154; *Asia Who's Who 1958* (Hong Kong: Pan Asia Newspaper Alliance, 1958), p. 217. Supplemented by interviews.

Mohammad Saleh LAHADE was born in Barru, South Sulawesi, the son of a school teacher. His first wife is the daughter of the nationalist educator, Ki Hadjar Dewantara; he later married into an aristocratic family in South Sulawesi. He was educated at a Dutch middle school (AMS) in Jogjakarta, and graduated from the Agricultural High School in Bogor. In 1944-45 he worked on the staff of SUDARA and the Pusat Keselamatan Rakjat with Dr. Sam Ratulangie. In 1945 he went to Java and joined the political arm of KRIS, and in 1948, Brigade XVI. He was appointed a member of the staff of the Military Commission for East Indonesia in December 1949, with the rank of major, and from 1950 to 1952 he was

Fifth Assistant (Civic and Territorial Affairs), on the TT-VII staff. He was placed in inactive status after 1952, and ran as a candidate of the Partai Kedaulatan Rakjat in the 1955 parliamentary elections. In October 1956 he was appointed chief of staff of KoDPSST, with the rank of lieutenant colonel. He was the principal drafter of the March 2 Charter, and was named chief of staff of the Permesta military government in March 1957. In February 1958 he was named Minister of Information in the PRRI Cabinet; he was dishonorably discharged from the TNI on February 17, 1958, and was arrested on May 20, 1958 and imprisoned in Den Pasar, Madiun, and Jakarta until 1963. In 1972 he was director of P. T. Utesco in Makassar, a firm associated with Sumual's Development Consultation group. *Propinsi Sulawesi,* pp. 223, 231; *Indonesia Timoer,* December 30, 1949; interviews, M. Saleh Lahade, Makassar, September and October 1971.

Bing LATUMAHINA was born in Makassar in 1926 of Ambonese parents. His father was head of the political department in the Sulawesi provincial office in 1957. He attended advanced primary school (MULO) in Makassar, and in 1941 received naval air training in Surabaya. During the revolution he fought with the Pattimura Division, a unit composed primarily of Ambonese. In 1950 he was appointed to the Military Commission for East Indonesia, with the rank of lieutenant, and then served as an aide to Colonel Kawilarang. From 1951 to 1955 he was a member of the intelligence staff at army headquarters in Jakarta, and in 1955 he was appointed First Assistant (Intelligence) on the TT-VII staff, with the rank of captain. He was also secretary of the Officers' Association for East Indonesia (IPRI). He was a member of the committee which planned the March 2 proclamation, and served on the secretariat of the Permesta military government until November 1957 when he was named secretary of the Permesta Supreme Council. He was dishonorably discharged from the TNI on April 15, 1958, and was arrested in May of that year and imprisoned in Jakarta and Madiun until 1962. In 1972 he was working with Development Consultation Ltd. in Jakarta, headed by H. N. V. Sumual. *PIA,* January 7, 1957 (p.m.), p. 3; and November 13, 1957, p. 6. Interview, Bing Latumahina, Jakarta, January 14, 1972.

A. C. J. "Abé" MANTIRI is from the Tonsea language group in Minahasa; his wife, a French language teacher, is a cousin of A. E. Kawilarang. He was a member of the PSI. Before the war he served as a merchant seaman, and from 1949 to 1958 he was a director of the shipping firm, Perindo. In 1957 he was named head of the Financial and Economic section (Finec) of the Permesta military government for North Sulawesi. From 1958 to 1961 he was Fourth Assistant (Logistics) on the PRRI/Permesta armed forces staff, with a rebel rank of lieutenant colonel. He was one of the principal negotiators for Permesta in 1960-61. Since the end of the rebellion he has operated a "mixed" farm in Airmadidi, near Manado, where he breeds race horses. Interviews with A. C. J. Mantiri, Airmadidi, November 1971 and March 1972.

Andi MATTALATTA was born in Barru, South Sulawesi, where his father and uncle were local rulers (rajah). His wife is the daughter of H. M. Junus Daeng Mile, Mayor of Makassar from 1956 to 1958. He attended the special school for local rulers (OSVIA) in Makassar, and became a teacher and athletic coach. He was a platoon commander in a militarized youth group organized by the Japanese in 1945. During the revolution he was responsible for the training in Java of expeditionary units sent to Sulawesi, and was a battalion commander, with the rank of major, in Brigade XVI. From 1950 to 1952 he commanded a battalion in the Expeditionary Forces sent to South Sulawesi and Maluku. In March 1952 he was named chief of staff of RI-23 and commander of Battalion 705, in Pare-Pare. From April 1954 until June 1957 he was commander of the Makassar city command, and from October 1956 to March 1957 was also deputy commander of KoDPSST, with the rank of lieutenant colonel. He was appointed commander of the South and Southeast Sulawesi Command established by the Permesta military government in March 1957, and was officially installed as commander of KDM-SST on June 1, 1957. He was replaced, by Jusuf, in November 1959, and attended the senior course at SSKAD, Bandung, from 1960 to 1962. In March 1960 he was promoted to colonel, and appointed a member of parliament. In 1968 he was promoted to brigadier general, and made a member of the central board of the Indonesian National Sports Committee (KONI). *Marhaen,* June 5, 1957; interview, Andi Mattalatta, Jakarta, March 1, 1971.

Abdul Qahhar MUDZAKKAR (Kahar Muzakkar) was born as La Domeng in the village of Lanipa, near Palopo, Luwu, South Sulawesi, on March 24, 1921. He attended an Islamic teachers' school (Mu'allimin Muhammadayah) in Surakarta from 1937 to 1940, and then returned to Luwu to teach in a Muhammadiyah school. When he was banished from Luwu in 1943 he returned to Surakarta, and was in business there at the outset of the revolution. He was the first secretary of KRIS, and was active in a number of youth and military organizations in Java during the revolution; he was made deputy commander of Brigade XVI in 1948. As commander of the Outer Island Command Group (Komando Grup Seberang) he returned to South Sulawesi in June 1950 to assist in negotiating with local guerrilla forces, but instead joined them. Negotiations to recognize the guerrillas as part of the National Reserve Corps (CTN), failed in 1951, and Qahhar again led the guerrillas into rebellion. In August 1953 he proclaimed Sulawesi part of the Indonesian Islamic Republic, and was named Deputy Minister of Defense of the RII. Negotiations with the TNI in 1961 again failed, and Qahhar resumed his rebellion in 1962. He was shot and killed on February 3, 1965. Radik Djarwadi, *Kisah Kahar Muzakar* (Surabaya: Grip, 1963); Bahar Mattalioe, *Kahar Muzakkar dengan Petualangannja* (Jakarta: Delegasi, 1965); Abdul Qahhar Mudzakkar, *Konsepsi Negara Demokrasi Indonesia* (n.p.: [1960]); *Tjatatan Sedjarah dari Gerilja ke Angkatan Perang* (Makassar: The "SS" [Sul-Sel] Publishing Office, [1951]).

Andi PANGERANG Petta Rani (Andi Pangerang Daeng Parani) is the eldest son of Andi Mappanjukki, the last rajah of Bone. He completed the special school for local rulers (OSVIA) in Makassar, and held a position in the council of chiefs of Bone in the 1930s. In August 1945 he was designated a member of the Sulawesi delegation to the Indonesian Independence Preparatory Committee, and worked with pro-Republican leaders until his arrest and imprisonment in November 1946. Sometime after 1950 he was appointed area head of Bone, a position which he held until 1955 when he was made resident-coordinator for South Sulawesi. On July 12, 1956 he was appointed governor of Sulawesi, a position which he held until April 20, 1960. He was one of the initial signers of the March 2 Charter, and was named military governor of South Sulawesi by the Permesta military government. He was officially appointed to this position on April 1, 1957, and was given the rank of titular colonel in the TNI. *Marhaen,* July 9, 1956; *Propinsi Sulawesi,* pp. 210-13, 234.

Jan Maximillian Johan "Nun" PANTOUW was born in Manado on January 20, 1925, and graduated from an advanced primary school (MULO) there. During the Japanese occupation he attended a Japanese naval school in Makassar, and was serving as a ship's officer in 1945. He joined the navy in December 1945, and served with ALRI Division VI in East Java until it was absorbed into Brigade XVI in 1948. He was involved in infiltration of Republican units into North and South Sulawesi, and in blockade running to bring supplies to the Republic from Singapore. In 1950 he accompanied Battalion Worang to Makassar and Manado as a liaison officer. From 1950 to 1952 he attended courses in military law, organization, strategy, and tactics given by the Dutch Military Mission to Indonesia. He served as chief of staff of RI-26, in Den Pasar, Bali, from 1952 to 1954, when he was appointed First Assistant (Intelligence) on the TT-VII staff, and was promoted to major. He was placed in a nonactive status in September 1954, following court investigation of TT-VII's involvement in copra smuggling. In 1955 he was named to head the Minahasa Coconut Foundation, set up unilaterally in Manado, and in about 1956 went to Singapore to establish the Eastern Produce Agency as an outlet for Minahasan copra. For a short period he was concurrently head of the Financial and Military section (FINEC) of the Permesta military government for North Sulawesi. In February 1958 he was designated Director of External Trade for PRRI, by PRRI Minister of Trade, Professor Sumitro. In May 1958 he went as chief of staff with the Permesta expeditionary forces to Morotai, and served briefly as PRRI/Permesta commander of the Maluku and West Irian region. On his return to North Sulawesi in January 1959 he was appointed First Assistant (Intelligence) on the PRRI/Permesta armed forces staff. In July 1961 he was named by Sumual to replace Somba as commander of Minahasa, but was captured by Permesta forces who had already gone over to the TNI. He was imprisoned from 1961 to 1966, and after his release established a copra trading firm in Jakarta. Angkatan Darat, *PRRI*, I, p. 150; *Sari Attensia*, VIII/6 (1961), p. 456; interview, J. M. Pantouw, Jakarta, January 23, 1972.

Henk RONDONUWU was born in Tondano, Minahasa, on September 9, 1910. He was married to Gadis Rasjid, a journalist and member of the PSI. Before the war he was a teacher in the Dutch-native school (HIS) in Pare-Pare, South Sulawesi. During the revolution he was one of the founders of the Pusat Keselamatan Rakjat, and of the pro-Republican newspaper *Pedoman Rakjat*, of which he was later managing editor. He was a member of the pro-Republican faction in the NIT parliament, and was appointed Minister of Information in the Putuhena Cabinet of 1950, which carried out the liquidation of the NIT and absorption of East Indonesia into the unitary Republic. He was a founder and the first secretary of the Partai Kedaulatan Rakjat, and later served as its general chairman. During 1957 he was one of the key civilian participants in the Permesta movement, serving as a member of the Executive Committee of the Permesta Central Advisory Council, chairman of the Bhinneka Tunggal Ika Congress held in Makassar in May of that year, and as a member of the Permesta Supreme Council formed in November 1957. He was later director of the Makassar city printing office, an instructor in the Hasanuddin University language program, and was affiliated with the firms P.T. Utesco and P.T. Development Consultation. He was active in the cultural field, particularly in drama and painting, in addition to his involvement in journalism and politics. He died on June 13, 1974. *Pedoman Rakjat,* July 14, 1974; *Propinsi Sulawesi,* pp. 171, 174, 511, 522; interviews, Henk Rondonuwu, Makassar, June 9, 1971 and February 23, 1972.

Daniel Julius SOMBA was born on July 26, 1923 in Central Java; his parents were from Tomohon, Minahasa. His first wife was Javanese; he has since married twice. He was a member of PETA during the Japanese occupation, and served in ALRI Division VI in East Java from 1945 to 1948. He was a company commander, with the rank of captain, in a battalion commanded by H. N. V. Worang in Brigade XVI, and in 1950 went with Battalion Worang to East Indonesia. In 1951 he was made commander of Battalion 702 in Makassar, and in 1953 was transferred to Ambon as commander of Battalion 707. He attended SSKAD, Bandung, in 1954, in the same class as Colonel Sunandar, commander of North Sulawesi at the time of the Permesta surrender. In 1955 he was appointed Third Assistant (Personnel) on the staff of TT-VII, and in December 1956 replaced Worang as commander of RI-24 in Manado. In March 1957 he was named military governor of North Sulawesi by the Permesta military government, and on September 28, 1957 he was officially installed as commander of KDM-SUT. He was promoted to lieutenant colonel (temporary rank) in January 1958. On February 17, 1958 he announced that North Sulawesi would recognize the rebel PRRI government and sever connections with Jakarta. He was dishonorably discharged from the TNI on February 18, 1958. During the rebellion he commanded Permesta forces in Minahasa. The bulk of the

Permesta troops ended their rebellion in April 1961 in accordance with an agreement negotiated under Somba's auspices with the TNI. After ten days' political quarantine in Jakarta, Somba resumed his official rank as major in the TNI. In 1971-72 he was lieutenant colonel on the staff of BAKIN (National Intelligence Coordinating Body). *Madjalah Brawidjaya,* VII/19 (October 5, 1957); interviews, D. J. Somba, Jakarta, August 15, 1971 and January 22, 1972.

Herman Nicolas "Ventje" SUMUAL was born in Rembokan, on the shores of Lake Tondano in Minahasa, on June 11, 1923. His father was a sergeant in the KNIL. His first wife was Javanese. He divorced his second wife, Henny Lie, sometime after 1961, and married Hetty Warouw Gerungan (former wife of Dee Gerungan). Sumual graduated from a Dutch-native school (HIS) and advanced primary school (MULO); he attended a merchant marine school in Makassar during the Japanese occupation, and the Law Faculty of Gajah Mada University in Jogjakarta during 1946-48. From 1945 to 1948 he was Jakarta liaison officer for KRIS, and was designated chief of staff of Brigade XVI in 1948, with the rank of major. He led KRIS units incorporated into Brigade XVI in the attack on Dutch-held Jogjakarta in January 1949. In 1950 he was appointed to the Military Commission for East Indonesia, with primary responsibility for North Sulawesi, and remained as commander of RI-24 in Manado until March 1952. He was head of the student senate in the SSKAD class of 1952-53. From 1953 until May 1956 he was in charge of training and education at the infantry inspectorate in Bandung. In May 1956 he was appointed chief of staff of TT-VII, with the rank of lieutenant colonel. On August 22, 1956 he was installed as acting commander of TT-VII. He proclaimed martial law in East Indonesia on March 2, 1957, and was one of the original signers of the Permesta Charter. He headed the military government established by the Permesta movement, and after the dissolution of TT-VII in June 1957, moved Permesta headquarters to Kinilow, in Minahasa. In February 1958 he was designated commander of PRRI ground forces, and was dishonorably discharged from the TNI on February 26, 1958. From 1958 to 1961 he fought with PRRI/Permesta forces in North Sulawesi and North Maluku. On October 20, 1961 (officially backdated to October 4 to meet amnesty deadline) he surrendered, and was imprisoned in West Java and Jakarta until July 1966. In 1971-72 he was director of the firm Development Consultants (P.T.

Konsultasi Pembangunan) in Jakarta, which had shipping and timber interests in East Indonesia, and which employed a number of people who had been involved in PRRI and Permesta. *Marhaen,* August 28, 1956; *Star Weekly* (Jakarta), XII/505 (March 16, 1957); *Angkatan Bersendjata,* October 8, 1969; interviews, H. N. V. Sumual, Jakarta, March 9, 1971 and April 13, 1972.

Her TASNING (Haeruddin TASNING Daeng Toro) was born in Sungguminasa, Gowa, South Sulawesi, on December 19, 1922. His father was from Gowa, his mother Buginese; his wife is Javanese. He attended advanced primary school (MULO) in Makassar, and graduated from the Agricultural High School in Bogor one year after Saleh Lahade. He worked as an agricultural official in Pekalongan, Central Java until the outbreak of the revolution, when he fought with the Diponegoro Division and the military police corps (CPM) in Central Java. From 1950 to 1953 he commanded a CPM battalion in Makassar, with the rank of captain, and was commander of CPM for South Sulawesi. He attended SSKAD, Bandung, 1953-54, and then taught at the CPM Training Center in Cimahi, West Java. In October 1956 he was appointed deputy commander of CPM for East Indonesia, with headquarters in Makassar; he was then a major. Although he was named chief of staff of the Permesta military government for South Sulawesi on March 2, 1957, he did not sign the Permesta Charter. He served as chief of staff of KDM-SST from its inception on June 1, 1957 until January 1959. From 1959 to 1961 he was military attaché at the Indonesian Embassy in Cairo, with the rank of lieutenant colonel. In about 1962 he attended the U.S. Army Command and General Staff College, Fort Leavenworth, Kansas. On July 28, 1966 he was appointed director general of Security and Communication Affairs, Ministry of Foreign Affairs; his rank was then brigadier general. In February 1972 he was promoted to major general, and in 1973 he was named Indonesian Ambassador to Australia. Roeder, *Who's Who,* pp. 452-53; interview, Her Tasning, Jakarta, February 1, 1972.

Jan TIMBULENG was from Tomohon, Minahasa. His wife was a younger sister of Minahasa area head, Laurens Saerang. He had been in the ranks of the KNIL, then fought briefly in a TNI battalion in 1950 in South Maluku. Late that year he joined a rebel movement in southern Minahasa, the Defenders of Justice Army (Pasukan Pembela Keadilan, PPK), becoming its commander in 1954. He and some 2,000 followers joined Permesta in March 1958, and Timbuleng and three PPK battalions went to Central Sulawesi with Somba in April-May 1958. He was shot and killed on or about October 9, 1960 (for his role in Permesta and the circumstances of his death see Chapter VI). *Pikiran Rakjat,* March 27, 1958; *Sari Attensia,* VIII/1 (1961), pp. 34-35; Staf Angkatan Bersendjata, *Sedjarah Singkat,* p. 140; supplemented by interviews.

F. J. "Broer" TUMBELAKA was born in Manado, but grew up in Surabaya and East Java. His present wife was head of the student council in Manado in 1961, and worked closely with him in the effort to bring the Permesta rebellion to an end. Tumbelaka attended a commercial secondary school (*middelbaar handelsschool*) in Surabaya, and worked there and in Jember, East Java, during the Japanese occupation. During the revolution he initially joined ALRI Division VI in East Java, then transferred to Battalion Abdullah in 1948. He went with Battalion Abdullah, which was formally under the Brawijaya Division, to South Sulawesi and South Maluku in 1950, becoming its commander in 1951. In April 1952 he was appointed Third Assistant (Personnel), on the TT-VII staff with the rank of captain. He was one of the principal instigators and organizers of the ouster of Colonel Gatot Subroto as Panglima of TT-VII in November 1952. In October 1955 he was placed in inactive status and moved to East Java, where he remained after his retirement in 1959, at the rank of lieutenant colonel. In 1960-61 he was the principal negotiator for army headquarters with the Permesta rebels. On May 25, 1960 he was installed as deputy governor of North Sulawesi; and from June 15, 1962 to March 19, 1965 he was governor of North Sulawesi. Radik Djarwadi, *Pradjurit Mengabdi: Sedjarah Bataljon "Y"* (Bandung: Pusat Sejarah Militer, 1959), pp. 118, 190; interview, F. J. Tumbelaka, Jakarta, April 15, 1972.

Joop F. WAROUW was born in Jakarta on September 8, 1917. His parents were from Remboken, Minahasa; his father was in the KNIL. Warouw studied military engineering at the KNIL school in Bandung, and was attached to a KNIL searchlight unit in 1940. He was a member of a Japanese-sponsored organization (Hantyo Ittokyu) in Surabaya during the occupation. In 1945 he led a Pesindo (Socialist Youth of Indonesia) battalion in Surabaya. From 1946 to 1948 he was deputy commander of ALRI Division VI in East Java, with the rank of lieutenant colonel, and in 1948 he was named commander of Brigade XVI. In the period

1950 to 1952 he was successively commander of TNI regiments in North Sulawesi and North Maluku (RI-24), South Maluku (RI-25), and South Sulawesi (RI-23). In March 1952 he was appointed chief of staff of TT-VII. On November 16, 1952 he ousted Colonel Gatot Subroto as Panglima of TT-VII in the aftermath of the October 17 affair in Jakarta. Warouw was installed as acting commander of TT-VII on January 3, 1953; he was recognized as full commander on August 1, 1954, and was promoted to colonel. In August 1956 he was assigned as military attaché at the Indonesian Embassy in Peking. He was named Minister of Construction and Public Works in the PRRI cabinet of February 1958; he was dishonorably discharged from the TNI on May 6, 1958 (retroactive to March 15, 1958). He was head of the PRRI/Permesta civilian government in North Sulawesi from 1958 to 1960. In April 1960 he was captured by troops under the control of Jan Timbuleng, and was imprisoned until October, when he was killed. Marpaung, *Almanak Angkatan Perang*, pp. 158-59; *Asia Who's Who*, pp. 248-49; *PIA*, May 10, 1958 (a.m.), p. 1; *Sari Attensia*, VIII/1 (1961), pp. 22-23, 34-35; supplemented by interviews.

Hein Victor WORANG is from the Tonsea language area of northern Minahasa. During the revolution he was in ALRI Division VI in East Java, and was a battalion commander of Brigade XVI in the Kediri-Blitar area. In April 1950, as a major in the TNI, he led Battalion Worang to South Sulawesi to augment the small TNI unit there. After the sending of an expeditionary force under Colonel Kawilarang overcame resistance from the NIT government to the landing of TNI units, Battalion Worang proceeded from Makassar to North Sulawesi, and then participated in the assault on Ambon in September 1950. From 1952 to 1956 Worang was commander of RI-24 in Manado; he supported Warouw's ouster of Gatot Subroto in November 1952, and was involved with Warouw in TT-VII sponsored smuggling of copra. In December 1956 he was transferred to South Sumatra as commander of RI-6/TT-II, in Tanjungkrang, Lampung. He served as an adviser to TT-II commander, Lieutenant Colonel Barlian, at the National Conference (MUNAS) in September 1957. In September 1958 he was assigned to attend SSKAD, Bandung; he was then a lieutenant colonel. From 1960 to 1966 he was a member of the parliament (DPRGR); during that time he was promoted to colonel, and then to brigadier general. On February 20, 1967 he was designated governor of North

Sulawesi, and in 1971 he was promoted to major general. Staf Angkatan Bersenjata, *Sedjarah Singkat,* pp. 90-94; *PIA,* September 9, 1957 (a.m.), p. 1; *Madjalah Angkatan Darat,* November 1958; *Sinar Harapan,* February 23, 1967; supplemented by interviews.

APPENDIX TWO
MILITARY COMMANDS IN EAST INDONESIA AND SOUTH SULAWESI MARCH 1, 1957

Tentara dan Territorium VII (TT-VII) Wirabuana, Makassar
    Commander - Lieutenant Colonel H. N. V. Sumual
    Chief of Staff - Lieutenant Colonel Jonosewojo (Brawijaya)
        First Assistant (Intelligence) - Captain Bing Latumahina
        Second Assistant (Operations) -
        Third Assistant (Personnel) - Major Lendy Tumbelaka
        Fourth Assistant (Logistics) - Major J. W. "Dee" Gerungan
        Fifth Assistant (Civic and Territorial Affairs) - Major Malady Jusuf (Diponegoro)
    Infantry Regiment 23 (RI-23), Pare-Pare, South Sulawesi*
        Commander - Major Andi Rifai
    RI-24, Manado, North Sulawesi
        Commander - Major D. J. Somba
            Battalion 714; Commander - Major Dolf Runturambi
    RI-25, Ambon, Maluku
        Commander - Lieutenant Colonel Herman Pieters
    RI-26, Den Pasar, Bali, Nusa Tenggara
        Commander - Lieutenant Colonel Minggu
        Chief of Staff - Major Joost Wuisan
    KMKB Makassar
        Commander - Lieutenant Colonel Andi Mattalatta
        Chief of Staff - Major Sjamsuddin
            Battalion 702; Commander - Captain John Ottay

Komando Pengamanan Sulawesi Selatan dan Tenggara (KoDPSST), Maros
   Commander - Colonel R. Sudirman (Brawijaya)
   Deputy Commander - Lieutenant Colonel Andi Mattalatta
   Chief of Staff - Lieutenant Colonel Saleh Lahade
       First Assistant (Intelligence) - Captain Komar (Siliwangi)
       Second Assistant (Operations) - Captain Tondomulo
       Third Assistant (Personnel) - Captain Sudjono (Brawijaya)
       Fourth Assistant (Logistics) - Captain Abdul Azis Bustam (TT-VII)
   Fifth Assistant (Civic and Territorial Affairs) - Major Abdul Manan (Brawijaya)
Operational/tactical command over the following units:
   RI-23, Pare-Pare; Commander - Major Andi Rifai[*]
       Battalions 703 (Brawijaya), 705 (Brawijaya), 709 (Diponegoro), and 711 (Brawijaya)
   RI-Hasanuddin, Maros/Malino; Commander - Major M. Jusuf
       Battalions 704, 708, 710, 715, 716, 717, 718
   On loan from TT-V, Brawijaya:[**]
       Battalions 509, 510, 511, 513, 514, 515, 516, 527, 528

---

[*] RI-23 and RI-Hasanuddin were administratively attached to TT-VII, but were under the operational command of KoDPSST.

[**] It is generally agreed that there were nine battalions from the Brawijaya Division on loan to KoDPSST. This listing of battalions is based on information provided by the Dinas Sejarah Militer, KODAM VIII/Brawijaya, Malang, in September 1971: "Daftar Tugar dari Kesatuan Braw[idjaja] di Sulawesi Selatan, th. 1950-1964." The dating on this list is not precise, but the battalions given above are those stationed in the areas in which the nine Brawijaya battalions were said to be located: Markas Besar, Komando Pemerintah Militer TT.VII Wirabuana, "Instruksi Bekerdja Pemerintah Militer diseluruh Wilajah Terr. VII" (Makassar, March 24, 1957).

Other sources: Interviews with H. N. V. Sumual, Jakarta, March 9, 1971; and Saleh Lahade, Makassar, October 4, 1971.

APPENDIX THREE
CHARTER OF INCLUSIVE STRUGGLE FOR THE REGION OF TT-VII WIRABUANA

I. Preamble:
1. We as Indonesian patriots are deeply aware that the situation in Indonesia, after experiencing a period of struggle/revolution lasting some twelve years, is at the present time very critical and a cause for concern.
2. To prevent ruin and destruction, caused by controversies and divisions among ourselves, it is deemed essential to take immediate, rapid and correct action, with full responsibility as servants of the country and people of Indonesia.
3. In this connection, it is necessary to adopt a policy of taking over all the unfinished work of the Indonesian national revolution, which is still plentiful in every field and at every level, and to employ revolutionary forces as a means of completing [these tasks].

4. In the interest of the welfare and safety of the people of Indonesia in general and the people of the region in particular, and in the interest of the goals of the [independence] proclamation of August 17, 1945, under the guidance of Almighty God, we who have gathered on March 2, 1957, from 3:00 a.m. to 6:00 a.m. at the governor's residence in Makassar, after deep consideration and discussion have unanimously pledged with pure spirits to take firm steps to carry out the carefully formulated program of struggle, in order to overcome the problems and difficulties flooding the land of our birth, Indonesia, at the present time.

II. Struggle Objectives

  A. Regional Level

   1. Defense Sector

     1.1 The area of East Indonesia as a military area defense perimeter cannot be fragmented and requires serious short and long range plans (see the program of Territory VII).

     1.2 In the struggle to Free West Irian, East Indonesia will form the essential military and political-psychological base area.

   2. Governmental Sector

     2.1 In the interest of defense and, in effect, development, the four provinces within the area of East Indonesia must immediately be given the widest possible autonomy.[1]

---

1 In the original draft of the charter this article read as follows: "In the interest of defense, and in effect development, East Indonesia must immediately be divided into five provinces, with wide autonomy: Province of South and Southeast Sulawesi, Province of North Sulawesi, Province of Maluku, Province of Nusa Tenggara, Province of West Irian.

2.2 Wide autonomy means for:
-- surplus regions: 70 percent of the revenue from the region is for the region, and 30 percent is for the Central Government.
-- minus regions: 100 percent of the revenue from the region is for the region, supplemented for 25 years by a subsidy from the Central Government for essential development projects.

3. Development Sector

3.1 Each Province requires its own five-year plan; immediate efforts for development and improvements must be undertaken in accordance with existing capabilities and opportunities.

3.2 The allocation of foreign exchange, home and foreign credits, and Japanese war reparations must be in proportion to the geographical extent of the area (not the total population) and the number of autonomous provinces.

3.3 East Indonesia must be made a 70-30 barter area to make development possible.

3.4 East Indonesia must be given a fixed quota for the admission of students to major educational institutions at home and for the sending of students abroad.

3.5 Soldiers, youth/students, and other key manpower will be directed to work cooperatively in constructing essential projects.

3.6 A semiofficial veterans and invalids corps will be formed in East Indonesia, and veterans and invalids will be guaranteed a proper living.

3.7 Government Regulation No. 41/1954 must also be valid for widows and orphans of members of groups which fought for independence before 1950, including the 40,000 victims in South Sulawesi.[2]

---

[2] See above, p. 26.

3.8 The care of heroes' cemeteries and places of worship must be the responsibility of the Government.

4. Security Sector

Guided by the program of the Seventh Military Region Command, it is essential that the Central Government provide:

4.1 A full mandate from the Supreme Commander/Government to solve internal security [problems] in accordance with the Government's security policy.

4.2 Finance and supplementary material support in a fixed amount for three years.

5. Personnel Sector

5.1 It is desired that the filling of important positions be by persons who are capable, honest, creative, consistently revolutionary, and devoted to the region.

B. Central Government (National) Level

1. Immediate elimination of the system of centralism, which is static and formal, and is the basic cause of bureaucratism, corruption, and stagnation in regional development.

2. Restoration of dynamism, initiative, and authority through decentralization of rights and powers as follows:

    2.1 Broad autonomy to the region:

    2.2 In the National Council envisaged in the plan of President Sukarno, 70 percent of the members must be representatives of First Level Autonomous Regions, so that the Council may eventually attain the status of an upper house (Senate), in addition to the People's Representative Council (Parliament).

    2.3 The Gotong-Royong Cabinet[3] must be Presidential in nature, and composed of honest, capable, and respected national figures, and be given a full mandate from the Parliament for at least five years.

---

3 Gotong-Royong—mutual cooperation, mutual aid; this was the designation which President Sukarno gave to the four-party cabinet which he proposed in February 1957.

2.4 Both the National Council and the Cabinet must be led by the Sukarno-Hatta Duumvirate as a symbol of unity, dynamism, and authority.
3. The leadership of the Armed Forces in general, and the Army in particular, must immediately be changed, reorganized, and replaced with young, dynamic leaders in accordance with the Jogja Charter.[4]

III. Struggle Methods
1. First of all, by assuring leaders of all strata of society that *we are not separating ourselves from the* Republic of Indonesia, and are struggling only for the improvement of the lot of the Indonesian people and the consummation of the unfinished National Revolution.
2. The Commander of TT-VII/Wirabuana together with the Concentration of Forces,[5] composed of leaders in politics and government, the police, armed forces, youth/students, workers, farmers, traditional and religious leaders, women, etc., assumes de facto authority in carrying out policies in the military field, in government, security, communications, finance, and economic/social fields, in the whole area of TT-VII, East Indonesia, through the proclamation of a State of War and Emergency and establishment of a Military Government, in accordance with article 129 of the provisional constitution, and Government Regulation no. 33, 1948, Republic of Indonesia, Jogjakarta.
3. Preparing for a "Bhinneka Tunggal Ika"[6] Congress in Makassar, and in Provincial capitals, which will be composed of leaders of the 1945 [revolutionary] struggle, political leaders who represent East Indonesia in the Parliament and Constituent Assembly, youth/student leaders, workers, farmers, traditional and religious leaders, women, etc.

---

4 See above, p. 31.
5 On the civilians organized into the Konsentrasi Tenaga, see above, p. 42.
6 Unity in Diversity Congress; see above p. 58.

4. Prepare for negotiations with [a] Central Government [representative] who has a full mandate from the Supreme Commander/President, in order to achieve and realize to the fullest the aims of this charter.
5. To begin to carry out the main tasks in all fields which have long been awaited and hoped for by the community, in accordance with [available] equipment and capabilities, and to block any efforts which would weaken the struggle.

IV. Conclusion
1. After discussing the main goals and the way in which they are to be realized, with complete conviction that these noble decisions which are supported by all strata of society in East Indonesia will receive full attention from the Central Government and the people of Indonesia, in order that the realization of the ideals of the Revolution of 1945 which have been and are being fought for may be experienced by the people of the region of East Indonesia in particular and the Indonesian nation in general.
2. This struggle of ours is a continuation of the struggle of 1945, thus the principle to which we hold continues to be the Proclamation [of Independence] of August 17, 1945, and our guides are:

"Unity in Diversity"
"The Youth Pledge of October 28, 1928"[7]
"Law in effect in the Republic of Indonesia and if necessary Revolutionary Law"

Makassar, March 2, 1957

Pledged with sincerity and firm faith by:

1. H.N.V Sumual	18. J. E. Tatengkeng	35. A. Mattalatta
2. A. Pangerang	19. M. Nur A.E.	36. H. Sholeh
3. H. A. Sulthan	20. A. R. Aris	37. Rauf Moo

---

7 The Youth Pledge, a key nationalist symbol, was to support a single country, nation, and language—Indonesia.

4. Abbas Dg. Mallewa
5. Mrs. M. Towoliu
6. Rafiuddin
7. E. Tadjuddin
8. Andi Mannapiang
9. Sun Bone
10. Sampara Dg. Lili
11. L. J. Rogahang
12. S. H. Ngantung
13. Abdul Muluk
14. Dr. P. Siregar
15. J. H. Tamboto
16. M. Riza
17. J. M. Hutagalung
21. H. M. Junus
22. Nurdin Djohan
23. J. Latumahina
24. B. Korompis
25. Andi Burhanuddin
26. Mustafa Tari
27. C. Kairupan
28. Haneng
29. K. Makkawaru
30. Dr. Towolioe
31. A. S. Dg. Masalle
32. Henk Rondonuwu
33. O. E. Engelen
34. E. Gagola
38. A. Hadjoe
39. W.G.J. Kaligis
40. Lendy R. Tumbelaka
41. M. S. Lahade
42. M. Jusuf
43. J. Ottay
44. Hasan Usman
45. Safiuddin
46. Bing Latumahina
47. M. Lewerisa
48. Maj. Sjamsuddin
49. H. A. Massiara
50. A. W. Rachim
51. Alimuddin Dg. Mattiro

APPENDIX FOUR
PERSONS ACTIVE IN PERMESTA, 1957-58

	1	2	3a	3b*	3c	4	5	6
Total	51	64	31	68	12	19	9	7
Occupation								
Government/ politics (total)	(24)	(21)	(14)	(35)	(4)	(7)	(1)	(2)
civil service	21	20	7	33	2	5	1	2
member of parliament or local council	3	1	2	1	2	2	-	-
hereditary position	-	-	5	-	-	-	-	-
political party official	-	-	-	1	-	-	-	-
Military (or police) officer	15	19	-	1	1	5	7	5
Business/banking/ the professions	6	9	5	9	4	1	-	-
Journalism	4	6	1	8	2	2	-	-
Education/cultural activities	-	7	2	5	1	1	1	-
Religion	-	-	2	5	-	-	-	-
Unknown	2	2	7	5	-	3	-	-
Political Party Affiliation†								
PNI	3	6	1	8	-	-	-	-
Masjumi	4	3	4	7	3	4	1	2

NU	-	-	1	-	-	-	-	-
PKI	-	-	-	1	-	-	-	-
PSII	2	-	1	2	-	-	-	-
Parkindo	-	-	1	3	-	-	-	-
Katolik	1	-	-	1	-	-	-	-
PSI	5	7	2	8	2	3	-	-
PKR	11	8	3	9	2	4	1	1
Other	2	1	1	4	-	1	1	-
None	1	3	3	1	2	1	-	1
Unknown[§]	22	36	14	20	3	6	6	3
Ethnic Identity								
Sangirese	3	2	-	3	1	2	-	-
Minahasan	13	18	2	10	2	3	7	2
Gorontalese	3	4	-	3	2	2	-	-
Toraja	-	-	1	1	-	-	-	-
Buginese/ Makassarese/ Makassar Malay	18	24	14	26	2	4	1	2
Mandarese	-	1	1	2	-	-	-	-
Southeast Sulawesi	-	1	-	1	1	-	-	-
Other Sulawesi	-	2	2	1	-	-	-	-
Ambonese	3	4	2	2	1	3	-	1
Nusa Tenggara (including Timorese)	-	-	-	2	-	1	-	-
Javanese	-	-	-	2	-	-	-	-
Batak	2	1	-	1	1	1	-	-
Minangkabau	-	-	-	1	-	1	1	1
Chinese	-	1	-	1	-	-	-	-
Dutch	-	1	1	-	-	-	-	-
Unknown	9	5	8	12	2	2	-	1

Key:
1. Signer of Charter of Inclusive Struggle, March 2, 1957.

2. Member of Permesta military government, including Team of Assistants (only those known to have accepted their positions, or to have been involved in Permesta activity).
3. Member of Permesta Central Advisory Council, formed in March 1957;
    3a. No record of participation in activities of Council.
    3b. Attended at least one meeting of Council, or participated in activities of Council.
    3c. Member of working committee of Council; includes the secretary general, a (Gorontalese) First Lieutenant, the only military member of the Council.
4. Member of Permesta Supreme Council, November 1957.
5. Member of PRRI Cabinet, or PRRI/Permesta military command (includes only those persons active in Permesta in Makassar during 1957).
6. Persons arrested in Makassar in May 1958 (who are known to have been active in Permesta in 1957).

Notes.

* A Javanese PKI member (Paiso) withdrew from the council after attending at least one meeting.

† Includes affiliated youth organizations.

§ The political affiliation of most of the military officers involved in Permesta is unknown.

APPENDIX FIVE
PERMESTA MILITARY ORGANIZATION, 1958-60

PRRI/Permesta Armed Forces Staff
    Chief of Staff   H. N. V. Sumual
    Deputy Chief of Staff   D. J. Somba
    First Assistant (Intelligence)   J. M. J. Pantouw
    Second Assistant (Operations)   A. W. Supit
    Third Assistant (Personnel)   Lendy Tumbelaka
    Fourth Assistant (Logistics)   A. C. J. Mantiri
    Fifth Assistant (Civic ξ Territorial Affairs)   Wim Najoan
    Air Force Commander   Muharto*
PRRI/Permesta Territorial Commands
    Maluku and West Irian   Abdul Kadir*
    Minahasa   D. J. Somba
        District I   Agus Tuwaidan
        District II   John Ottay
        District III   Wim Tenges
        District IV   Joost Wuisan
    Bolaang-Mongondow ξ Gorontalo   Dolf Runturambi
    Central Sulawesi   J. W. Gerungan*
Autonomous Units
    Brigade 999   Jan Timbuleng
        Battalion 1   J. Lisangan
        Battalion 2   Goan Sankaeng
        Battalion 3   Hans Korua (Korowa)
        Battalion 4   B. Mandang
        Battalion 5   Benny Pandeiroth

Battalion 7	R. Parengkuan
Brigade Manguni	Laurens Saerang
Battalion Sumbernjawa	Daan Karamoy
Brigade Anoa Djantan	J. Lumingkewas
Brigade Sinobatu	W. Siregar

* Existing on paper only.
Sources: *Sari Attensia*, VII/9 (1960), pp. 580-82, VIII/1 (1961), p. 33; Chart of Permesta military organization as of March 1, 1960 (a copy of which was lent to the author by Mr. H. M. Taulu); interviews: A. C. J. Mantiri, Airmadidi, November 5, 1971; H. N. V. Sumual, Jakarta, April 13, 1972; D. J. Somba, Jakarta, August 15, 1971.

GLOSSARY

ALRI	Angkatan Laut Republik Indonesia
	Indonesian Navy
anak buah	younger associate, follower, dependent
anak daerah	child of the region, native son
anak mas	"golden child"; favorite pupil or follower
AUREV	Angkatan Udara Revolusioner
	Revolutionary Air Force (or PRRI/Permesta)
AURI	Angkatan Udara Republik Indonesia
	Indonesian Air Force
bapak	father, patron, leader
CPM	Corps Polisi Militer
	Military Police Corps
CTN	Corps Tjadangan (Cadangan) Nasional
	National Reserve Corps
Dewan Nasional	National Council
Dewan Pemuda Sulawesi	(later Dewan Pemuda Indonesia Timur)
	Sulawesi (East Indonesia) Youth Council
DI	Darul Islam
	the world of Islam; the Islamic State
DPP	Dewan Pertimbangan Pusat
	Central Advisory Council (established by Permesta military government in March 1957)
Dewan Tertinggi Pemuda Permesta	Permesta Youth Supreme Council

Dewan Tertinggi Permesta	Permesta Supreme Council
Dwitunggal	Duumvirate, two-in-one; Sukarno-Hatta
IPRI	Ikatan Perwira Republik Indonesia Republic of Indonesia Officers' Association
Jajasan (Yayasan) Kelapa Minahasa	Minahasa Coconut Foundation (established unilaterially in January 1955)
Jajasan (Yayasan) Kopra	Copra Foundation
kabupaten	district; second level of government administration
KADIT (KOANDA-IT)	Komando Antar Daerah Indonesia bagian Timur Inter-regional Command for East Indonesia
KDM (KODAM)	Komando Daerah Militer Military Area Command
KDM-SST	Komando Daerah Militer-Sulawesi Selatan dan Tenggara South and Southeast Sulawesi Military Area Command
KDM-SUT	Komando Daerah Militer-Sulawesi Utara dan Tengah North and Central Sulawesi Military Area Command
KNIL	Koninklijk Nederlands Indisch Leger Royal Netherlands Indies Army
KoDPSST	Komando Pertempuran (Pengamanan) Daerah Sulawesi Selatan dan Tenggara South and Southeast Sulawesi Battle (Pacification) Command
Komando Pemuda Permesta	Permesta Youth Command
Kongres Bhinneka Tunggal Ika	Unity in Diversity Congress (Makassar, May 8-12, 1957)

konsepsi	plan; in particular Sukarno's proposal of February 1957 for restructuring the government
KPM	Koninklijke Paketvaart Maatschappij
Royal [Netherlands] Steamship Company
KRIS	Kebaktian Rakjat Indonesia Sulawesi
Loyalty of the Indonesian People from Sulawesi (youth group, 1945-49)
KRU-Hasanuddin	Komando Reserve Umum-Hasanuddin
General Reserve Command-Hasanuddin
laskar seberang	Outer Islands militia
Manipol	Manifesto Politik
Political Manifesto; essence of philosophy of Guided Democracy
Masjumi	Madjelis Sjuro Muslimin Indonesia
Consultative Council of Indonesian Moslems
Muhammadiyah	modernist Islamic social and educational association
MUNAS	Musyawarah Nasional
National Conference (Jakarta, September 10-15, 1957)
NASAKOM	Nasionalism-Agama-Kommunism
nationalism-religion-communism; one of the slogans of Guided Democracy, which indicated the acceptance of communism/the PKI on a par with nationalist and religious parties
NIT	Negara Indonesia Timur
State of East Indonesia (Dutch-sponsored, 1946-50)
NU	Nahdatul Ulama
Council of Moslem Scholars
Panca Sila	the five principles of the state philosophy of Indonesia
panglima	commander
panglima besar	commander-in-chief

Parkindo	Partai Keristen Indonesia
	Indonesian Christian (Protestant) Party
Partai Katolik	Catholic Party
pejuang	fighter, struggler (implies fighter for independence)
Permesta	Piagam Perjuangan Semesta Alam
	Charter of Inclusive Struggle (March 2, 1957)
PESINDO	Pemuda Sosialis Indonesia
	Socialist Youth of Indonesia
PETA	Pembela Tanah Air
	Fatherland Defense [Force]
PKI	Partai Komunis Indonesia
	Indonesian Communist Party
PKR	Pusat Keselamatan Rakjat (1945-46)
	Center for People's Security
	Partai Kedaulatan Rakjat (after 1946)
	People's Sovereignty Party
PNI	Partai Nasional Indonesia
	Indonesian Nationalist Party
PPK	Pasukan Pembela Keadilan
	Defenders of Justice Army (rebel group in Minahasa)
PRRI	Pemerintah Revolusioner Republik Indonesia
	Revolutionary Government of the Republic of Indonesia (proclaimed in Padang, West Sumatra, February 15, 1958)
PSI	Partai Sosialis Indonesia
	Indonesian Socialist Party
PSII	Partai Sarikat Islam Indonesia
	Indonesian Islamic Union Party
PWP	Pasukan Wanita Permesta
	Permesta Women's Unit
RPI	Republik Persatuan Indonesia

	Indonesian Federal Republic (successor to PRRI in February 1960)
sabrang (Javanese)	the lands across the seas
seberang (Indonesian)	the Outer Islands
SSKAD (SESKOAD)	Sekolah Staf dan Komando Angkatan Darat
	Army Staff and Command School
Sudara	Sumber Darah Rakjat (Kenkoku Doshikai)
	Source of the People's Blood (Nation Founding Friendship Association; established in Makassar in June 1945)
TKR	Tentara Keamanan Rakjat
	People's Security Army (here a rebel group in South Sulawesi, 1952-56)
TNI	Tentara Nasional Indonesia
	Indonesian National Army
TRI	Tentara Republik Indonesia
	Republic of Indonesia Army (here a rebel group in South Sulawesi, 1952-56)
TT	Tentara Territorium
	Military region
zaken-kabinet	business-like (professional, nonparty) cabinet

www.ingramcontent.com/pod-product-compliance
Lightning Source LLC
Chambersburg PA
CBHW020645230426
43665CB00008B/326